TWO YEARS ON TREK

TWO YEARS ON TREK

BEING SOME ACCOUNT OF THE

ROYAL SUSSEX REGIMENT

IN SOUTH AFRICA.

BY THE LATE
LT.-COLONEL DU MOULIN.

WITH A PREFACE BY
COL. J. G. PANTON, C.M.G.
Commanding 2nd Battalion Royal Sussex Regiment, 1903-1907.

EDITED BY
H. F. BIDDER,
Captain, 3rd Battalion Royal Sussex Regiment.

MURRAY AND CO.,
THE MIDDLESEX PRINTING WORKS,
180, BROMPTON ROAD, S.W.
1907.

THIS BOOK

WRITTEN FOR THE MOST PART BY THE LATE

LT.-COL. DU MOULIN

HAS BEEN COMPLETED AND PUBLISHED

BY HIS COMRADES

AS THE MOST FITTING MEMORIAL

TO A GALLANT SOLDIER.

DULCE · ET · DECORUM · EST · PRO · PATRIA · MORI

CONTENTS.

Chap.		Page.
I.	To Bloemfontein.	1
II.	The 21st Brigade. The Trek Begins....	13
III.	To Zand River.	28
IV.	The Fight at Zand River.	39
V.	Across the Vaal.	50
VI.	Doornkop.	60
VII.	Pretoria.	69
VIII.	Diamond Hill, First Day.	79
IX.	Diamond Hill, Second Day.	84
X.	To Springs.	95
XI.	To Reitz.	105
XII.	To Meyer's Kop.	117
XIII.	Retief's Nek....	126
XIV.	To the Boer Laager.	144
XV.	To Winburg.	162
XVI.	Up and Down.	173
XVII.	To Lindley.	185
XVIII.	The Railway Needs Repair.	202
XIX.	To Bothaville.	215
XX.	Ventersburg Road....	225
XXI.	Back to Lindley.	234
XXII.	In Garrison.	247
XXIII.	The Raising of the Mounted Column....	257
XXIV.	Two Districts.	273
XXV.	De Put.	282
XXVI.	To Vlakfontein.	291
XXVII.	Abraham's Kraal.	301
XXVIII.	Northwards—and the End.	308
XXIX.	The Third Battalion.	319
	Appendices.	

INDEX TO MAPS.

Seven of the eight maps illustrating actions are from sketches made in South Africa at the time of the War, the first six being by Col. J. G. Panton, C.M.G. In most cases they illustrate only that phase of the action in which the Royal Sussex Regiment took part. For the country round De Put, the map issued by the Intelligence Department has been used.

	Page.
ZAND RIVER	46
DOORN KOP	66
DIAMOND HILL	82
DIAMOND HILL	92
RETIEF'S NEK	138
VENTERSBURG ROAD	230
DE PUT	288
ABRAHAM'S KRAAL	306
FOLDING MAP	

PREFACE.

Louis Eugène du Moulin was of French descent. By birth he was a New Zealander. He passed through Sandhurst and entered the army in 1879, joining the 107th Regiment—now the Second Battalion of the Royal Sussex Regiment. With this battalion all his service was spent, until his promotion in 1899 as second in command of the First Battalion Royal Sussex Regiment (the old 35th).

He served in the Black Mountain Campaign of 1888, in the Chin-Lushai and Manipur expeditions of 1889-91, and in the Tirah Campaign of 1897-98. Alike among the dark pine woods of the Himalayas, in the dense jungle of Manipur, or on the bleak, stony ridges of the Hazara country the name of du Moulin became a byword in the Regiment, and far beyond the Regiment, for restless energy, never-failing resource and cool daring. He became known all over India as a musketry expert. Many of his ideas were adopted, and are in universal use by those who may never have heard his name.

Perhaps his real genius was for organization. This quality came conspicuously into notice in South Africa during the war. Many men who served in the 21st Brigade under General Bruce Hamilton had reason to bless the forethought and unstinted labour of the man who carried out so thoroughly the idea of the Brigade commander, and supplied the Brigade with those welcome additions to bully beef and biscuit which were obtainable at the Brigade Canteen. Often after a hard day's march and a tough fight have I admired the unselfish spirit in which, disdaining fatigue, he would set to work with his coat off to open stores and arrange the wagons lighted with "dips," which served as a "coffee shop" for famishing Tommy.

A tall, spare man, with keen, dark eyes, a courageous nose and a harsh-toned voice—such was the outward du Moulin. Feared not a little, loved greatly by those under him, afraid of no one, despising precedent and precaution, dependent only on his own iron will and keen intellect, he had a brilliant career before him when he fell gloriously at Abraham's Kraal on January 28th, 1902. He had gone through the campaign from the advance to Pretoria of Lord Roberts' army, down to the pursuit of De Wet and of the broken commandos after De Wet's time, without a wound, and, as far as I can remember, without a day's sickness—and with very few days' rest from marching and fighting.

He always knew what it was he wanted and how to get it, and how to make others help him to this end.

One anecdote I may here relate:—

Worn out with much marching, ragged and hungry, the half battalion under du Moulin halted at Kroonstad to refit. Supplies, and especially clothing and boots, were hard to get. Some tired subaltern returned, repulsed from the Ordnance Store, empty handed.

The matter quickly reached du Moulin's ears, and he disappeared for what seemed a few minutes. Presently out of a cloud of red dust emerged a mule wagon at a hand gallop. Standing up, driving, cracking a long whip, and yelling at the Kaffirs to clear the road, came " *Mullins*," *as he was familiarly known to all. His grey regulation shirt was rolled up to the elbow, showing a pair of red muscular arms like copper wire. He shouted as he turned his team into the camp, and we hurried to his wagon, to have bundles of new clothes, white shiny rolls of waterproof sheets, and thick soft blankets rapidly alotted to our men;* **and** *to save time (for we were moving next morning)* "*Mullins*" *himself hurled out the bundles into our arms.*

At another time, when we were at Ventersburg Road Station in one of the brief intervals of rest allowed by Boers who blew up the railway line three times a week (this was in 1900), *the siding leading to the dock for entraining horses or cattle was completely blocked by the burnt remains of a train of trucks, rusty and apparently immovable.*

The railway staff smiled incredulously when du Moulin offered to remove the entire train of trucks. Without cranes or appliances they declared it was impossible.

Collecting all the spare rails, sleepers and fishplates that could be found about the station yard, du Moulin started work, and a branch railway some 100 *yards long was quickly laid leading into the veldt, with proper points connecting it with the siding. A hundred willing hands hauled at the ropes—the rusty axles, well greased, revolved. In half a day the siding was clear, and the ruined trucks were standing on the veldt, where they probably stand to this day!*

Another picture of du Moulin under fire, and I have done.

On the 12th of June, 1900, at Diamond Hill, " B " Company was sent to support the three companies of the Royal Sussex under du Moulin, about midday. These three companies were lying under the scanty shelter of a few rocks at the edge of the flat-topped hill facing the main Boer position, at a distance of about 900 yards. The hail of bullets was incessant, the noise of guns and thousands of rifles deafening. As we arrived breathless, having crossed the 200 yards of flat open ground amid a " rush " of bullets, I sought du Moulin to ask where we were most wanted. He was standing up, a conspicuous figure amidst a " feu d'enfer "—pounding with the butt of a rifle a prostrate man, who would not move from the imagined shelter of a stone about as big as a Dutch cheese, and who could not see to fire from his position.

I got a very curt, lurid rejoinder, and promptly subsided behind a very inadequate rock myself.

Colonel du Moulin was shot through the heart, leading a charge against the Boers who had rushed his camp. Always in front—always the first to face the foe. " Felix opportunitati mortis." May he rest in peace.

J. G. PANTON.

Crete,
November, 1906.

EXPLANATORY.

It was the design of Col. du Moulin to write an account of the doings of the Royal Sussex Regiment in South Africa, which should both serve to remind those of the Regiment who went through the campaign of the incidents in which they took part, and should also put on record another chapter of that Regimental History, made through many years in many lands, of which all who serve in the Regiment may be so justly proud.

During the months of November and December, 1900, he found, in the comparative quiet of the occupation of Lindley, an opportunity of completing his account up to date. His manuscript is typed (he managed to obtain a machine from somewhere) upon the only paper available—the backs of invoice sheets from a store in the town.

From the evacuation of Lindley in January, 1901, to his death a year later, Col. du Moulin was far too much occupied with his work in the field to do more than make a few notes for his book. And it is from these notes of his, and from the diaries, letters, and personal reminiscences of other Officers, that the later chapters have been compiled.

It has been thought better to leave Col. du Moulin's work practically untouched, although it was never subjected by him to a final revision, and although he had no opportunity of modifying anything he wrote, in the light of subsequent history. As it stands, it gives a vivid picture of events that had only just occurred—drawn with a firm hand, while the impression was fresh upon the author's mind.

In compiling the subsequent chapters, the object has been merely to give a slight sketch of the experiences of the Regiment during the latter half of the war. It has not been attempted (nor would it have been possible) to enter into detail to the same extent as was done by Col. du Moulin, writing upon the spot. If one or two scenes are preserved, it is the utmost that can be hoped.

The Appendices contain the stories of the 13th and 21st M.I., on which several officers and a number of men of the Regiment were serving. The former is kindly contributed by Capt. G. P. Hunt, of the Royal Berkshire Regiment.

H. F. BIDDER.

December, 1906.

CHAPTER I.

TO BLOEMFONTEIN.

Malta—Orders for South Africa—The Pavonia—Cape Town—Port Elizabeth—Bloemfontein—Glen.

The senior regiment in the 1st Brigade in the 1st Army Corps at Aldershot and the first regiment on the roster for foreign service at the time war was declared in South Africa in 1899, we might fairly have expected to be one of the earliest regiments to embark for active service; but it was not to be. We saw our old friends in General FitzRoy Hart's Brigade—The Black Watch, the Welsh, the Northamptons—and almost every other regiment in Aldershot receive their orders to mobilise, and with heavy hearts we proceeded to pack our kits for—Malta!

Even in this festive island our ill luck seemed at first to follow us unceasingly, and, notwithstanding all our field training at Mellieha and the numerous occasions upon which we defended Naxaro against overwhelming hordes of invaders, still we were not among the chosen. Our old friends the Sherwood Foresters took themselves off also, via the Suez Canal, for the seat of war, with a nice fat draft of seasoned soldiers from their Second Battalion, and we were left lamenting, to troop the Colour on the Palace Square, and to go on guard with five nights in bed.

The very bad news which arrived soon after the opening of the campaign in Natal had a depressing effect on all of us, which soldiering in Malta is not calculated to remove, and any fresh news issued by Bartolo, the printer, was eagerly sought after. A glimmer of excitement was caused by the offer of His Excellency the Governor to the

Secretary of State to provide a fully equipped company of Mounted Infantry from the troops in garrison, of which company the Royal Sussex hoped to form a large part; but in this again we were doomed to disappointment, as we were not even asked to send in our names.

Things were in this unhappy state—everyone with long faces and villainous tempers—when the New Year was ushered in and found us at Verdala Barracks. From there, towards the middle of the month, five companies were sent to the new barracks at Imtarfa and the other three were put out into various holes and corners at Zabbar, Salvatore and other undesirable residences. We all thought this was putting the climax on our misfortunes, but we little knew then that in another five days we were to be raised to the seventh heaven of delight by the news that we were at last selected to proceed to South Africa.

This welcome news was hurriedly brought out to the exiles at Imtarfa by Captain Aldridge, his face fairly beaming again, and shortly afterwards we heard that we were to go home to be mobilised for active service, and that we were to be relieved in Malta by the Royal Berkshire regiment. Immediately everything was hurry and bustle, and we were all writing to our friends and making our arrangements for a prolonged absence, except, alas, some of the younger soldiers, who could not reasonably expect to fulfil the conditions of being over 20 and having completed a year's service.

Shortly afterwards the glad tidings arrived that we were to mobilise in Malta, that our reservemen would join us there, and that we should proceed straight to the Cape.

On one occasion, whilst at Imtarfa, when an unusually stirring account of the battle of Colenso appeared in the *Daily Telegraph*, one of the officers went down to the Recreation Room at night and read it to the men. Mr. Bennett Burleigh, the writer of the vivid piece of word painting, would have been flattered if he could have seen the great crowd of men in the room, absolutely still and motionless, following with breathless interest the splendid description of the gallant behaviour of our gunners on this fatal day, when they bravely tried to work their guns within 600 yards of the enemy's riflemen, and the magnificent story of how young Roberts, Captain Congreve and others endeavoured to save the guns.

On the 16th of January after a prolonged field day over the rocks beyond the Victoria Lines, which lasted from 9 a.m. to 3 p.m., we marched off to Pembroke to execute the annual course of musketry, which we succeeded in doing in some of the most villainous weather which it has ever been a soldier's lot to experience. This concluded, back the five companies went to Imtarfa, being relieved by the other three from Headquarters; and now a constant succession of field days and route marches of a more or less interesting character opened for us and continued until the 12th of February, when the whole regiment was collected together on the Cottonera side of the water, and those who were not to go to the Cape were definitely weeded out.

Sir Francis Grenfell inspected the Battalion on parade at Zabbar Gate a day or two before we embarked, and was good enough to make some very complimentary remarks. The " Pavonia," a big Cunarder, which arrived early on the morning of the 19th of February with our reservemen on board and no end of our mobilisation stores, impressed us very favourably, and our liking for her as a comfortable ship increased with our acquaintance of her.

She was crowded with old comrades and new friends, both officers and men, and we gave each other a cheery reception—not quite so cheery, however, as the send-off from Chichester, which we had all heard about by the mail a few days previously, and regarding which a large amount of good natured chaff continued to pass for a long time. Many is the time since then that some of us have longed, and with some reason too, for one of the Mayor's famous pork-pies!

The reservemen, especially those of Section D, were a fine lot, and made one's heart swell with pride to think that at last the reward of years of parades and routine would be reaped, and that a battalion of thoroughly seasoned soldiers, second to none serving Her Majesty, was to have an opportunity of showing what it could do in the field.

Major Scaife, who had been left at home on the sick list when the battalion embarked for Malta, but who had succeeded in passing a medical board, was on the "Pavonia," as well as Captain Gilbert and Lieut. Wroughton, of the Second Battalion. Both these had been attached to this Battalion for duty during the campaign; so also had Captain Blake of the Third Battalion, who had volunteered for duty as a subaltern. Lieut. Harden, who had been promoted into the regiment from a West India Battalion and had already seen considerable service on the West Coast of Africa, and Lieut. Gouldsmith from the Depôt, with four new officers, 2nd Lieuts. Paget, Anderson, Montgomerie and Leachman, had also come to join. These latter young officers were to purchase their experience somewhat dearly as after events proved, but luckily with no fatal results to themselves.

The send-off of the battalion from Malta, although not equalling in magnificence that accorded to our reservemen by the generous citizens of Chichester, was no less cordial. The battalion concentrated in Margharita Square and marched to the Bakery Wharf, the scene of endless similar departures, played down by the band of the 3rd Royal West Kent regiment and by the civilian band of Cospicua. We embarked about mid-day, but remained in harbour that night to complete the loading of the mobilisation stores and also to embark the Malta Company of Mounted Infantry, which some weeks before we had been so chagrined at our inability to join. This company was commanded by Captain Pine-Coffin of the Loyal North Lancashire regiment, and he had with him a fine lot of men of the Derbyshire, North Lancashire and Warwickshire regiments.

At half-past ten on the 20th of February the screw made its first revolution on its long journey, and we were fairly moving at last. The Baracca and the fortifications overlooking the harbour were crowded with people to see us off, and there was a scene of great enthusiasm as we slowly steamed past St. Elmo, the bluejackets on the ships in harbour giving us cheer after cheer.

Between Malta and Gibraltar a great many stowaways turned up, some of them having succeeded in bringing their full kit on board. Unhappily for them the "Pavonia" called in at Gibraltar in obedience to signals from the shore, the Malta authorities having telegraphed ahead; so our friends were hunted up and taken ashore, terribly dejected at their ill-luck. One or two, however, were 'cute enough to hide again, and this time succeeded in coming with us all the way.

The voyage was a slow and uneventful one. Absolutely nothing occurred to vary the monotony or to increase the speed. The "Pavonia," although an Atlantic liner, was not by any means the flyer that we had anticipated, and performed all her duties with deliberation even to coaling. This was carried out in a slow and stately manner in two days at St. Vincent, many of our men, who volunteered for the purpose, being utilised in assisting, owing to the dearth of coolies. Crossing the line on the 8th of March we had the usual visit from Father Neptune, who arrived on board about 7 p.m., and proceeded to hold his court according to ancient custom, when numbers of his young subjects were presented to His Majesty in due form and greeted by him in proper sea style.

During the voyage every endeavour was made to give the men exercise and to keep them in condition, no easy matter with such a large number of men on board and so little room. However parades were held every day, and signalling and semaphore classes were kept going, which relieved the monotony a little. When we could not think of anything else for the moment it was always easy to have a roundup amongst the kit bags or a worry around the helmets on the lower deck! The band played on deck pretty often, and so the weary time passed slowly away until the 20th of March, when Table Mountain was at last sighted. We should never have believed it possible that it was to be our fate to remain six days at anchor, but such was the fact. The number of ships—mostly with troops, but many with horses, cattle and coal—lying in the harbour was prodigious, and we had of course to wait our turn before going into the docks. This we did on the 26th, and we were enabled to give the battalion a run ashore in the shape of a route march. Passing through the streets of Cape Town we excited a good deal of comment owing to our strength, which was over 1,200 and caused people to think we were two battalions. A certain amount of liberty was accorded the men to go ashore which they were not slow to avail themselves of, though they took no undue advantage of the permission. Numbers of men seized the opportunity to remit various sums to their families at home, and a draft, one amongst several, for over £242 was sent to the Depôt on account of these small remittances. The Depôt

authorities sent out these sums to the families, but
for some idea best known to themselves, informed
them that the money was part of a subscription
from officers and men, which led to endless correspondence, as the families immediately with one
accord wrote and demanded to know what had
become of their husbands!

Cape Town is a fine city and contains some
splendid public buildings, whilst its situation at the
foot of Table Mountain is magnificent. The
suburbs at Green Point and Wynburg are excellently laid out, and it is very pleasing to see the
way trees are planted in the streets, and how open
spaces are encouraged. The electric trams are
splendid, and many of the battalion amused themselves by riding on the top of a car as far as it went
and coming back again. There is no better way
of seeing a town.

The streets were crowded with soldiers of all
sorts. Every kind of corps, Horse, Foot and Artillery, was represented, not only of the Regular Army
but of Colonials also. Here were Canadians, Australians, New Zealanders, men from India and
Ceylon, men from Malta, men from the West
Indies, men from Natal and all parts of South
Africa, and crowds of adventurers and dare-devils
from every quarter of the globe, who had enlisted in
various local corps. Not only the Army, but the
whole British nation, owe to Mr. Kruger a debt of
gratitude that can never be repaid, inasmuch as
the South African war has brought about such a
reorganisation and betterment of the Army and
such a magnificent outburst of patriotic feeling
among our vast colonies as could never have
been excited by any other means. The ordinary
individual who remains in England all his life or
potters about the Continent cannot, unless he is a
man of an open mind and phenomenal intelligence,
grasp the enormous size and resources of our

colonies such as India, Australasia, the Cape Colonies and Canada, and it has remained for Mr. Kruger to compel this fact to become startlingly patent to the minds of many men, both at home and out in the Colonies, who had never given any attention previously to the subject.

On the 30th March orders were received to proceed to East London to disembark there, as apparently the traffic on the Cape railways was congested to a degree, and some of it must be diverted on to the East London line. So we steamed out again, passing round the Cape of Good Hope in the afternoon and arriving on the 2nd of April at East London, where we lay off the harbour, as we drew too much water to pass over the bar and enter the channel.

Captain Pine-Coffin and his Mounted Infantry were the first to disembark, and were followed by A, B, and C companies under Major O'Grady. F, G, and H companies under Major du Moulin were the next to land on the 3rd of April, and were followed by Headquarters and D and E companies the same evening. Each of these parties were entrained on successive days with their kits and rations and ammunition, and were despatched up country, meeting with great demonstrations from the residents along the line. Some ladies at Fort Jackson were kind enough to turn out late at night and provide tea for us, than which nothing could have been more acceptable. A run of about eighteen or nineteen hours brought us to Bethulie Bridge, where the fact that we were actually at the enemy's country became as evident as a slap in the face when we saw the railway bridge with its piers destroyed and its enormous arches blown into the river. The Railway Pioneer regiment, a local corps composed mostly of railway men and miners, was hard at work making a diversion over the road bridge, which, luckily for us, had been saved from the enemy by Major Shaw and Lieut. Popham of the Sherwood Foresters a short time previously.

The road bridge had had a line of rails laid along it, and trucks were pushed over one by one, as the bridge was not strong enough to bear the weight of an engine. This method of procedure was slow, but the advantages of a through line were enormous; and considerable precautions had to be maintained to guard against the likelihood of any further disaster, since it was possible at any time that the enemy might try and blow up the sole remaining bridge over the river, and it was, therefore, needful to take especial care. Each party of troops arriving detrained in succession and marched over the river about a couple of miles to the railway station, where, in due course, they were entrained and despatched up country.

Head Quarters and D and E companies, however, remained for some little time at Bethulie, relieving the Royal Scots on picket, and performing the usual garrison duties. Alarms were several times raised that the advance of a party of Boers, bent on wrecking the bridge, was imminent, and all the troops stood to arms and reinforced the pickets; but nothing further was ever heard.

At last, on the 20th April, these two companies started on their march to join the remainder of the battalion, which about this time was concentrating at Ferreira, a siding on the railway a few miles south of Bloemfontein. However after marching about 60 miles, and reaching Edenburg at the end of a long and trying tramp of fully 24 miles, orders were received to go on by train to Bloemfontein; and on arriving there the two companies were sent on at once to Glen, which they reached early on the 27th of April. Headquarters had detrained at Ferreira in passing, and had joined the remainder of the battalion.

Meanwhile, A, B, and C companies had been

having some adventures, B company having been fetched out of the train at Edenburg and ordered to place the little town in a state of defence, as the advent of the enemy was hourly expected. The Boers, however, failed to turn up, and B company was then, on the 6th of April, ordered off to Bethany, about 10 miles distant, where the company entrained, reaching Ferreira Siding late at night. They stayed here and took their share of picket duty until the end of the month.

A and C companies, under Major O'Grady, after dropping B at Edenburg, went on by rail to Bloemfontein, arriving there on the 5th April, and receiving orders next day to camp on a hill about 2 miles south-east of the railway station. This was in a dangerous neighbourhood, as about this time the Boers were threatening the Waterworks and Springfield, which is not far to the East; so a defensive work was laid out on this hill by the Royal Engineers, which these two companies amused themselves by erecting. Lord Roberts visited the site on the 10th of April and christened it "Sussex Hill." The usual picket precautions were taken by day and night, and the men were kept busy with pick and shovel; but a good deal of rain interfered with the work, which was not completed until the 17th of April, when orders were received to move to Ferreira and join the remainder of the battalion.

F, G, and H companies arrived at Bloemfontein on the 5th of April, but after waiting some hours were entrained and moved down the line about 6 miles to Ferreira Siding, where the pickets of the Royal Scots on Leeuberg and the surrounding kopjes were relieved, and a guard mounted on the bridge.

At Ferreira, close to our little camp, a brother of Mr. Steyn, the late President of the Orange Free State, had a sort of country residence, and we saw a good deal of him, as he and his wife were very civil in allowing the men to purchase bread, butter, and other things from their farm.

Mr. Steyn was a typical Boer, a fine, big man, with a long, black beard; he was a solicitor in Bloemfontein, and of course an educated man, who had travelled over England and the continent. Both he and his charming wife used to be astonished, or pretended to be astonished, at the never ending succession of troops daily passing their house on their way up to the front, and used to ask us where all the troops came from. We, naturally, did not give the show away, and explained carefully that there were lots more where they came from, and that there was our magnificent Indian army behind them again, only waiting to be called on.

Around the Steyns' farm French's cavalry had encamped during Lord Roberts' dash on Bloemfontein, just before entering the town, and there was ample evidence of the fact in the shape of dead animals and empty biscuit tins strewn for miles over the veldt.

Mr. Steyn had, of course, been made a prisoner by the first arrivals of our cavalry, but had taken the oath of allegiance, and had been given a special pass to enable him to reside peacefully on his farm and to prosecute his business in the town.

He was occasionally subjected to a good deal of annoyance, it is a pity to relate, from our own troops, and had several times to send over to our detachment and ask for a sentry to be posted on his house. The intruders were usually men of the Colonial forces who apparently thought they had a right to order meals to be prepared and fowls to be handed over at any time, and that they could remove Mr. Steyn's horses and wagons in defiance of the written permit to retain them which he used to show.

On the 7th of April B company arrived, and also a battalion of the Scots Guards and a squadron of Mounted Infantry. G and H companies went to Kaal Spruit during the night, and from that date to the end of the month the outposts were furnished by the Scots Guards and ourselves.

On the 21st of April A and C companies arrived from Sussex Hill, and a new camp was formed and tents pitched in anticipation of the arrival of the remainder of the battalion. The Volunteer company arrived somewhat unexpectedly early on the 24th, and went off to take their turn on picket the same evening. The Colonel and the regimental staff arrived the next day, and the battalion was then almost complete.

Orders were shortly afterwards received to proceed to Bloemfontein; at 3 p.m. on the 27th of April the seven companies left by road, and on arrival camped in the Highland Brigade camp just south of the town. The men's blankets and baggage had been sent by rail, and, as no transport could be procured until late, the blankets did not reach camp until nearly midnight. However the men were in tents, and the bivouac poles came in handy for making tea, no fuel of any kind being procurable in camp.

Lord Roberts, accompanied by Major General Kelly, who had served many years in the battalion, inspected us on parade the next day at 10 a.m. preparatory to marching off to Glen. This march, a long and tiresome one, gave us our first experience of the veldt, and we were not sorry to find ourselves at Glen after our 16 miles tramp. D and E companies were already there, and had camp pitched for us; our baggage, however, did not turn up until the early morning, so we had to put in the night the best way we could, under bags and tent walls, in the absence of blankets. The whole Brigade was camped here, and the next day we fairly started on our travels.

CHAPTER II.

THE 21ST BRIGADE. THE TREK BÈGINS.

Composition of the Brigade—Start from Glen—Transport arrangements—To Jacobsrust—Rations—Halts—Pickets—Tobacco—Tea.

The 21st Brigade was composed of four regiments, of which the Royal Sussex (under Col. Donne) was the senior. Next came the Sherwood Foresters, under Major Gossett (commanding in place of Colonel Smith-Dorrien, who was then in command of the 19th Brigade), who had under him a splendid body of men, the majority having served in their Second Battalion during the Tirah campaign. The experience gained in this war against the Afridis was extremely valuable to the officers and men, as the system of fighting adopted by the crafty Pathan bore many points of similarity to that carried out by brother Boer. The next regiment in the brigade in order of seniority was the Cameron Highlanders, commanded by Lieut.-Colonel Kennedy. This regiment was practically just off one campaign, as they had served in the last Omdurman expedition and had not left Egypt until ordered to the Cape. The men were in magnificent condition, hard as nails, and, throughout the campaign, they amply justified the opinion formed of them at first sight. The remaining battalion in the brigade was the famous regiment of the City Imperial Volunteers. They were, of course, men of fine physique, having been especially selected for their physical fitness and their soldierly qualities, and I think it has been allowed by everyone who has marched and worked in the field side by side with this battalion of citizen soldiers that their conduct and bearing has at all times been equal to that of the best infantry battalion in the Regular Army.

They had a cyclist section with them, but this was too small to be of any use except as orderlies, or despatch riders.

I think there is a great future before the cyclist soldier, and I should like to have seen a cyclist battalion, 1000 strong, employed in this campaign with the Mounted Infantry Brigades. There is one point I am quite positive about, and that is, that after having trekked over 1,500 miles in all parts of the country, from Pretoria to Bethulie, and in all weathers, I have seen no district, not even in the Caledon Valley, where cyclists in large numbers could not have been utilised in place of or in addition to Mounted Infantry.

The Brigade was commanded by Colonel Bruce Hamilton of the East Yorkshire regiment, who was promoted to Major-General before the conclusion of the campaign. General Hamilton has a long record of active and staff service, having taken part in the Afghan war, the Burma war, and campaigns in Ashanti and on the West Coast of Africa; one of his earliest experiences of active service being in the Boer War of 1881, when he was A.D.C. to Sir George Colley and was present at the historic fights of that campaign, Laings Nek and the Ingogo. He afterwards served on the Staff at Bombay and at Simla, and, at the time our battalion was at Aldershot in 1899, he was an A.G. to General Lyttleton's Brigade, eventually going out to Natal as an A.G. when the war broke out, and later receiving command of the 21st Brigade.

Major Shaw, the Brigade Major, belonged to the Sherwood Foresters and was in Malta with us in that regiment, with which he also served in the early part of the campaign in the Orange Free State, distinguishing himself at the capture of the bridge at Bethulie. The General's Aide-de-Camp was Lieut. Fraser of the Cameron Highlanders, who was afterwards assisted in his duties by Lieut. Clive Wilson of the Yeomanry. The Brigade Transport Officer was Major Cardew of the Army Service Corps, and the officer in charge of Supplies was Lieut. Lloyd of the same corps, who had lately returned from active service on the West Coast.

Our medical officer was Major Dundon, R.A.M.C., who had accompanied us from Malta, and who on board ship had inoculated a great many officers and men of the battalion against enteric fever. Major Dundon's own health, however, gave way, and he suffered so much from fever that he had to be admitted to hospital and sent down country, so that he did not afterwards return to the regiment.

On the 29th of April we started from Glen on our travels, but we did not move until one o'clock, as there was a good deal of work to be done first, leaving extra kit behind and issuing rations, of which we carried two days' supply in our haversacks and four days' on the wagons. Some of us have often, on after days when we were hard up for a bit of breakfast, looked back on this morning at Glen and wished we could lay hands on the piles and piles of biscuits which were thrown away by the men.

At Glen our transport was issued to us; there were nine wagons altogether, but as it was impossible to obtain mules, our four ammunition carts, which we had brought out from home with us, and the great casks of harness, had all to be left behind. We had no water-carts either, except the one which had been lent to the detachment at Ferreira, and which, under the circumstances, it was thought advisable to retain. We should also have had led mules to carry ammunition, the medical panniers and the signalling gear, but none were available for this purpose; so all this gear had to be loaded on the nine wagons, which were pretty full in consequence.

One wagon was allowed to every two companies to carry blankets, great-coats, cooking pots, ration baskets, etc. Our nine companies thus took four and a half wagons, leaving the same number to carry all the miscellaneous gear, the officers' kits, the ammunition, entrenching tools, and two days' rations, besides the reserve ration of bully beef.

It always struck us as being somewhat ironical having to carry a reserve ration of bully beef while on the march, as the country was full of cattle, which could have been driven in if required. If the worst had come to the worst we could, in an emergency, have eaten the trek oxen, which were quite as tender as the slaughter bullocks.

The company wagons were terribly overloaded; each company was about 120 strong, so the wagons had to carry 240 blankets and waterproof sheets and 240 great-coats, besides the other impedimenta.

As time went on, Major Cardew succeeded in getting us other wagons, and some small carts were picked up at farms and utilised to carry our reserve ammunition, the signalling gear, the doctors' boxes and the tools; but the difficulty was to find animals to draw these carts. There were plenty of carts at the farms, but the only beasts that we could get were such stray mules as we encountered on the road, or which were found in camp. They were mostly quite unfit for work and had been abandoned on that account, but, anyhow, we had to put them in harness and get what work we could out of them until we found better ones.

Each large wagon was drawn by ten mules, and looked after by two black boys as drivers, and one soldier as wagonman, who applied the brake when necessary. The wagons were large and heavy, and the wheels too light and spidery to stand much rough usage; and each wagon was cumbered with a huge box or driving seat which must have weighed at least one hundredweight, the use of which was not very obvious.

All wagons, and indeed all the transport carts, and the guns too, were fitted with the South African brake, which is applied or taken off by means of a hand-wheel at the back of the cart. These powerful brakes are very necessary owing to the steep descents sometimes met with, and the erratic behaviour at all times of the mules. These animals gave much trouble at first, but soon, with hard work and scanty feed, became more docile.

The native drivers had been enlisted evidently because they were natives, not on account of what they knew about mules or oxen. Many of them were quite ignorant of how to treat the mules, and flogged them all day without cessation, until at last the use of long whips was forbidden.

The mules suffered a good deal from the want of water on the march. They will not drink before about eight o'clock in the morning, and by that time we were on the road usually, and there was no opportunity, until we arrived at our destination, of watering the animals. This was a pity, as they would have travelled much the better for it. Sometimes we had a rest of a couple of hours in the middle of the day, when the animals were allowed to water and graze; but more often the exigencies of the campaign would not allow of our halting for long.

Some of the artillery baggage wagons were of the old box pattern which, it is understood, was condemned in 1881, after the first Boer war, as being quite unsuitable; but now they appeared again. The artillery used to mount a driver on the leading mule of the team and this plan seemed to have many advantages. There is always much trouble in starting a team of mules, as the natural perversity of the animals prevents them from all pulling at once and together, until they are fairly started.

To humour the wretched beasts it is sometimes necessary to get men to give the van a shove along, so that the ten mules, when they find the wagon moving, get at once into their collars and step out together in the most docile fashion. Give a mule a slight ascent in the road in front of him and the extraordinary creature is in his element at once, and puts all his weight into his work; but on level ground or on a down grade, a good deal of attention is necessary to keep the traces taut and the mules from hanging back and getting their legs over them.

We crossed the river by a footbridge and marched about eight miles to Klein Ospruit. The baggage wagons had some adventures at the drifts and did not arrive till fairly late, so that we had some trouble sorting out our kits and other property in the dark.

Next day we marched to Schanz Kraal, a short march over grassy veldt. The Volunteer company had the honour of being the first to come under the enemy's fire on this occasion, as they were plugged at by one of the Boer guns whilst they were acting as escort to our battery. The shells, however, dropped short and did no damage. The 1st of May saw us up at 6.30, and on the tramp on an exceptionally long march to Jacobsrust, or Steynspruit as it is sometimes called. The weather was the most charming that could be wished for, a true South African day, and, had the march been 12 miles instead of the 18 or 19 that it actually was, we should have been better pleased. Arriving on the top of a nek, or dip in the hills, we saw a huge plain in front simply covered with troops, all dismounted and resting. These were Broadwood's Cavalry and Ian Hamilton's Mounted Infantry, and, after a while, they moved off in advance of us, we following in an hour's time and reaching Jacobsrust just before dusk.

Our first business on arrival in camp each day was to see to the provision of wood and water for cooking purposes, no easy matter in a treeless country like the Orange Free State. When there were trees, wood parties were sent out under an officer, and sometimes wooden fencing posts were brought in from round the fields. Later on, when we moved further North and wood became more scarce, men used to pick up these fencing posts on their march home into camp, but, as they never knew where camp was to be until they reached it, sometimes they were let in to carry these logs of wood for miles. Occasionally, but very seldom, a few small houses were ordered to be destroyed, and in that case the troops were allowed to take the wood out of the doors and windows, floors and ceilings. This did not often happen, though, as great precautions were always being taken not to do any unnecessary damage or to alarm the people of the country needlessly. A better substitute for firewood was also found, under the guidance of stern necessity, to be dried cowdung, and towards the close of the campaign the men used this in preference to wood, as it was easier to get and lighter to carry.

Whilst the wood and water parties were out, there was nothing more to be done except to wait until the wagons arrived with the blankets. This was a matter, sometimes of minutes, sometimes of hours, and it was in order to guard against any possible delay in the movements of the wagons that every man was ordered to carry, in addition to a blanket, two days' rations of tea, sugar and biscuit, and one day's ration of meat in his haversack and canteen, which were regularly replaced when consumed. Thus every man had in his possession the wherewithal to make a meal, either in the middle of the day when a halt took place with the intention of allowing the men to cook, or on arrival in camp.

The meat ration was driven with us in the form of slaughter oxen, and immediately on arrival in camp the butchers, who rode on a wagon and did not have to walk, set to work and killed sufficient oxen to supply the Brigade. It is said that sometimes the butchers killed a tough old trek ox by mistake for a young heifer, but this statement is, I am sure, a libel. The butchers were allowed to sell the liver, heart, head, etc. of the bullocks and sheep killed, at a certain fixed price; so, when the slaughtering was going on, there was sure to be a small crowd of would-be purchasers waiting.

Sometimes when the Brigade arrived late in camp the issue of rations would take place several hours after dark; but as every man had that day's rations carried on his person in addition to the next day's groceries and biscuit, there was not really anything to complain about, except the inconvenience, which was unavoidable. Many men did not at first, however, realise that they had two day's biscuit in their haversacks, and used to eat it all, or most of it, on the first opportunity. There came a time, also, when, without notice, *flour* was issued for the second day's ration, and our improvident friends were fetched up with a round turn.

Owing to the difficulties of transport and to the fact that every mortal thing had to be carried with us—the country furnishing nothing but cattle and forage—the ration question was always a troublesome one to the regimental officer. No doubt it is an awkward thing issuing fresh meat on the march, but what could be done? Preserved meat could not be carried owing to the weight, and so the trek ox had to be cut up and served out at no matter what hour. No doubt the pound-and-a-half of meat, when cut up into portions, looked very small, and was often so uninviting, that many of the men threw away their meat ration, such as it was. Personally I do not think that the meat ration issued in this way is nearly large enough, and it might with advantage be doubled at the very least. By the time the bone, scraps, skin and dirty pieces are cut away from a portion of meat representing the rations of a section calculated at three pounds per man, and this again is subdivided into each man's little chunk, it will be found that what was originally considered as three pounds has dwindled to a pound-and-a-half or less. The Boer prisoners, whom we rationed, laughed at the idea of existing on the soldier's ration of a pound-and-a half of meat, and complained to the General and got more.

Whilst on the march it was impossible to make any other arrangement than that each man should be responsible for his own cooking. This was necessary in consequence of the liability of any man to go off on picket, on guard, or on any duty where he might be detached from the bulk of his comrades. The utmost that the company cooks could do to be of benefit was to occasionally boil the water for the tea and let each man make his own brew. Not that he could make many brews out of his ration; far from it. In a laboratory, no doubt, carefully weighed rations of tea will make a certain quantity of quite a respectable drink, but in the field when the soldier has to carry his tea, tied up in a bit of rag, it certainly does not go far enough, and the man has to drink water, with every possibility of enteric supervening. Again, tea made in bulk as in military kitchens at Aldershot is quite a different matter to the same article made in a canteen out of the miserable pinch which constitutes one man's ration for one day. Similar arguments apply to the coffee and sugar ; in fact the whole question of rations in the field needs revision. What we would have done without the Brigade Canteen which the General started, I do not know; but the quantity of tea, sugar and foodstuffs generally sold in that institution was only limited by the amount that could be purchased in the towns.

On the march, the column usually halted at the regulation intervals of time as prescribed in the drill books, of five minutes after the first half-hour's marching and ten minutes on the completion of each succeeding hour. There is some slight modification needed in this regulation, as experience gained in marching, not only in South Africa, has shown : the first halt is not long enough and should be at least ten minutes or even longer, to enable men to fall out if they wish it. After that, the halts should be for five minutes on the completion of each half-hour's marching.

A full hour is too long to continue moving, carrying the heavy weight that men do on the march, and a few minutes rest after half an hour's walking is better than a long spell after an hour's march. The weight of the blanket and the other equipment on the shoulders, which may not appear to be great on first putting it on, soon reminds one of its presence, and the half-hourly halt enables the men to sit down and relieve their aching shoulders.

According to the regulations the proper place for the stretchers of a battalion is for all of them, with their stretcher-bearers, to move in rear under the medical officer, but common sense points to each stretcher being always kept with its own company.

In South Africa, movements were so extended and companies so far apart, sometimes, that the stretchers would have been useless if kept together ;

and it is much more reasonable for the two men to go with their company, wherever it might be, on picket or baggage guard, or escort to guns, or any similar duty.

All regiments did not do this, however; and once during the mid-day halt, we were much amused at the antics of a very military Volunteer doctor, who was in charge of a squad of stretcher bearers, and was trying to move them off with due decorum and a proper observance of their importance. After falling-in and telling-off, they took up and laid down their stretchers several times, just to wake things up a bit, and then they received the order—" Stretcher party, r-r-right—form ! "

This not being satisfactory, the doctor exclaimed " As you were ! Now on the word ' Right ' ! the right hand man turns to the right, the remainder at the same time making a half-turn in the same direction, " etc., and he delivered the order again; upon which, this intricate manœuvre being executed to his satisfaction, the whole party solemnly moved off, followed by the smiles of our men and a few muttered remarks, such as " 'e must 'ave thought 'e were in 'Ide Park " !

When our baggage wagons arrived in camp they were unloaded at once, and the rolls of blankets and great-coats taken off to the sections that owned them. The men then proceeded to erect their bivouacs, if they were particular, or to spread their blankets on the ground, if they were tired.

Sometimes it was our duty to furnish the pickets to protect the camp during a halt, and when this was the case the companies used to go off, as soon as they arrived in camp, to the spots pointed out by the Brigade Major, and make themselves comfortable there until daybreak the next morning; when either they were relieved, or else the column marched off and the pickets followed behind as a rear guard. The wagons used to go out to the pickets, if they were any distance off, with their blankets and great-coats; but if they were at all close to camp, as they frequently were, then the men used to carry out their bundles themselves. As a rule, we camped in a hollow close to water, which was either in a dam or a spruit (small stream), and the pickets were posted in prominent places on the surrounding hills. We had early learned to consider these pickets as really defensive posts, put out to hold certain prominent features, with a view to preventing the enemy from occupying them with guns and riflemen and from annoying us in camp, and not as outpost pickets with their visiting and reconnoitring patrols by day and night.

Cover from view was as much to be desired as protection from bullets and possible shell fire, and every man was told off to his own little position some distance away from the next man. Permanent objects like sangars and walls in exposed positions might serve to draw the enemy's fire more than was desirable, so, to deceive him, other positions were whenever possible utilised. At early daybreak every man stood to his arms for a while, watching especially points from which fire might be opened by the enemy. Cordite being smokeless, we, of course, never knew where the enemy actually was concealed, and could only fire at likely places, in the hope that he *was* there and that our bullets would make him keep his head and rifle safe under cover. Double sentries, especially at night, were of course an absolute necessity, and signalling communication was invariably maintained between the pickets and the camp, both by day and by night.

In the field there ought to be a weekly issue of tobacco, which should be considered as part of the rations : it is impossible, sometimes for weeks on end, for the men to purchase tobacco for themselves, and the loss or absence of this luxury is very severely felt. Tobacco is certainly procurable at some of the Supply Depôts at the bases, on payment, and twice during the nine months of our wanderings an issue was made to those companies which had money on hand with which to pay for it; the amounts which were due from the individual men were then charged through their accounts and, after a good deal of clerical labour, the transaction was concluded.

Owing to the greater necessity for carrying food, our Supply wagons usually had no room to carry tobacco; so that it was not often, in fact only twice, as has been said, that it was procurable.

The price was very inconvenient too; in a land where copper coins are unknown and the smallest coin is a "tikky," or threepenny piece, to charge 1s 4d. for an article means that there is always trouble over the change, which is increased if only half the quantity is asked for.

Smoking before food has been taken as productive of eventual thirst. It is extraordinary how men will smoke at all hours of the night, in fact whenever they are awake; but it is a practice which ought not to be allowed on the march, as the effects are surely felt later in the day when the heat and consequent thirst rapidly increase: this engenders drinking, and the water bottles are soon emptied before there is any chance of replenishing them.

Undoubtedly, men require careful training and education in these little matters, and, if they are properly attended to, as a result a long march may be comfortably carried out and the men brought in to camp in good physical form, not exhausted to the last stage, as they frequently are.

Our water supply when we were on the march was usually procured from the spruits or streams, but in the Orange River Colony we frequently had no other water than that procured from pools, more or less stagnant, and of a dirty yellow colour from the suspended impurities. The section of the Royal Engineers with our Brigade had a couple of hand pumps in their carts with the picks and shovels, explosives and other things that they carry in the field; and these pumps, immediately on arrival in camp, were fixed up at the water supply, and a sentry posted to keep off cattle and to see that the water was not contaminated by men washing in it.

Whilst on the march there was very little sickness from bowel complaints. No doubt the constant daily exercise in the magnificent climate and the excitement combined to render the men somewhat innocuous to the attentions of the enteric microbe, or, more probably, the water that we drank had not, up to then, been poisoned with these germs, although it was dirty enough in all conscience.

What with the constant smoking and want of self control, men usually drank a good deal of water on the march and during the day in camp or on picket : were the ration of tea increased in the field, as it might well be, to three times the present quantity, men would drink considerably less water on service and would save themselves a good deal of sickness. Men will not go to the trouble of preparing boiled water for their bottles ; but if they have sufficient tea to spare, they will often fill up their bottles with it.

There is nothing better to drink on the march than cold tea : it is an excellent mild stimulant, it is a gentle aperient, and it is also a febrifuge in a small way, besides being somewhat astringent : it clears the brain, too, and leaves a clean taste in the mouth. Veldt water, on the other hand, besides being a breeding establishment for the germs and microbes of nearly all the diseases under the sun, is nasty to look at, horrid to smell, and disgusting to drink : it invariably pours out in the form of sweat if the weather is at all warm, and it clogs the mouth and tongue with a mawkish taste which speedily requires more water to remove it.

Why the microscopic ration of tea should be increased on the same day by equally minute portions of coffee and cocoa has always been a puzzle. The advantage and necessity of varying the drink ration is understood, but why issue three kinds in one day, instead of tea one day, coffee the next, and cocoa the third? At the best of times the men had no place in which to stow the small portions of each of these articles which comprised the daily ration, and were, perforce, compelled to wrap each lot up in bits of rag and carry them in their haversacks.

Ration baskets were provided in which one day's groceries could have been carried in bulk by each company, but, as an order had been issued for each man to carry his own, these baskets proved to be useless lumber.

CHAPTER III.

TO ZAND RIVER.

On the march—Formations—Protection—Necessity of Mounted Troops—Engagement at Welkom Farm—Capture of Winburg—Soldiers and their Boots—Naval Guns.

In order to enable the force to be concentrated, the 21st Brigade halted on the 2nd of May at Jacobsrust, continuing their march the following day to Isabellafontein. The names of some of the farms are very curious and depend greatly on local conditions. The thick-skulled Boer farmer when he first arrived and selected his farm lost no time in dubbing it with a title, which, in after years, appears somewhat incongruous and confusing, as numbers of farmers hit upon the same happy idea of naming their locations Klipfontein, Doornberg, or Leeukop; and the result is that there are hundreds of places in the Orange River Colony with the same name—Doornkops are as common as dirt, whilst Deelfonteins, and farms called Modderfontein, or Muddy Spring, are quite numerous. Then, again, the settler, instead of naming his farm from the physical properties of the land or the quality of the water, frequently called it after his vrouw, so that one often came across farms called Ellensrust, for instance. Many others are named after animals, such as Hartebeestefontein, Wildebeeste Hoek, or Quaggafontein, while others are called Welkom Rust or Wonderfontein, the meaning of which is apparent.

The farms are all fenced with barbed wire, of generally three strands, with posts of wood or, more usually, of big slabs of quarried stone. These wire fences were of course a great hindrance to all mounted men and had to be cut in all directions.

On the march we used to move in column of fours, unless the veldt was broad and open, when we still kept our fours but moved the companies out to the right and left, so that we were really in a column of double companies moving in fours to a flank. This was a very good and simple formation, since the companies could open out or close in to the centre without difficulty, and at any time they were all handy and ready to move in any direction without the slightest delay. The battalion seldom or never moved in column of companies, as it was found that this was the most tiring formation of all in a long march, especially when the men were carrying a full kit. This full kit consisted of rifle, with magazine charged; haversack, with one day's complete rations and one day's issue of tea, sugar and biscuit; canteen and water-bottle; sidearms and equipment with 100 rounds of ammunition; and a blanket, strapped on the waistbelt at the back. All this totals up a good load, but there was nothing that could have been dispensed with, the blanket, which was most cumbersome and unwieldy, being really as necessary as anything.

The officers wore equipment the same as the men, and nearly all of them carried a rifle or a carbine. This was a most necessary precaution, as there is no doubt the enemy invariably directed their fire on the officers, and of course anyone seen to be dressed differently to the men, or not carrying a rifle, would be immediately spotted by the Boers. I asked some of the prisoners this question when we were escorting them from the Golden Gate, and they said at once that they always concentrated their fire on those who appeared to be the leaders.

The advanced flank and rear guards were always found by the mounted troops, who kept well away from us; as indeed they ought to, if they intend to keep the column beyond rifle shot of the enemy, which may be taken as fully 2,000 yards, or about a mile and a quarter. It will easily be seen what a farce a flank guard of infantry must be, unless it can move at such a distance from the column as will enable it effectually to protect that column, without hampering it or checking its progress. On the other hand, if the flank guard gets too far away from the column, it is liable to be cut off itself, whilst if it remains too close in, it does no good and merely masks the fire of the main body. It is a difficult question to answer—how is a column to protect itself in these days of long range rifle fire unless it has mounted men?

I saw a column on the march once which consisted of an infantry battalion with its full complement of transport and with a couple of guns, with their wagons, and the way the flank guards were put out was a study in how *not* to do it. Imagine an enormous rectangle, stretching along the road and extending about 200 yards on each side of it, the ends and sides of this rectangle being composed of men moving in single file and about three or four paces apart. Inside this rectangle was the main body, the baggage and the guns; and it is easy to conceive that, owing to so many men being used to form the ends and sides of the rectangle, there were hardly any left to make up the main body or to act as a reserve, while, from the formation adopted, nothing could be done by the men forming the sides, except to lie down if they were attacked. I never saw a more hopeless instance of slavish adherence to the drill books and utter want of common sense and adaptability to the conditions of service in this country. The commanding officer, who was a Staff College man, has since been badly stellenbosched.

A story is told of General Smith-Dorrien which is very characteristic of that gallant officer and worth repeating.

It seems that on one occasion, somewhere in South Africa, the officer commanding a certain battery of artillery was somewhat chary of getting too close to the enemy : perhaps he was thinking of his horses.

Getting tired of finding the battery to be always out of effective range, the General sent an order that the battery was to be brought up to where the 19th Brigade flag was planted. So the Major limbered up and advanced his battery up to the General, who promptly galloped on, flag and all, another 600 yards nearer the enemy, where he stuck his flagstaff into the ground and waited for the battery to carry out their orders, to come " up to where the flag was ! "

On the 4th May, whilst on the march northwards, we had our first experience, as a battalion, of shell fire at the engagement of Welkom Farm, or Wellow as it is sometimes called. The brunt of the fighting was borne by the Cavalry and Mounted Infantry, but the enemy dropped several shells in our direction, two of which burst at the the head of the battalion, but luckily did no damage. The battalion had advanced in column of companies, extended of course, in support of the mounted troops, who were manœuvring on our front and on our left. To our right and left front the hills converged and were held by the enemy's riflemen, who were, however, out of range. A couple of companies were detached to guard our right flank, moving parallel with us and keeping the enemy behind his cover, whilst a couple more advanced against the hills on our left front, which had by this time been cleared by our cavalry, not before they had come under shell and pom-pom fire and had experienced a few losses. One of our men,* was severely wounded on this occasion.

After climbing the low hills on our left front, we sat and watched the remainder of the Brigade

---

* Private D. Downer of A company.

coming along, and waited until the Cavalry had scouted some miles to our front before we finally left our position.

A very good view was obtainable from this hilltop, and it was disgusting to have to sit still and watch the Boer convoy trekking away in a north-easterly direction and about 4 miles off. We could see the wagons and long lines of bullocks distinctly, and little specks, which were probably mounted men, darting about up and down the road. However, nothing could be done to stop them, and so they slowly passed out of sight.

It was very interesting to see, watching from the top of the hill, one of the other regiments of the Brigade advancing in attack formation, in column of companies extended about ten paces; and, even at the very great distance they were away, it was curious to notice how the officers and section commanders showed up in the intervals between the long extended lines. They were, of course, in their proper places and only a few paces in rear of their sections, but, even two miles away, one could recognise the black speck in front of the centre of the company, and the other tiny atoms moving along in rear of the half-companies and sections.

There is no doubt it is a sound principle that, when extended, officers, supernumeraries and buglers should invariably march in the extended line amongst the men, from whom, if this is done, they are practically indistinguishable. The companies and sections can just as well be controlled from the ranks as from any other position half a dozen paces in rear, and the reduction in the size of the objective which the enemy is looking at is worthy of consideration.

During the afternoon we went on to the farm near the river and there camped, but after this long day's work we still had the pickets to furnish, and sent out several companies to the hills to the north and west of the camp for this purpose. However, picket duty, except for the slight extra marching entailed, is no great hardship on a fine night when wood and water are plentiful, and one has always the consolation of knowing that some other regiment will be on duty the day after.

Winburg was reached on the evening of the next day after a long and tiresome march. We camped near the railway station, and found the piles of wooden sleepers very easily split and very useful for our fires. The town is situated at the end of a branch railway which joins the main line at Smaldeal Junction, about 20 miles off, and which will in time, no doubt, be prolonged to the north-east and connect with Senekal, which is distant about 34 miles. Winburg is a small town of the usual description—Church in the middle of the market square, a couple of small hotels, two or three decent-sized general stores and a few small houses. The railway makes a curious curve when entering the town, and runs round three parts of a circle before it finally pulls up at a tiny station.

The line and the station buildings were untouched when we arrived, but no engines or rolling stock were left for us. The Boers had not long been gone when our cavalry entered the town and demanded its surrender, but our horses were too much done up for the mounted troops to continue the pursuit. The Boer forces were so very mobile—as they naturally would be when moving about in their own country and acting always on the defensive—that to allow our mounted troops to get too far in front and away from the infantry would have been a tactical error. It might have resulted in the separation of our columns and their attack in detail by the Boers, who would then have had a great advantage.

The battalions in the Brigade were ordered to

be weeded out of all men unable to perform steady and continuous marching, and we accordingly had to leave a goodly number of lame ducks behind in charge of Major Panton.* Some of them had bad and worn-out boots, ruined, most likely, by the salt water on board ship, and by the want of dubbing but the large majority were suffering from sore feet, caused in nine cases out of ten either by badly-fitting boots or by want of attention to the feet. These had occurred in spite of orders and warnings without number, but it seems impossible to get the soldier to pay any attention to his feet.

There is not a medical man or a pedestrian who will not say that it is absolutely necessary to change the socks frequently and to wash the feet invariably at the end of a march. There is not a soldier in the service who will not insist that this practice softens the feet and leads to blisters and subsequent falling out.

Until some very drastic measures are introduced preventing men from receiving boots too small for them, and legislating for their better preservation and for proper cleanliness of the feet, our army will never be able to march any better than it does at present. The man to blame is the man who wears the boots, but he cannot be brought to see that, or to listen to words of experienced men who were marching with soldiers when he was in his cradle. The agonies which some men will endure from a badly-fitting boot are beyond belief. I have seen, in Ireland, a man draw out his foot, covered with blood, from his boot, after a 5 miles' walk, and be unable to march for weeks afterwards.

The pluck and endurance and indomitable perseverance shown by men with ill-fitting boots

---

* Major Panton ultimately succeeded in marching these men (drawn from all four battalions) up to Irene, where they rejoined the Brigade on the 9th of June, three days before Diamond Hill. They had covered 15 miles a day, acting as escort to a large ammunition column.

proves devotion worthy of a better cause, but it has been a marvel to me for the last twenty years, why bitter experience has never taught the foot soldier to wear boots large enough for him. It is a well-known fact that after some marching has been done, a larger size in boots is required, as the feet swell and need more room; but the soldier, with an 8-2 foot when he joins, will go on asking for 8-2 boots until doomsday, and will have a grievance if he is compelled in the field to wear a pair of 9-3's, as he should be.

Whilst on the march we were compelled to resort to individual cooking, since every man carried his own ration, and this practice worked well, although a great deal of time was taken up by each individual which might have been better employed in sleep or rest. The men seemed to be always cooking; what with looking after the fires, collecting wood and *mest*, or dried cow-dung, and fetching water, the whole camp seemed to be perpetually moving round their camp fires, frying and boiling until a very late hour at night. The issue of flour instead of biscuit was responsible for a great deal of the time wasted in cooking. Some of the companies used to arrange for the cooks to prepare, in the camp kettles, hot water for the men to make their own tea, but it was impossible to arrange to cook the meat in this way, as each man had his own portion served out to him by his section commander.

Many men cooked and ate their scrap of meat in the early morning, others finished it off at the mid-day halt, whilst a great number threw away their little bit of tough trek ox rather than carry it all day, steaming and jostling about in a smelly canteen, or wrapped in a dirty piece of rag and crammed into a haversack, cheek by jowl with some tobacco and a pair of socks, perhaps.

This canteen was the only cooking pot the

men had, although in the course of time many of them procured tin cans, the Australian " billy," to assist in making their tea or coffee. The canteen is not an easy thing to keep clean at the best of times when it is in constant use, and we had no opportunity of replacing those which wore out by the constant cooking.

We had to thank De Wet for this. One of the trains which was wrecked by him contained many thousands of new canteens which, months afterwards, could be seen lying by the side of the line, reduced to their original factor of sheet iron.

After leaving Welkom Farm the rearguard was overtaken by the Highland Brigade, who were following in support to our Brigade; with them were two of the famous 4·7 naval guns, manned by a party of bluejackets—at least the men wore straw hats, but the rest of their kit was the same as ours.

The guns had been rigged up on temporary field carriages, designed by some bold man, which would have made an official in the Royal Gun-carriage Factory turn ill with horror.

First of all came bullocks—about forty of them—dragging an absurd-looking gun, mounted on an equally curiously-made limber, with enormously broad wheels. This was dragged muzzle first, contrary to all precedent, with the gun pointing over the bullocks' backs. The trail was supported on a little low carriage with a boom sticking out behind like a tiller; and a tiller it was undoubtedly, for two bluejackets hung on to it, and, by shoving it to port or starboard, guided the gun in the proper direction.

Whilst in Winburg the following order was issued by General Ian Hamilton, commanding the entire force, which was henceforward called the Winburg Column :—

Extract from Brigade Orders. Winburg,
5th May, 1900.
"The G.O.C. Winburg Column has much

pleasure in informing the troops under his command that he has received from the F.M. C.-in-C. in South Africa a telegram, in which Lord Roberts expresses his high appreciation of the good work recently performed by all ranks in the Winburg Column. His lordship has yet to hear of the further success achieved by the capture of Winburg. During the past thirteen days a portion of the Winburg Column has marched over 100 miles, fighting the enemy on nine separate occasions, and capturing two important towns. The other portion of the column has borne at least its full share of the very successful operations which have followed the battle of Houtnek. The G.O.C. cannot therefore but feel that his column has fairly earned, not only the praises of the F.M. C.-in-C., which are published separately, but also a day or two of comparative rest. In the same message, however, in which Lord Roberts expresses his high appreciation of the successes we have achieved, he directs us not to slacken our efforts for several days to come. The enemy is hurrying northwards to concentrate, and it is of nothing less than national importance that his movements should be impeded, and his guns and convoys if possible captured. Thanks to the good work which has already been accomplished, this column now finds itself better placed to carry out the Field-Marshal's wishes than any other portion of the troops under his command. The opportunity is a great one, and Gen. Ian Hamilton confidently appeals to the officers and men of the Winburg Column to make the very best of it, regardless of the fatigue and privation which will probably have to be undergone before success is secured."

The next day—the 6th of May—we made an

afternoon march, together with the 19th Brigade, Smith-Dorrien's, and the Cavalry and Mounted Infantry, of about 9 miles, to a farm called Dankbarsfontein. The "fontein" in this instance belied its name, and instead of being a gushing spring of clear, sparkling water, which would have pleased the heart of Sir Wilfred Lawson, it was a succession of dirty puddles which would have created dismay among the ranks of the A.T.A. had there been any of their members left!

We remained a couple of days at this festive spot, but marched on the 9th of May to Bloomplaats. This was a well-to-do farm, with plenty of water and good grazing, and with a herd of halftame buck which careered about all round the camp at 40 miles an hour, raising clouds of dust. Of course some sportsmen went out and stalked these frolicsome animals, and were followed by others, the result being that in a short time there was a good deal of indiscriminate shooting going on, and life hardly became worth living; so that these keen *shikaris* had to be fetched back. The amusing part of the show occurred later, when a Mounted Infantry picket, who were lying about on the look-out a mile or so away, had a shell dropped close to them by the Boers. They scattered with promptitude, and a few more shells came over in the same place. We could not see the Boer gun, which was fully two miles away, for a long time, but at last we caught the flicker of the sun on the breech block as it was swung into position.

In addition to all the firing at the buck every time they raced round our camp, there had been a good deal of desultory firing going on all the afternoon between the Mounted Infantry, who were on our right, and the Boers, who were holding some low hills some miles from us. We could see a few mounted Boers riding about now and then, but their guns were well concealed, and their men did not show themselves.

CHAPTER IV.

THE FIGHT AT ZAND RIVER.

Description of the Action—The Final Charge—Necessity of continuing to Advance—Prisoners—Their Impressions—Fire Tactics.

On the 10th of May we made an early start from Bloomplaats, leaving the camp at 4.30 a.m. This means being up at three o'clock, and it was pitch dark at that hour; but the General's object was to reach the drift, a few miles away, before daybreak. This we did just before early dawn, and found a company of the Derbyshire Regiment holding it on the far side. There was water, about a couple of feet, in the drift proper, but boldly—and like fools—we waded across and clambered up the other side, and extended among the mimosa bushes. Fools we were, indeed, as a few yards further up the sluit we could have crossed dry shod, and saved ourselves the tender feet from which most of us suffered, brought about by a long day's marching with wet socks—which resulted in our poor feet being simply boiled in our boots.

It was just after dawn and fairly cold, so that we were glad to see the sun rise and to get on the move ourselves again. Bye-and-bye an order came for us to pass on through mimosa bushes which were scattered about on the north bank of the Zand stream, towards the hilly ground on the east. Towards the north the ground was open and level and treeless for a couple of miles; then it rose a little, and ended on the skyline with a biggish kopje to the north west. To the east the ground also rose a little, and about 2 miles away culminated in a ridge running across our front from north-east down to east, gradually getting higher, and ending in a confused jumble of black hills running down to the river; somewhere among these black hills being the gun, which I have previously mentioned as having dropped a shell or two into the Mounted Infantry picket, near our camp at Bloomplaats. The whole of this ground was treeless and grassy, but a few mimosa bushes were scattered about on the hills to the east, and there was a good fringe of these prickly bushes down on the river banks.

Through these bushes, and past a couple of isolated houses, we were working our way in column of companies, extended, towards a low hill, an underfeature which jutted out towards us from the higher hills beyond. Having gained the shelter of this, we closed in a bit, ascended the slope, and lay down in quarter column, the leading company just below the top of the hill, and the rear company at its foot.

So far all had been peaceful and quiet, and some of the hungry ones had already started on their biscuits, when phit, ping-boom, phit, phit, came the Mausers, and we woke up to try and grasp the situation. The General had sent forward a few men over the hill-top to the other side, Captain Robinson and some of C company had gone, and the enemy, who, up to now had lain low, had greeted them with every demonstration of affection, and continued to do so for some little time. Our men could do nothing but take cover and return the fire of the invisible Boers: they had played their part, had drawn the fire of the enemy, and had induced him to show his hand.

Apparently expecting that a column of troops would soon advance against them over the top of the hill, following on the track of our few men of C company, the enemy now maintained a heavy rifle, shell and pom-pom fire on the edge of the crest line, a few feet above us. We, sitting on the ground close under the lee of the hill, were perfectly safe, and could not be touched by any Boer shell so we had nothing to do but to listen to the bursting of the shells and to watch for the fragments striking the ground beyond. The noise was terrific, and at one time there was a perfectly awful outburst of roars and screams and pounding, as the pieces of shell went shrieking and whizzing over our heads, while, throughout the fearful din, we could hear that infernal pom-pom-pom-pom-pom, five times, which denoted that the Vicker's-Maxim, belonging to the Boers, was hurling its disgusting little shells at us.

The whirring and the shriek of these spiteful little beasts, as they strike the ground and burst into hundreds of vicious, stinging fragments, is, at first experience, the most disconcerting sound that I know. Throughout the whole of this pandemonium—which lasted perhaps ten minutes, and then settled down into the occasional dull roar of a bursting shrapnel, and the whiz and flop of the fragments—the Mausers were going ping-boom, ping-boom, and the enemy's Maxim was in full blast at frequent intervals.

Sitting under the side of the hill, we could see to our rear, most of the other troops of the Division, all advancing to take their part in the attack, and hastening lest they should be too late. Following in our path through the mimosas, and in similar formation, came one of the regiments of our Brigade; they had just reached an open space half a mile in rear, when, being apparently spotted by the Boer gunners, plump came a shell, close in front of the column. A little to the left it was, so the bursting fragments flew harmlessly onward, while the onlookers drew a deep breath of relief, and the regiment quickened its pace, well knowing what was to be expected next. Soon it came, plunk-plunk, and we held our breath; two shells, two clouds of dust, in rear of the hastening battalion

Luckily the Boer gunners had not allowed sufficiently for the distance advanced by the regiment, while they were laying the guns.

Following in rear of this battalion came the Camerons, but they wisely led off to their right, and got under shelter of the high banks of the river—not, however, without being spotted and plugged at by the enemy, harmlessly as it turned out; and so they passed on beyond us.

Far away out in the open veldt dashed a battery of our Artillery: round it swung and unlimbered: in a second or two off trotted the horses to shelter, and the gunners began to drop their shells, at 3,000 yards, on to the ridge held by the Boers—not, however, without reply, as the enemy shelled that battery with vigour for some little time. Over and over again did we, from our shelter, see a cloud of dust rise amongst the guns, now in front, now between them, now in rear; and yet the little black specks ran unconcernedly from the guns to the limbers and back again, and every now and then, with a sheet of flame and a muffled roar, did the gunners send back their defying answer to their hidden enemies.

A similar game was being played on the other side of the river, where, miles away, came a battery in column of route, heading unostentatiously for the drift: suddenly the enterprising Boers flopped a shell, followed by another, first on this side of the battery, then over their heads. "Action-right" was the yell, round wheeled the guns, and boom-boom, came the answer to the Boers. A few shells exchanged places, and then the battery limbered up and trekked on quietly to the drift.

In the far distance, towards the south-west, came acres of troops, clouds of cavalry, columns of infantry and the dense dust of great baggage lines, while over the sky-line sailed peacefully a huge balloon, looking unconcernedly down at us pigmies below, striving to oust each other from tiny little kopjes. This was Tucker's Division, coming up from the railway on our left rear, and by this movement causing the Boers, in due course of time, automatically to fall back from their right flank.

About this time, we also began to move—half of B, the rear company, being sent out to our left front, where a battery was coming into action behind the hill by indirect laying, and the other half moving along about a mile to our left, and slightly to the rear, to a point where the ground rose gradually in a long gentle swell until it joined the ridge above. This half company was sent by way of keeping an eye on the other side of the grassy slope, and it soon reached the ground and lay down in extended order. Letter A Company was then dribbled out, man by man, each about ten yards apart, in the same direction, with orders to move towards the end of the ridge: they came under some long range fire as soon as they quitted the shelter of our hill, and, bearing off rather too much to their left, eventually got round where B company was, lay down and opened fire. The Volunteer company was then sent on in the same way, and worked along to the spur, where A and B companies were gradually creeping along, upwards towards the ridge. Meanwhile D and E companies had moved out about a quarter of a mile to their left, and then turned and advanced towards the ridge. C company remained where it had halted earlier in the day, and was joined by F, both companies being held in reserve. The Maxim gun had been sent to a low spur on our left, where it came into action at 2,200 yards against a sangar on the top of the ridge, so as to cover the advance of the other companies; and the remaining two companies, G and H, were brought along behind the Maxim, and then sent forward in front of it.

This was the situation at about the middle of

the morning. The battalion was extended over about a mile and a half of front, facing a ridge occupied by the enemy and distant some 1,500 yards, the companies being, in order from right to left, thus: D, E, ½B, G, H, Vols., A, with C and F and half B in reserve. Our right was on a spur rising up towards the ridge, the centre was lined across a large open valley, and the left was on another spur which also ran up the ridge.

There was a round kraal on the summit of the ridge, at about the centre, in which the enemy had a gun, and where one or two men could be seen moving. The battery, over our heads, shelled this spot briskly, but without much effect, and we, from a closer range of 2,200 yards, turned our Maxim on to it, and searched the whole hillside in the neighbourhood. After a while a man, shown up distinctly against the sky-line, walked calmly out of this kraal, passed along and disappeared over the hill. One or two more followed, and then a little clump with, presumably, the gun in their midst, moved slowly out and away beyond view. All this time a heavy fire was being kept up by all the companies in the firing line, the Maxim was stuttering out bullets like mad, and the guns were dropping shells along the ridge, whilst these plucky Boers calmly and deliberately moved their gun clean away.

The instant it was gone, our slow and cumbrous Maxim hitched in its mules and advanced to a closer position, where, behind a wall at about 1,600 yards, its fire again searched out the slopes of the hill, especially to the left of the circular kraal—the spot where the enemy's gun had been—where a number of stone walls, rising in tiers, seemed to point out a likely hiding-place for Boer sharpshooters. Meanwhile the firing line had been gradually closing up nearer to the foot of the hill, and we had spotted, at 600 yards, a Boer using black powder behind one of these stone walls, and were making it warm for him. Another advance or two, and we were nearer still to the ridge, when suddenly, like a flock of pigeons, up rose a crowd of men from behind the tiers of stone walls, and bolted up the hill. With a roar, our men were on their feet and after the Boers, racing madly up the hill, shouting, cheering, cursing the heavy blankets bumping at their backs, yelling with delight, regardless of the shells from our battery in rear screaming and whistling over their heads and plumping on the ridge.

Panting and blowing, the heavy equipment dragging them back, our fellows struggled on, and when close to the top of the ridge, with a final rush (headed in the centre by Markwick, Treagus, and H. B. Mills), gained the summit and paused to take breath. A few Boers had waited too long and now remained for ever, one with Mobsby's bayonet in him, whilst the others were trekking as fast as their ponies could carry them away from the cursed rooineks.

Numbers of loose ponies were about, and a few Boers opened fire on us from a knoll about 600 yards to our right front; while many others could be seen riding rapidly away. To hasten their departure, we fired a few volleys at 1,100 yards at these gentry, the squad who fired at them being rather a mixed one, consisting as it did of the Second in Command, the Adjutant, a Second Lieutenant, and four or five men hastily scratched together—the whole under command of Lieut. Ashworth, who had only enough breath remaining to yell "Fire!" It is said that the oldest soldier of this squad "pulled off" and spoiled a volley; but perhaps he did not know very much about musketry!

The advance was continued very shortly afterwards, as soon as the men had got their breath;

and soon all firing ceased, the Boers disappeared, and we devoted ourselves to looking about us and wondering where the Cavalry had got to.

After a few minutes, by which time most of the battalion had come up, we continued our advance as we were, without reforming, down the slope of the hill, across the valley, and up the gentle slope of the opposite hill, where we posted look-out men and reformed the companies.

Those that were on the right originally had been pushed off slightly to the right front, after occupying the hill we attacked, in order to search a kopje some little way off. Coming down the hill, after the rout of the Boers, everyone was on the look out for loot, as there were all sorts of articles strewn about, such as rifles, saddles, bandoliers, blankets, and great-coats; while there were numbers of loose ponies, ready saddled and bridled, quietly cropping the herbage. Quite a dozen of these were promptly annexed and mounted by the captors, who rode along in great pride. Each had a great coat and a blanket rolled on the pommel, with a horse blanket under the saddle, and a couple of saddle-bags, usually containing a quantity of Mauser cartridges in addition to some food. One man was lucky enough to find a bag of coffee and a bag of sugar on one saddle, and others found Boer tobacco, dried fruit and other small articles. Several dead Boers lay about on the ridge, and a number of dead and wounded horses were on the reverse slope of the hill, whilst our Volunteers, when they came in with A company from the left flank, brought about a dozen prisoners, who had surrendered.

It was a fortunate thing for us that we did not remain on the top of the ridge, but continued our rapid advance without delay, as this prevented the Boers from collecting and opening fire on us. That they attempted to do this is certain, as one

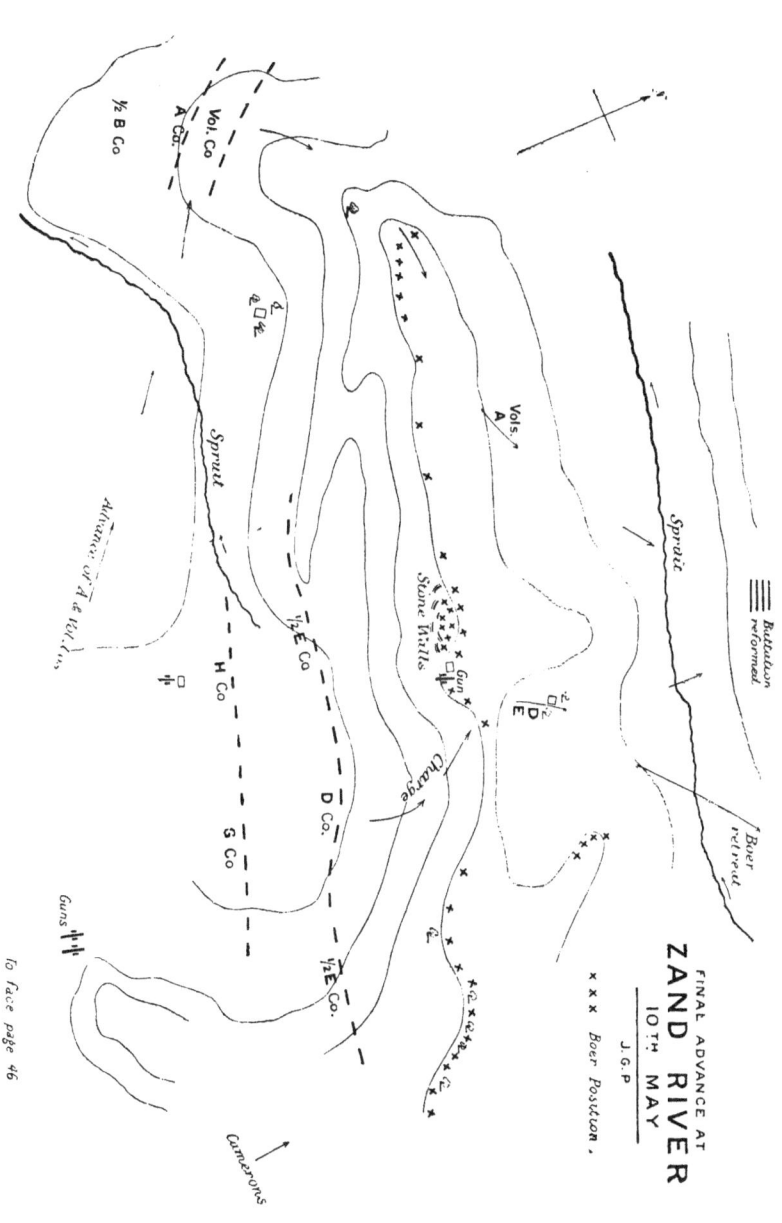

man of ours was shot dead on the top of the hill, and Second-Lieut. Paget was severely wounded, about the same time. The sharpshooters, however, who caused us these casualties, fled and left us in peace, when the companies on the right advanced towards them.

The usual practice at a field day is for the operations to conclude when the final charge has been delivered. Everyone then stands about, prefferably on the skyline, in full view of the supposed retreating enemy, who may perhaps be merely removing to a better position in rear.

To do this on active service is, I think, criminal. The advance should certainly be continued by some, if not all, of the first line; or at any rate the first arrivals should push on so as to cover the advance of those behind them. There should be no stopping; the enemy should be kept on the run, unless, of course, he has taken up another position in rear, in which case a bold front should be shown and he should be attacked at once while he is disorganised. There is always, however, the possibility of a trap having been prepared, and it has been a favourite trick of the Afridis to draw on our men to a position where they can be shot down at known ranges; so that considerable caution is necessary.

After forming up the whole battalion and calling the rolls, we joined the rest of the Brigade, and moved on a few miles to Erasmus Spruit, a nice little camp with good water and shade, and plenty of grass and wood. Now that the excitement was over we all felt pretty tired, and were glad to rest and get a meal.

The next morning we had some conversation with the prisoners, one or two of whom spoke English. They were the usual farm hand sort of type, some of them being young lads, of about the stamp of the recruits whom we get. They did not seem to mind having been captured, and were very grateful for what tobacco, coffee and other little luxuries we could give them.

One of them told me that the Maxim fire was terrible—*they dared not put their heads up to fire.*

I have never forgotten that remark, since the man made it to me, and there is a great deal in it to which the attention of company officers and section leaders might with advantage be drawn. The main point is that we Infantry do not fire nearly enough ammunition when delivering an attack. Of course we see no enemy: we only hear the crack of his rifle and the whiz of his bullets: but we sometimes see the splash of the bullet on the ground, and can from that obtain some slight idea of his position at the time. Having found that, a constant hail of bullets should be directed at all parts of the position, high and low, at rocks, at bushes and at all places likely to afford a hiding spot, with the object always in view of making the enemy keep his head down behind his cover.

For this purpose volley firing is useless, and what should be adopted is controlled individual firing, using the magazine *always*, and refilling it behind cover when, and as often as, an opportunity occurs of so doing. There should be no breaks or intervals, either in the firing or in the advance: the latter should be continuous, as in the old skirmishing days, until the last possible moment, when, if the men cannot advance any further, they should take cover and employ themselves in firing as rapidly as possible.

The wretched system of false economy in the use of blank ammunition at instructional field days, when a man carries perhaps five rounds in his pouch and five in reserve, is responsible for the fact that men cannot be got to fire fast enough in the field, and that they lie under cover and husband their ammunition, firing only occasional shots, as they have been taught in peace time. They forget that they are now more widely extended than formerly and that one man now occupies as much space as was formerly allotted to five, and that he should, therefore, fire five times as fast as before. The present system of widely extended lines is merely what was learned by the troops employed in the Chitral and Tirah expeditions, two or three years ago; and the system of fighting adopted by the Afridis is practically the same as that used by the Boers in the Free State and the Transvaal.

Owing to the widely extended lines adopted by us in our advance at Zand River, and to the steady shelling by the batteries which the enemy received during the attack, our casualties were not very heavy.*

The following order was published by the General on the day after the battle :—

Twistniet, Zand River,

The Major General Commanding desires to express his pleasure at the behaviour of the brigade yesterday. The good leading of the officers and the conduct of the men enabled a strong and numerously held position to be captured with a slight loss.

---

* Our losses on this day were as follows :—

KILLED.

Private W. Webb   D Company.
   „   G. Merritt   H   „
   „   W. Goodes   E   „

WOUNDED

Second Lieut. R. E. Paget
Corpl. W. Backshall   B   „
Private E. Cam   B   „
   „   W. Osborne   G   „
   „   P. O Connell H   „
   „   G. Shepherd   C   „
   „   H. Overy   E   „

CHAPTER V.

ACROSS THE VAAL.

Kroonstad—The Road to Lindley—Drifts—Lindley—Heilbron—Elysium—The Vaal at last.

The day after the Zand River fight we had a long rest, and did not start on the march again till after mid-day; and a terribly long march it was, the Brigade not getting into camp till considerably after dark. It being our turn to be advanced guard, we had to find the pickets as soon as we arrived in camp. The worst part of all night marches is the slowness of the pace; the troops creep along with frequent halts, either to rest or to reconnoitre the road, and what appears to have been a twenty mile march, has in reality not been more than half that distance.

On the 12th May we started off after breakfast at about nine o'clock, with another long march of 17 miles before us; but this one was done in good style, as we halted for three hours in the middle of the day to rest and cook a meal. Eventually we fetched up in our new camp, a few miles outside Kroonstad, about six in the evening.

This town is, after Bloemfontein, the largest and most important in the Orange River Colony; it is well situated on the main line of railway, and is a popular resort in the summer owing to the boating on the river. There is one large hotel and several smaller ones, some large stores and the usual public buildings—landrost's office, post and telegraph office, bank, etc. The Boers had on their retreat done considerable damage in this town by burning the goods shed at the railway station, and by blowing up the railway bridge; but the latter was the most serious by far, as the loss of the goods shed did not affect the military situation in the least. The bridge was a fine lofty structure with huge stone piers and enormous steel girders ; two of the piers were blown to pieces, and we found the girders hanging down into the water. There is another large railway bridge about a mile away, but luckily the Boers made no attempt to destroy it.

Our engineers were soon on the spot, and at the end of a few days (certainly under a week) had found and repaired the old deviation which was in use before the bridge was built, had made a low bridge of sleepers over the drift, and had trains running without any more trouble. These old deviations exist at every river where there is now a bridge, and were made years ago when the line was building ; so that all our engineers had to do when a bridge was blown up, as they were at Glen, Vet River, and many other places, was to find the deviation, clear out the weeds, lay the rails, and repair the line where it required it ; and trains were running again in, probably, a day or two. One great drawback, however, was the want of engines and rolling stock, as the Boers had removed all they could take away up country, and we could not get nearly enough engines and wagons from the Cape railways to satisfy our requirements.

There were a few supplies left in the town, and a wagon load was bought for the regimental canteen, most of the contents, milk, jam, tobacco, matches, sugar and eatables generally, being sold out the same afternoon. The Staff Officer for Supplies had been round the town before our canteen people got in, and had collared nearly all the tea and sugar; but we managed to get a good quantity. After having been on three-quarter rations for the best part of a fortnight, our men were quite ready to buy any amount of foodstuffs, especially tea and sugar.

Two days did we halt here and enjoy our well earned rest, but on the 15th of May we were off again on the road to Lindley—and such a road! Even now, after many months, one remembers as in a nightmare that cursed road to Lindley, with its ever recurring drifts and its messages—" The General wishes you to send a company to the drift to assist the baggage," or to repair the road, or to pull wagons out of the mud. The drifts were the steepest and the worst that we experienced in perhaps all our trekking. The full distance to Lindley was about 48 miles, but, the first march being only a short one, we made the last two average over 15 miles each, both of which had more than their proper allowance of drifts.

It might be as well at this stage of the proceedings to describe what a bad drift looks like to an unprejudiced and impartial mind.

A drift is really a crossing place over a river, which latter is called a sluit, if it has water in it, or a spruit if it is dry; and whether the drift is easy or difficult for wagons to cross depends on the banks and the bottom. Thus, a shallow drift gives no trouble at all; but if the banks are steep, the mules and oxen go down one side with a run, even if the brake be well screwed up on the wagons, and invariably get mixed up at the bottom, getting their legs over the traces and pole chain: or perhaps one is pulled down, when there is much confusion and delay. If the bank is very steep on the other side, fatigue parties have to come and push the wagons up by main force, or else a team of bullocks is brought from another wagon and hitched on in front of the team which is in difficulties. Even then there is more delay, as the business is to get all the thirty or thirty-six oxen to pull simultaneously; and to induce them to do this, half a dozen drivers with their enormous two-handed whips, like huge fishing rods, flog the wretched animals unmercifully, yelling and screaming all sorts of insults in Basuto at the trembling beasts.

If there is mud or water at the bottom of the drift, the difficulty is increased enormously, as the banks become slippery. It is doubtful which are the worst animals to have in your wagon when crossing a bad drift, mules or bullocks. The mules generally get mixed up with the harness, but on the other hand, when once they are started pulling all together, they certainly do tug all they know, and need no more incentive than a row of men on each side of the path yelling at them. Bullocks, however, are faint-hearted and difficult to manage, as they will lie down when they have had enough of it, and nothing will induce them to pull when they think they cannot do any good. There is one good point about bullocks, and that is that if they can only be induced to lean into their yokes, all together, their enormous bulk and weight will move anything. The greatest abomination of all in a drift or on a road is sand, as that causes trouble with both mules and bullocks; and our worst drawback has been the native drivers, as, owing to the enormous number of wagons in use by the troops, the supply of good drivers ran short, and any coolie was accepted. It was the same with the conductors, or civilians in charge of wagons, who were all supposed to be experienced transport riders; but one little man confided to me that he was nothing more or less than a baker out of employment!

The Boers, when trekking with their wagons under ordinary circumstances, take things very leisurely at drifts, and hitch on an extra team at once if there is the slightest sign of trouble; but this, although the best plan, wastes a lot of time, and we never had any time to spare on the march.

Lindley, like most of the towns we visited, is situated in a hollow, and on topping a rise in the ground we saw it at our feet. It is a small town, but has* given more trouble than any other in the colony, as it and the neighbourhood has been nothing more than a hotbed of rebellion for months; in fact since we first entered it, when the majority of the surrounding burghers took the oath of allegiance and surrendered what old guns they had—of no use even to scare crows with. It is built on the same river, the Valsch, that runs past Kroonstad, and in its most palmy days contained only a few hundred inhabitants.

On the 19th of May General Ian Hamilton issued the following information in the Winburg Column Orders of that date :—

"With the occupation of Lindley, the provisional seat of the Free State Government, the first part of the task allotted to the Winburg Column has been accomplished to the satisfaction of the Field Marshal Commanding in Chief.

"The next task allotted to the Column is to lead the advance northwards and to capture the important town of Heilbron."

Our entry into Lindley was entirely unopposed, and we camped a mile south-west of the town, about four o'clock in the afternoon of the 18th of May. There was an immediate rush into the town of all those who could get passes in search of bread, besides butter and other delicacies to ameliorate the condition of the regulation biscuit, which by this time had become harder than usual. However, the Canteen cart got private information, and secured a cask of butter and several boxes of eggs, which were duly sold to the men of the regiment early next morning. There was nothing else procurable in the town, except a little fresh bread.

After a day's rest at Lindley, we trekked off again on the 20th of May, starting at

* December, 1900.

seven o'clock; and fortunate it was that we did start so early, as there was a considerable amount of firing on the rear guard, and a fairly lively action going on until about midday. We were with the main column in front of the baggage, and had of course to regulate our pace by the rear guard; but we heard afterwards that as they were leaving the neighbourhood of the town they were followed up by a large number of mounted Boers, whose presence was not expected by the Mounted Infantry forming the screen in rear of our troops; these Boers pressed our men rather closely, one or two of the Mounted Infantry, who found themselves hung up at a barbed wire fence, being captured, and a few men being wounded. There were some narrow escapes, Lieut. Lloyd, the Supply officer, having to ride all he knew to get clear, and the mess cart belonging to the Mounted Infantry being abandoned; the men in charge had only just time to take out the ponies and bolt for their lives.

We did not get into camp until after dark, and the baggage was later still, as there was a nasty drift over a sluit at the entrance to the camping ground; fires had to be lighted to show the wagons the way across. The 19th Brigade and some of the Mounted Infantry camped a few miles lower down, where there was another drift over the same stream.

After a march of seventeen miles, on the 21st of May, we found Heilbron in front of us; and the next day, after a short spell of ten miles, we camped to the south-east of the town, such as it is. Heilbron comes distinctly under the category of "one horse" towns, notwithstanding that it is connected by rail with important cities, and hopes in due course of time to have its railway prolonged to Bethlehem; but until that happy occasion Heilbron is vegetating. It is a Mark IV town of the usual pattern—

Dutch Reformed Church in the middle of the square, one or two melancholy streets stretching slowly away at right angles to each other, a hotel, conspicuous for the entire absence of anything which, in happier climes, constitutes refreshment for man and beast, a despondent-looking shop or two with a large stock of lemons, medicines, sheep dip and ironmongery, and some tired-looking inhabitants holding up the door-posts of their houses.

We headed off towards the railway main line on the 23rd of May, and camped that afternoon at a place called Spitzkop.

Next day, the Queen's Birthday, the band turned out at reveillé and played " God Save the Queen," causing the greatest outbursts of cheering from the other regiments, which was taken up and continued by the Cavalry and Mounted Infantry. That day we marched to the railway and struck it, and then trekked off, some miles north, to the neighbourhood of Elysium, where we camped on a great rolling plain, extending for miles in every direction. The march was an unpleasant and a lengthy one, as the whole surrounding country was either a burning grass fire or a place where there had been one, and we walked over dust and ashes, which parched the mouth and interrupted the breathing. In many places on the veldt the grass grows in small clumps, somewhat isolated from each other, and although this looks pleasant enough to walk upon, you soon find that these little grassy bunches put you out of your stride and upset your balance time after time. This is, if anything, rather worse than when the grass has been burnt off.

The following Brigade Order was published on the 26th of May :—

" The G.O.C. wishes to express his appreciation of the fine spirit and excellent marching shown by the troops composing the 21st Brigade since it was formed at Glen on April 29th 1900. Since then the Brigade has marched 250 miles, and the effect of this long and rapid march has been that the enemy has been unable to complete his preparations for defence, and has been repeatedly compelled to retreat in front of us after a weak resistance. The force is now a few miles off the Vaal River and not 50 miles from Johannesburg, and the Major-General is sure that every man of the 21st Brigade wishes to share in the entry into that town, and that every possible effort will be made by all ranks to attain that object."

After starting on that day, the 26th of May, we halted for several hours to enable a part of Lord Roberts' main column to pass us, so that our baggage should not become intermingled. We were crossing their path, which led them to the north, while we were heading north-west.

The country is marvellously open between the the railway and the Vaal River; not a tree was to be seen, hardly a farm—nothing but endless rolling veldt as far as the eye could reach, covered with grass. There was no view, nothing to rest the eye or give the fatigued brain a little relief. As soon as a gentle rise was topped, the same expanse was to be seen in front, with some slightly rising ground in the far distance, from which the same view of interminable veldt would, in due time, be procurable.

After many, many miles of this sort of travelling, we at last saw, from the top of a rolling down, a silvery streak winding in and out on our left front, fringed with a few scattered green bushes.

At once everyone's spirits rose, and we stepped out briskly, and, sure sign that camp was near, all the men began to chatter; and with reason too, for was not this silvery streak the great Vaal River, dividing us from Paul Kruger's territory, and would not we be over it before we halted? Certainly we would; we would get that far at any rate; no more camping for us till we had secured a sound footing in the Transvaal, which we had come so many thousand miles to see and conquer.

A couple of hours afterwards, under a setting sun, we were at the drift, and what a sight was there! We were fording a crossing at a shallow bend of the river, and it had been necessary to cut down the banks and improve the approaches, so that the wagons might have some chance of getting over. Meantime the south bank was crowded with wagons and vehicles of all kinds, guns, baggage-wagons, Cape carts, water-carts, ox-wagons, ammunition-carts, mule-wagons, drawn up in long rows, patiently waiting their turn to be dragged and pushed across.

The infantry troubled themselves not the slightest about all this, but passed stolidly down to the water's edge, stripped off their boots and socks by companies, and stepped gingerly into the eighteen inches of dirty water. On their left, within a few feet, was an endless succession of wagons streaming across; a little further down was a wagon with ten jibbing and obstinate mules, who had got into deep water and heeded not the yells and whip cracks of their two black boys, themselves unwilling to go further into the water than they could help. On the farther side fires were being lit to show the drivers what was land and what was water, and superhuman efforts were being made to keep the wagons moving ahead up the steep, rocky bank so as not to block the road.

Never was there a more weird military scene. Every nigger was yelling like a fiend, and cracking his whip like mad over the flanks of his wretched animals, soldiers were shoving at the wheels of every wagon, Staff officers, cool and collected, were dispersed at intervals directing operations, the worried baggage-master, dancing with rage, was using the most dreadful language on a jutting bank, and the infantry, with their boots slung round their necks and their socks in their pockets, were trying to avoid the sharp stones of the bottom.

So it continued without intermission till about midnight, by which time nearly all had been got across. Our footing in the Transvaal was gained.

CHAPTER VI.

DOORNKOP.

On the way to Johannesburg—29th May—2 p.m.—Attack begins—The advance—Checked by flanking fire from One Tree Hill—Attack of this position—Through veldt fire—Final charge—Boer retreat—Gordons attack simultaneously — Main attack pushed home —Casualties.

On Sunday, the 27th of May, we started at 8.30 a.m., and marched some sixteen miles before camping. Bitterly cold it was that night, and we felt it a good deal the next day, when we started at 6.45 a.m. and trekked 10 miles to a small hill a little south of Cypherfontein; here, during most of the afternoon, we heard shells and pom-poms and other indications of a brisk fight going on towards the north. Away to the south we could see dimly Lord Roberts' troops, who had crossed the Vaal at Vereeniging, higher up than we did, pressing on to the junction of the railways at Elandsfontein. Our business, we now learned, was to push off to the left and make an enveloping movement on the enemy's right, whilst General French delivered his blow in front and Lord Roberts fell on the Boer left.

We therefore made an early start, and were under way at 6.30, despite the severe cold, and, with the 19th Brigade leading, headed north-west, so as to come up on the left of Johannesburg. We spent the earlier part of the day marching and halting and moving on again, and watching the cavalry on our right, and the shrapnel and pom-pom shells bursting; until about two o'clock we were moved out from behind a hill, upon which was a battery busily engaged in shelling the enemy's guns, one or two of which were in position on some low hills about a mile and a half away. We lay down in the open grass with big intervals between companies. At the same time the City Imperial Volunteers had pushed on to the left of the guns, and the Derbyshire had also gone out in companies in widely extended order. And so we lay and watched and waited.

We were at the end of a long grassy valley, with smooth, rolling hills rising on our left and on our right, these latter separating us from Smith-Dorrien's Brigade; in front of us and blocking the end of the valley the hills swung round from the left and trended off to our right front, leaving a sort of gap in what might be called the right top corner of the picture; this we afterwards found to be the nearest way to Johannesburg. The smooth hills on our right rose gradually and ended in a cluster of rocks, surmounted by a solitary tree—an ideal position, in which we afterwards found that the enemy had a field gun, a Maxim and endless riflemen.

In front of us, the low hills which seemed to close in the valley, and indeed part of the valley itself, had suffered from a grass fire, and only an occasional ant-hill showed up grey against the black soil.

We had moved slightly to our right and had extended a little, and were again lying down in the grass; suddenly the enemy's guns spotted us and sent along a couple of shells, clear of us, luckily, but near enough to the lagging water-cart to make it increase its pace somewhat abruptly.

We had watched the C.I.V.'s pass out of sight along the ridge to the left, and then we had seen the Derbyshire moving along in the same direction. The enemy's gun, right in front of us, up the valley, we could with difficulty locate, but it was carrying on a plucky duel with our battery.

At last we got orders to move: D company led off first, followed by E, both in widely-extended lines, officers and all supernumeraries being in the ranks; and, with intervals of some 80 or 100 yards between the companies, after these followed F and G, and, behind them again, came H, the Volunteers, A, B and C. The Maxim gun went with the leading company, and, under charge of Captain Green, operated on its left. Soon after the companies led off they began to come under the long range fire of the Mausers, and the little spirts of dust were rapidly becoming more numerous as the lines of skirmishers diminished the distance between themselves and the enemy. At last it became necessary to subdue the enemy's eagerness somewhat, and the leading lines dropped down on the veldt and opened fire on the invisible Boers. After a while the skirmishers rose to their feet and advanced. whereupon the enemy's fire redoubled in intensity : regardless of the bullets, which were falling pretty thickly by now, a few men having been hit, our men pushed on, and, with the supporting lines which came up in rear, rapidly drew nearer to the enemy's position. Soon shots were observed to be coming from a new direction, from our right front, where, a long distance away, was the cluster of rocks and the solitary tree, which we had previously noticed as being a likely position for the enemy's sharpshooters.

After a little while there was no possible doubt upon this question, because, as our leading lines crept forward, the dropping shots from the right front became vastly more numerous, while one or two more casualties occurred. All this time the enemy on our front were keeping up a brisk rattle of musketry, but as our men were fully seven to ten paces apart this shooting had little effect upon them ; not so however, the cross fire from our right front, which caught us diagonally, as it were, and caused a few more casualties. The machine-gun had come into action on the left, but was soon spotted by the Boers, who concentrated a pretty heavy fire on the unfortunate Maxim, which, with its big wheels, and the huge shields to the limber boxes sticking up in the air, provided the Boers with a target that they did not often get. Sergeant Funnell was shot in the head almost immediately the gun came into action, Archer and Hunnisett were knocked over, and only two men left to work the gun, which ceased firing for some minutes until Corporal Weston and two men from the nearest company, D, volunteered to assist. As it was so palpable that the enemy's fire was being concentrated on the gun, Captain Green ordered the detachment to lie down and use their rifles.

The wheel mule, an acquisition of the battalion dating from Bethulie (where the animal, a fine specimen of its kind, was found wandering in an ownerless state), was hit in two places, while the lead mule was so alarmed at this untoward accident to his stable companion, as to be quite petrified with fear and unable to move. When the advance took place he had to be abandoned, and the gun went on with " Bethulie " alone.

The leading companies had by now been reinforced by some of the supporting companies in rear, but had reached a limit from which further advance would not have been possible without very serious loss, so they lay down and blazed at the rocks and clumps of bushes which concealed the enemy. For some little distance now the advance had been carried out over the scene of the grass fire, which was even then still burning away on our right, and the only cover the men had was an occasional ant heap ; but even this was but little protection from the stinging flanking fire which was whistling over from the right.

Noticing that the firing line seemed to be checked temporarily, and soon discovering the cause, an officer from the rear succeeded in turning the flank sections of F and G companies, together with some men of E company, and making a demonstration against our friends on One Tree Hill. These fellows, however, were quite wide awake, and made it hot for this small party, who were attempting to create a diversion in the state of affairs.

Their firing increased in intensity; Corporal Hollington and one or two others were shot, and our men, who were only about 800 yards from the position, soon abandoned the drill-book style of advancing by alternate sections (which only caused the enemy's fire to be doubled and redoubled as they gleefully took aim at the full-length figures of our soldiers), and continued their advance by crawling on their hands and knees through the long grass, and by keeping up a continued dropping fire on the rocks concealing our enemies. Not a single Boer had any of us seen since we started, and, at this stage of the proceedings, none of the enemy were likely to show themselves. Looking back, we could see heads behind us—a long way, certainly, but they showed that the Colonel had observed our flanking movement and had despatched a company to our support.

Emboldened by this, we pressed on, but our crawling progress through the grass was brought to a sudden end by our reaching the edge of a rapidly-advancing grass fire, while before us stretched a waste of burnt ground, with a few, a very few, grey ant heaps showing up. There was only one thing to do, and that was done quickly; springing to their feet, the two or three officers with this little party yelled to their men, who dashed on with shouts and cheers, through the flickering fire and the smoke, on to the bare ground beyond. They raced on rapidly, the faster runners outpacing the others, until breath began to go and knees to totter; and after a couple of hundred yards or so, we were glad to drop into a schanz, or long trench, which we found suddenly at our feet, and halt there to regain our breath.

We still kept up our fire, and the enemy's began to slacken, and at last almost ceased ; there was no time to waste if we wanted to see a Boer, so we jumped out of the schanz and dashed on as fast as our heavy equipment and cumbrous roll of blanket would permit us towards the rocks, now silent as the grave.

Bearing off a little to the left to some slightly rising ground, we found ourselves alone ; but what a sight was in front of us !

The ground dipped and rose again in a gentle slope of grassy fields with a rocky patch on the summit, about 1,100 or 1,200 yards away ; and these grassy fields, about twenty or thirty acres in extent, were alive with fugitives moving rapidly towards the rear. Among them (and this is a curious circumstance which puzzled us not a little at the time and afterwards) were a number of mounted men, dashing furiously amongst the runaways. The sight of these riders careering wildly among a crowd of flying Boers stayed our volleys for some moments, while we overhauled the scene with our glasses. Could these mounted men be our cavalry suddenly appearing from the right flank, where we had left them ?

No, they could surely not have travelled the distance in the time, so we formed up what men we had at hand and poured several volleys at 1,200 yards into the retreating enemy. After ten or a dozen volleys had been fired, a Highlander appeared among the rocks on our right, and, holding up his hand, shouted to us to stop firing. Wondering at this, reluctantly we complied, and the enemy quickly dwindled away ; we had serious thoughts of following them rapidly, but, seeing how few men of ours were actually on the spot, and in view of the possibility that the Boers would hold the rocky patch on the summit, we decided against it, and proceeded to overhaul the rocks on our right, which but a short time before had been teeming with riflemen.

In a cunningly-selected nook was the spot where the enemy's gun had been at work; all round the ground was strewn with empty shell boxes, fifteen or twenty of them, and the grass was thick with the little cardboard boxes in which Mauser ammunition is issued. Several large tins still had a quantity of rusk biscuit remaining in them, but these soon disappeared into our fellows' havresacks; a few blankets were lying about, and the usual camp litter and rubbish showed that a party of some strength had had their head-quarters on that spot since the day before. Two or three dead horses were in the vicinity, and a couple of wounded ones were put out of their agony; while several others browsing on the short grass were quickly collared.

Ensconsced among the rocks were two or three Boers, shot dead behind their cover by the bullets of our little flanking attack, as was proved conclusively by the attitudes of the bodies. All around, scattered in the most ingenious clefts among the rocks, were heaps and heaps of cartridge cases, Mauser, Lee-Metford, Steyr, and Martini, showing exactly the well-chosen positions of their former owners, and convincing us that thousands of our bullets might splash and splatter on the rocks close by without disturbing the occupants, until the fixing of the bayonets and the unrestrained advance of British soldiers caused that cold feeling down the back which no Boer could afford to disregard.

In a most ingeniously selected corner between several big rocks, improved by the addition of a few stones into a bullet-proof sangar, had been the enemy's Maxim, luckily for us not laid in our direction, but pumping forth lead against the

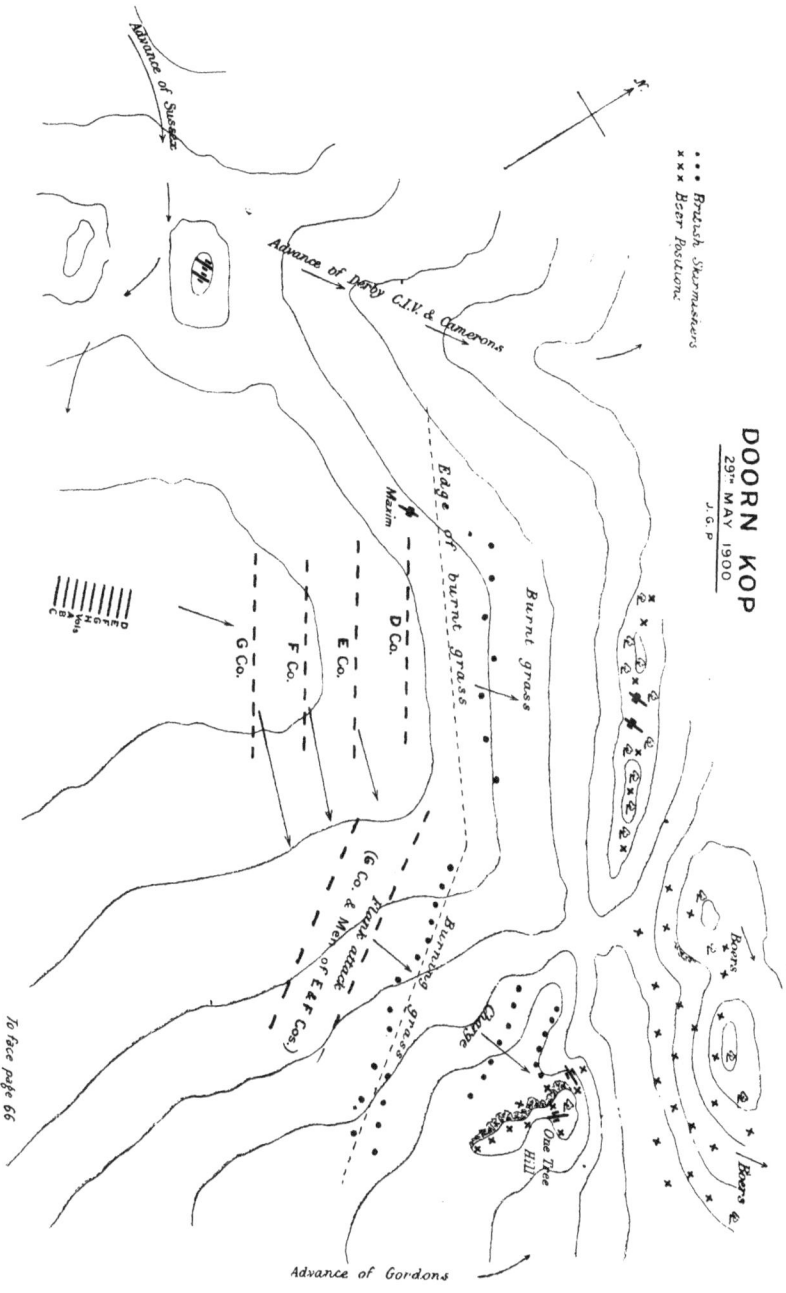

attack of the Gordons, which, unknown to us, had been carried out on the other side of the ridge separating the two regiments. Apparently the dashing 800 yards' charge of the Gordons, in which they suffered such severe loss, had been taking place about the same time as our advance from the schanz, across the burnt grass; but whether it was our appearance so close to them, or the sight of the Gordons, so gallantly pushing on, which caused the enemy to retreat in such a hurry, none but the Boers themselves can decisively say.

Anyhow, we claim for the Royal Sussex the honour of being the first to reach One Tree Hill. When we originally rushed up to this spot, some few minutes were wasted in searching with glasses the crowd of flying Boers, one or two more minutes before men could be hastily gathered together on the knee ready to fire, and about a dozen volleys had been hurriedly got off before the Highlander, to whose appearance I have before alluded, came out from among the rocks and waved to us to stop firing.

Dusk was closing in, so we reformed the companies which had taken part in this attack on One Tree Hill; they were principally the flank sections of E, F, and G, with a few men of D and some of the rear company, C, who were following in our support; and we moved off to join the remainder of the battalion.

We found that they had been at first checked by the cross fire from One Tree Hill, and by a considerable fire directed on them from the front, but had held their own, pouring in a constant fire, until the pressure on the right weakened somewhat the intensity of the Boer musketry, and enabled our men to continue their advance over the bare, level, burnt up ground.

The advance became quicker and quicker, the men came up with a livelier step and at last could be restrained no longer, and, with cheers and yells, which were taken up by the supports in rear, they dashed up the slope.

Here, amongst the rocks on the summit, they found the usual signs of recent occupation, cartridge cases and so on, and traces of the gun, which had evidently been removed some time earlier, besides a number of loose ponies, whose owners had apparently been unable to ride or unwilling to waste time in mounting.

The companies then formed up and joined hands with those who had been engaged on the right; the rolls were called,* and we moved off to find the Brigade, eventually discovering that our camp was to be just beyond One Tree Hill and practically on the field of action. Here in the dark we sat and waited for our baggage: no water, no wood was procurable, and we had eaten nothing except a scrap of biscuit since six o'clock that morning. Those who had husbanded their water during the day now scored, and, with what bits of wood they had secured from the Boer shell cases, and had since carried on their backs, soon had their canteens boiling.

Later, the baggage arrived, and the water carts, the contents of the latter being divided among the companies; and the men soon settled down, tired out and hungry, and dropped off to sleep among the piled arms.

---

* Our casualties were as follows :—

KILLED :—		DIED OF WOUNDS :—	
Private J. Simmonds,	D Co.	Corporal J. Hollington,	E Co.
„ H. Braiden,	G Co.	Private W. Lucas,	F Co.
		„ G. White,	G Co.
		„ H. Wells,	Vol. Co.
WOUNDED :—			
Sergeant W. Funnell,	C Co.	Private G. Pelling,	F Co
Corporal W. Backshall	B Co.	„ E. Colwell,	„
Private J. Archer,	C Co.	„ G. Fuller,	G Co.
„ C. Ellis,	D Co.	„ E. Young,	„
„ E. Honeysett,	.,	„ A. Vitler,	H Co.
„ E. Cooper,	E Co.	, H. Wells,	Vol. Co
„ T. Smith,	F Co		

CHAPTER VII.

PRETORIA.

Johannesburg—Pretoria—An abortive conference—The entry and march past—The people—The town—Irene—Botha again fails to appear.

A few miles march on the 30th May cleared us from the scene of the battle of the day before and brought us into one of the mining suburbs of Johannesburg, Florida, where we camped in the midst of mining shafts and engine houses. Some few of the pumps were going, clearing out the water, but the majority of the mines were shut down and in charge of the Kaffir Mines Police; no damage had been done to any of them that we could see.

On the 31st of May the following Divisional Order was published:—

The G.O.C., has much pleasure in publishing the following extract from a letter just received from Lord Roberts:—

"I am delighted at your successes and grieved beyond measure at your poor fellows being without proper rations; a trainful shall go on to you to-day. I expect to get the notice that Johannesburg surrenders this morning, and we shall then march into the town. I wish your column, which has done so much to gain possession of it, could be with us."

Two days we rested after our heavy day's work on the 29th, but we changed our camp to a new spot, more to the north and closer to the town. This was Bramfontein, and we were allowed to go into the town and inspect it, and make such purchases as we could.

Lord Roberts wired to the War Office on the 30th of May as follows:—

"The brunt of the fighting yesterday fell on

Ian Hamilton's column. I had sent him, as already mentioned, to work round to the west of Johannesburg in support of French's cavalry, which was directed to go to the north, near the road leading to Pretoria. I have not heard from French yet, but Hamilton, in a report which has just reached me, states that about one o'clock in the afternoon he found his way blocked by the enemy strongly posted on some kopjes and ridges three miles south of the Rand. They had two heavy guns, some field guns and Pom-poms.

"Hamilton at once attacked. The right was led by the Gordons, who after capturing one extremity of the ridge, wheeled round and worked along it until after dark, clearing it of the enemy, who fought most obstinately. The City Imperial Volunteers led on the other flank and would not be denied, but the chief share in the action, as in the casualties, fell to the Gordons, whose gallant advance excited the admiration of all.

"Hamilton speaks in high terms of praise of the manner in which Bruce Hamilton and Spens of the Shropshire Light Infantry handled the men under Smith-Dorrien's direction."

Johannesburg is a fine town, a long way superior to Pretoria or Bloemfontein : it owes its sudden rise and wonderful growth to its situation on the Witwatersrand and to the enormous development of the mining industries within the last few years.

No doubt when all the shops are open and the streets filled with the usual well-dressed crowd, it must make a fine appearance. When we first entered the town it looked quite desolate, with the magnificent plate glass windows boarded up and the doors covered with corrugated iron, evidently in anticipation of severe rioting and looting. Johannesburg has a most magnificent town railway station at the Park, with waiting rooms and offices, all of ornamental brick, mahogany and plate glass, fitted up in the most gorgeous style with silk curtains, marble floors and decorated ceilings. This is where the millionaires condescend to embark on the train, when they think of honouring one or other of the South African cities with their presence. The contrast between the elaborate Park station and the hovels that serve for stations at Elandsfontein and Bramfontein, is too absurd for words.

On Sunday, the 2nd of June, we were off again at seven o'clock; and the next day found us still heading off towards the north-west of Pretoria, apparently with the intention of circling round, and descending on the capital from the north or northwest. However, while we were on the march, our direction was changed, and we came back on our tracks, having received orders to march straight on Pretoria. When this order was passed by the mounted officers, there was a certain amount of excitement, naturally, as Pretoria was our goal and destination. The band struck up a march and there was a scene of much enthusiasm, one regiment in particular cheering madly, and some individuals producing Union Jacks, which they flourished with all their might.

So on we went, and about three o'clock reached the shelter of the hills outside Pretoria. The 19th Brigade went up the hills a little way, and the rest of us lay down and waited to see if we were wanted. Some of the men fell out and wandered away to the reverse flank, but quickly came running back, as bullets were dropping over the hills, apparently fired at long range and considerable elevation. Indeed, a couple of the City Imperial Volunteers were hit by these spent bullets. Later, the Brigade camped close by, and in the dark, to our astonishment, we found, alongside of us, some of the Sussex Yeomanry; and then we heard of the unfortunate accident to the Duke of Norfolk, which precluded his taking any further part in active operations, and which, unfortunately, prevented our seeing him either.

The 5th of June was the great day of the campaign, culminating in the withdrawal of the enemy and the entry of the victorious troops into his capital.

Very early in the morning, De Lisle's Mounted Infantry had pushed on into the town from the position gained by them the previous evening, and, meeting with no opposition, had demanded its surrender, but were received by Commandant Botha with a request for an armistice and a conference. This was of course agreed to by Lord Roberts, and nine o'clock was the hour fixed for the meeting. Towards that hour, therefore, all the troops who had marched with the 19th and 21st Brigades under General Ian Hamilton, were entering the pass which wound through the hills into the valley of Pretoria. This pass was quite two miles in length, and the surrounding country was composed of a succession of low, broken hills, which, if they had been held by a determined enemy, would have given us considerable trouble to capture. It has always been a marvel why the Boers did not defend Pretoria, surrounded, as it is, by a network of hills, topped by several strong forts built, I suppose, for that purpose; but probably the fact was that they would have been unable to get their big guns dragged up and mounted in sufficient time to oppose our advance, and therefore thought it wise not to risk them. Undoubtedly, Lord Roberts' rapid advance, or rather his dash from Bloemfontein to Pretoria, will be recorded in history as one of the remarkable military achievements of the century; and the breathless rapidity with which his movements were planned and executed had possibly paralysed the Boer commanders, and influenced their decision to sacrifice Pretoria, and to fall back to the east on the railway, as this would leave open a convenient line of retreat and an easy means of departure, whenever necessary, for Mr. Kruger and the foreign mercenaries, through Komati Poort and Delagoa Bay.

About nine o'clock, the hills opened out, and a mass of buildings could be seen in the dim distance: this was Pretoria, and, forming up on a low hill, a mile or two closer in, we were enabled to have a long look at the town about which we had heard so much of late years.

Between us and the town, and among a multitude of iron-roofed houses, was the famous racecourse where so many of our unfortunate prisoners had been confined: we could just distinguish with our glasses the big enclosure with its high fence of corrugated iron, but it was too dim and misty at that hour of the morning for us to make out much more.

Nine o'clock came but no Commandant Botha, and no signs of him, or of anyone else. We were all ready for a durbar or a conference, formed up in three sides of a hollow square, and everyone who could raise a kodak had produced it and pushed himself up into a prominent position, ready to take snapshots of the celebrities. And so we waited for an hour, speculating idly as to the cause of the commandant's non-appearance, and inclining to the belief that he was merely bluffing, to gain time to get his guns away; whether he was or not we have never heard, but it was a very suspicious circumstance that he played a similar game on another occasion, and caused us to wait two days, which would have been valuable time to us had we been able to advance.

Eventually the troops moved on, and camped to the west of the town and just outside the notorious race-course, where merely a few sick prisoners were now left, the majority having been moved some time previously to Waterval; while the officers had been confined in the Model School and other places in the town. On our approach, these officers, over a hundred in number, had succeeded in bouncing the few of their guards who still remained, and had effected their escape. They came and reported themselves to Lord Roberts, who afterwards inspected them on parade and congratulated them on obtaining their freedom.

The Brigade paraded in the early afternoon and formed up to march through the streets of the capital; the Derbyshire were leading, as it was their turn, and, headed by their band, they moved off in column of route; we followed, what was left of our band showing the way, and after us came the Camerons and then the C.I.V.

The streets were crammed with troops, as the Mounted Infantry and their baggage were passing along with us, and moving to their camp on the other side of the town; but when we approached the centre of the city they branched off to the left. The Guards' Brigade had preceded us and had left a number of men to keep the ground clear, as we entered on to the square. There, facing the Union Jack, floating (never again to be removed) proudly on the Town Hall, sat Lord Roberts on his charger, surrounded by the officers of his staff; while on the other side of the square, stood a dense, sullen mass of people—a few British subjects, but mostly foreigners who had business interests in Pretoria, with many women and children. What impressed us most was their silence: many of the women were in tears, and most of the men glared at us with anything but friendly glances. And so we passed on, saluting Lord Roberts, and meeting General Kelly's friendly glance, and marched away down the principal street, named Kerk or Church Street.

In a prominent position behind Lord Roberts, and surrounded by a mass of scaffolding, was a pedestal, where work had been carried on to erect a statue of the President of the Transvaal Republic. That pedestal, destined to remain unfilled, stood there, a monument of disappointed ambition.

Down Church Street we went for half a mile, swung off to the right, and returned by a parallel road to our camping ground, passing the Electric Lighting Company's tall chimney, where the enterprising mechanics had, with much danger and trouble, hoisted the British flag at the summit, and stood at their gate cheering us as we went by; one of the few marks of enthusiasm with which we were greeted.

The square in the centre of the town contains the most important buildings, the Town Hall and the Raadzaal being large and lofty modern erections; a large hotel, three banks and several minor buildings complete the list. In Church Street are numerous splendid shops, which then showed signs of trouble, most of them being blocked up with corrugated iron, which, in compliment to the troops, as heralding the approach of safety, the owners were commencing to remove as we went by. The rest of the town, which is well laid out, with broad streets running at right angles and planted with trees, consists of smaller shops and native stores, or of private residences—many of the latter built in the Indian style, with broad verandahs and large compounds, well planted and laid out. Further out to the west of the town are the suburban residences of the wealthier townspeople, in great contrast to the humble-looking dwelling of the President, which we passed on our way before we entered the square. Mrs. Kruger was still residing in the, to her, now lonely house, upon which an officer's guard had been mounted to ensure proper respect being paid to the old lady

Cleanliness was not a great point of the housekeeping, as may be understood from the fact that the sergeant of the guard was compelled to go and buy a bottle of Keating's Powder and some other disinfectant, the whole of which he had to sprinkle in the room allotted to the men as a guardroom, before it could be lived in.

We only stayed a day and a half in Pretoria, as on the 6th of June we were sent by half battalions to Irene, about 12 miles off, the first party moving at three o'clock in the afternoon and the others some hours later. The road winds for the first few miles, through a pass in the hills, in and out among dusty rocks, and then opens out on to the usual interminable veldt. Irene cannot be seen until the traveller is close upon it, as it lies in a fold of the ground; but it is not much worth seeing, anyhow, consisting merely of the railway station buildings, and some cement works. There is, however, a very successful irrigation farm in the neighbourhood.

Captain Maguire joined us here from England, looking very cheery, and full of keenness and eagerness to see some of the show before it was all over.

Lord Roberts issued a special Army Order in Pretoria which may be of some interest; it ran as follows:—

Extract from Army Orders, 7th June, 1900.

"In congratulating the British Army in South Africa on the occupation of Johannesburg and Pretoria, the one being the principal town and the other the capital of the Transvaal, and also on the relief of Mafeking after an heroic defence of over 200 days, the F.M.C. in chief desires to place on record his high appreciation of the gallantry and endurance displayed by the troops, both those who have taken part in the advance across the Vaal River, and those who have been employed on the less arduous duty of protecting the line of communication through the Orange River Colony. After the force reached Bloemfontein on the 13th March it was necessary to halt there for a certain period. Through railway communication with Cape Colony had to be restored before supplies and necessaries of all kinds could be got from the base. The rapid advance from the Modder River, and the want of forage *en route*, had told heavily on the horses of the Cavalry, Artillery and Mounted Infantry, and the transport mules and oxen, and to replace these casualties a considerable number of animals had to be provided. Throughout the six weeks the Army halted at Bloemfontein, the enemy showed considerable activity especially in the south-eastern portion of the Orange River Colony; but by the beginning of May, everything was in readiness for a further advance into the enemy's country, and on the 2nd of that month active operations again commenced. On the 12th May, Kroonstad, where Mr. Steyn had established the so-called Government of the Orange Free State, was entered. On the 17th May Mafeking was relieved. On the 31st May Johannesburg was occupied, and on the 5th June the British flag waved over Pretoria. During these thirty-five days the main body of the force marched 300 miles, including fifteen days' halt, and engaged the enemy on six different occasions. The column under Lieut.-Gen. Ian Hamilton marched 400 miles in forty-five days, including ten days' halt. It was engaged with the enemy twenty-eight times.

"The flying column under Colonel B. Mahon, which relieved Mafeking, marched at the rate of 15 miles a day for fourteen consecutive days, and successfully accomplished its object, despite the determined opposition offered by the enemy. During the recent operations, the sudden variations in temperature between the warm sun in the daytime, and the bitter cold at night, have been peculiarly trying to the troops, and owing to the necessity for rapid movement, the soldiers have frequently had to bivouac after long and trying marches without firewood and with scanty rations.

"The cheerful spirit with which difficulties have been overcome and hardships disregarded, are deserving of the highest praise, and in thanking all ranks for their successful efforts to attain the objects in view, Lord Roberts is proud to think that the soldiers under his command have worthily upheld the traditions of Her Majesty's Army, in fighting, in marching, and in the admirable discipline which has been maintained through a period of no ordinary trial and difficulty."

We moved off, after a day's halt, in a north easterly direction, but halted on the 9th and 10th of June, when it was said that Botha, the Boer Commander in Chief, was arranging a Conference which, however, seemingly fell through.*

---

*As to these abortive conferences, it was subsequently learnt from Boers on Gen. Ben Viljoen's staff that after the fall of Pretoria Botha urgently advised President Kruger to make peace on any terms he could, on the ground that the farms of the Transvaal had not yet suffered from the war, the issue of which was no longer doubtful. Kruger was persuaded, and the conference arranged; but at the critical moment De Wet brought President Steyn up to Waterval, and they insisted that the war, by which the Free State had already suffered so much, should be continued.—ED.

CHAPTER VIII.

DIAMOND HILL, FIRST DAY.

The attack begins—Description of ground—Capture of Boer advanced position—Night-fall.

On Monday, the 11th of June, began two days' heavy fighting; the operations were on a large scale against a strong and well-found enemy, posted, as we saw afterwards, in a position almost impregnable, along a front of six or eight miles, with his line of retreat open.

On the first day, the 11th of June, we were the leading battalion of the column, the Camerons being on baggage and rear guard and the Derbyshire and C.I.V's. with us. We marched at six o'clock and moved off towards the west; after trekking for a few miles we halted for some time under cover of a rise in the ground, from which we could see that the mounted troops were pretty heavily engaged in our front, over a considerable area. Away to our right front there was a plateau of great extent with a kopje of some size rising out of it; this kopje was being shelled with much spirit by the enemy, and on looking through our glasses we could see a fairly large party of mounted troops, either cavalry or mounted infantry, who were ensconced under cover of the kopje. To all appearance they were hung up in a state of compulsory inaction, as they could neither leave its cover nor take any offensive steps. They appeared to be quite safe, however, as regards shell fire, for the shrapnel seemed to burst beyond them or on the far side of the hill each time.

After a time we were put in motion again, but now in extended order, moving in columns of companies at wide intervals, G company, under Lieut. Nelson, leading, followed by H under Captain

Wisden and A under Captain Blake (Major O'Grady being temporarily on the sick list), and the remaining companies in the usual order.

The three leading companies moved along towards a deep ravine, at the head of which they halted in accordance with orders; but from there G and H, under command of Captain Wisden, were directed to advance across the open and occupy a kopje to the left front. On the left of this ravine were some farm houses lying under the lee of two small hills, from the summit of which a fairly extensive view would be obtained. The ground in front of these two hills was quite open for about a mile, but to their left a smooth grassy range of hills rose and extended back for some considerable distance, swinging round, about a mile and a half away, to the left and diminishing in elevation until the plain was reached, and thus forming a deep re-entrant angle, the inside of which was very fairly wooded and looked rocky on the top.

On our left the ground remained open, though undulating; but a wooded kopje rose out of the plain about a mile away, with two other kopjes of a lesser elevation on its right, and bearing off towards the re-entrant angle already mentioned.

This wooded kopje was the one that Captain Wisden was ordered to seize, and accordingly he sent off his companies in succession, in the usual widely extended formation, while Captain Blake followed with A company as a support, at a considerable interval. Captain Wisden met with a pretty wide and deep donga when he had gone about half way, and, while crossing this, a dropping fire was opened on him, but at a very considerable range (perhaps, 1,200 or 1,500 yards), apparently from the thickly wooded range of hills on his right. One or two sections were promptly formed to the right and replied to this fire, being relieved by A company, who came up very shortly and devoted themselves to pouring in a steady fire on the enemy, thus leaving Captain Wisden's two companies at liberty to continue their advance.

Just about this time, five mounted men were seen to leave this kopje and to move towards the range of hills, so G and H companies pushed on, while our battery, from the rear, opened fire and shelled the kopje over their heads. The companies led on steadily, and, when the guns had finished shelling, they rushed the hill and climbed to the top, where they remained, holding it for some little time.

Directly they showed that they were in possession of the hill, a move was made by A company towards the low kopjes on the right of that held by Captain Wisden; in this they were supported by the advance of B, C, and D companies under Major Panton, with Lieut. Nelson and Lieut. Ashworth in command of the latter two companies; the machine gun under Captain Green came along also. A company reached and occupied these small hills, and, the other companies coming up, fire was opened on the wooded and rocky hill beyond, which, it was now seen, was separated from us by a grassy valley about half-a-mile in width. The Maxim came into action also, and remained at this spot firing over our heads and covering our advance for some little time, after which it followed us. A consistently steady dropping fire was maintained on us all the time, and nothing could be done except to rush across the open, gain the end of the spur in front, and then, turning to the right, swarm up the hill in the hopes of taking the Boers in flank. We moved down the valley and across, and, when within a long run of the foot of the spur, the bugle sounded and off we dashed, shoving on our bayonets as we went, yelling and shouting like fiends. Breathless, we reached the foot of the hill, turned to our right, and commenced to climb it; the enemy had gone, and we were quite free from annoying Mauser bullets for a time; at least so we thought, until someone went a little too far and showed himself on the edge of the hill, facing the east, when one or two shots soon came whistling over his head.

Seemingly, the majority of the enemy were in position on an appalling high and continuous range of hills, stretching to north and south, as far as we could see. A deep and grassy valley about 1,500 to 2,000 yards in width separated us, but we had no time to waste in looking about us, as we had yet to reach the top of the spur, at whose foot we had only just arrived; so, keeping on the lee side of the hill, we ascended the spur until we reached the top, where we halted to await orders. In our rush across the little valley three or four men had been wounded.

While this little attack was being carried out, the Volunteer company had moved out in support of G and H companies, then in occupation of the wooded kopje, but had somehow left the kopje on their right and had gone off in a north-easterly direction towards the tremendous range of hills to which we found that the enemy had retired. The Volunteers met with some firing on their way, but were allowed by the enemy to come within about 800 yards, when suddenly a furious outburst of fire descended on the unfortunate company, compelling it to retire somewhat precipitately, until it got beyond range. The Boers must have watched their approach and concentrated their fire in anticipation of the Volunteers coming within medium range, for the number of rifles employed against the Volunteers was very large: the ground all round and amongst the men was covered with spirts of dust, while the noise was perfectly deafening and reminded one of the

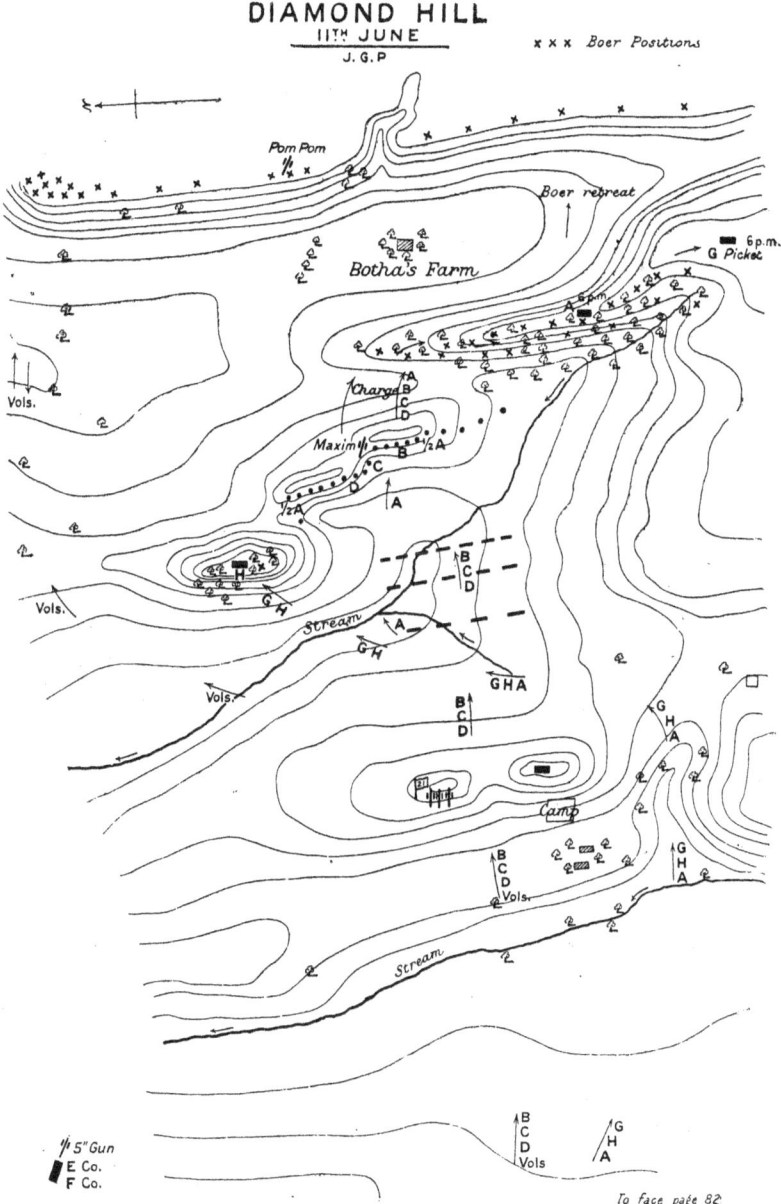

last stage of the attack at a field-day when every man is anxious to finish his ammunition. Wonderful to relate, only two men were wounded; but this was doubtless due to the very extended line maintained, both in the advance and the retirement. The enemy had a pom-pom on the hill which also contributed its quota of noise and clouds of deadly fragments and flying splinters.*

The battalion, after remaining until dusk on the top of the hill, received orders to march back to camp near the farm from which it had, earlier in the day, advanced to the attack. Three companies, however, had to remain on picket, including H company, which was to stay on the kopje it had originally occupied. G company was therefore sent for and posted on the top of the hill, and A was directed to remain about half way down the spur, while the remaining companies made the best of their way back to camp, which they reached about six o'clock.

We had to wait some time for our baggage; E and F companies, who were escort to the two five-inch guns, did not come into camp at all that night, but joined us late the next morning.

---

*Our casualties during the day were as follows:

WOUNDED.

Lce-Cpl. G. Washer, B Company.
Private A. Hobden, C ,,
,, J. Clapshaw, B ,,
,, E. Baker, Vol. ,,
,, J. Caldwell, Vol. ,,
,, J. Miles, G ,,
,, T. Gainsford, A ,,

MISSING.

,, Ebsworth, F Company.

This man of F Company seems to have wandered off, without permission, to a farm, where he was promptly sniped by some Boers, wounded and taken prisoner: a lesson to others: some men, however, will only learn by bitter experience.

CHAPTER IX.

DIAMOND HILL, SECOND DAY.

Boer main position—Reconnaisance by Lieut. Morphett—Advance of C.I.V.'s—General advance—Failure of Boers to occupy outer ridge—They hold the second crest in force—No further advance possible—Nightfall.

The following day, the 12th of June, we did not start very early, but moved after breakfast up to the hill we had attacked and captured the previous day, where A company was still on picket. Arrived there, we waited for some time, until the afternoon in fact, before we moved again.

In front of us, across the valley, was a long ridge, steep of access on our side and, apparently, flat on top ; this ridge on our right ran down into the valley in a grassy slope, becoming less and less steep as it trended further away; but on our left it became more and more precipitous, until, in the far distance, it appeared almost like a wall. There were no signs of the enemy on it, but they were there all the same.

There was a farm in the valley below us surrounded by trees and vegetation, said to belong to one Botha, and the road wound along from our left rear past this farm, and disappeared in a cleft in the hills in front of us. We all realised that the position held by the enemy was a terribly strong one, and on the flanks it appeared, as far as we could see with our glasses, to run for miles in a similar way; and there did not seem to be any break or change in the surface of the ground opposite to it, which continued to present the same grassy undulating slopes as far as we could see.

On our left, miles away, we could hear an occasional gun fired, and on our right there had been a shot or two from the Artillery; but for the moment all was still and peaceful, so we sat and nibbled our biscuits and waited.

About one o'clock the five-inch gun, from somewhere in our left rear, began shelling Botha's farm and the ridge near it and beyond: they made excellent practice, and searched the slopes of the hill thoroughly. Near the farm there was a sort of cleft in the hills, into which the road ran: we could trace its existence for some little way back into the hill by the brushwood growing on the edge of the cleft, and just now we were watching this place, some of us, with exceeding great interest. The General had ordered two companies to proceed in a short time towards this cleft, to move up it, and then to swing round to the right and take the hill in flank, thus covering the advance of the remainder of the Brigade, who were prolonging the line on our right, and were to attack on the part of the hill previously mentioned, where the grassy slopes were more gentle and ran easily up to the summit.

Now, for all we knew, this cleft might have been full of Boers on all sides, before and behind, and we were not looking forward to what was evidently going to be a nasty piece of work; but the matter was settled, we had got our orders, and we meant to carry them out to the best of our ability, somehow or other. So we watched with renewed interest the shells of a cow gun dropping about on the ridge and the slope of the hill, experiencing feelings of much satisfaction when one or two, as they occasionally did, fell plump into the cleft in the hill, where we hoped crowds of the enemy were concealed. Although not visible, we knew they were there, as shots occasionally came over and struck the ground near us, when anyone incautiously went too far forward, to look at the position.

Towards two o'clock, the General wished a few men sent over in the direction of the farm, to feel our way; so Lieut. Morphett and a section of E company went out, widely extended, and with orders to go to the Farm and signal back any information, and to occupy the walls and hold out at the Farm until reinforcements arrived.

Directly this small party showed themselves over the ridge behind which we were lying, fire was opened on them by the enemy, who on this occasion showed their stupidity in wasting their ammunition in firing at extreme ranges. We could not, of course, see from what point of the hill the firing was coming, but from the direction in which the bullets were dropping and the way the dust flew up, we could see that those of the enemy who were firing were somewhere on our left front. So we got some men out and opened a steady dropping fire on the slopes of the hill to our left, and especially on a row of poplar trees which looked a good place in which to conceal sharpshooters. Our maxim gun came up too, and rained a hail of bullets all over the hillside at varying ranges. This is about all the good this machine gun is in the advance, because, when the actual forward movement takes place, the gun cannot keep pace and is left behind : of course a gun on a light field carriage could be brought on by hand, but, during the campaign, the gun we were supplied with was a huge, cumbrous affair, as big as a field gun and about as heavy. It took two mules to draw it, and all sorts of manœuvres and operations had to be gone through before a single round could be fired. In this respect the pattern of machine gun needs considerable improvement before it will ever be of any sound practical use in the field, with infantry and in the advance, at any rate.

After a while the enemy's fire lessened, although it still continued to some extent, and we could see Morphett and his few men working their way through the trees, and up to and beyond the farm. Soon they signalled to us that all was clear and no enemy at the farm, but reported some to be on a ridge in front of the farm, and in the row of trees to the left, which we had already searched with our fire. So we peppered this row of trees again with the Maxim, but were unable to develope any rifle fire on the ridge, as the distance was rather too great for us to fire over the heads of our men in front—some of the shots might have dropped short.

During this little episode the Derbyshire had been sent miles away to the right, and the City Imperial Volunteers had moved against the slopes of the hill, some way to our right. It was pleasant to watch their advance party skirmishing up the slopes, which became steeper near the top. They did it very well, and we watched them with much interest, pushing their way, well extended, moving slowly so as to keep their breath, going steadily on advancing and gaining a firmer footing all the time, although they must have been in momentary expectation of being engulfed in a torrent of fire. We could see their advanced scouts out in front creeping up to the crest line, and we waited, breathlessly, fearing to hear at any instant the infernal din and clatter of a heavy musketry fire opened on their column. Still they crept on and the supports got closer up, and we were in dread that the Boers were waiting only until the supports came closer up yet, before they opened a furious and disorganising fire as they did at Magersfontein.

At last the skirmishers gained the crest line, and we could see them run forward and disappear over the ridge, followed by the supports and the remainder of the regiment. Curiously enough, the ridge was not held by the Boers, and the advance of the Brigade could take place at once. Our little scheme of attack in the cleft was not, therefore, required, as the C.I.V.'s had gained the summit;

but the General sent forward two companies to occupy the hill overlooking the farm.

Why the Boers had neglected to occupy this long ridge and splendid position, I have never been able to understand: there was every point in their favour, except one, and we should have been compelled to make frontal attacks all along the line, at very great loss, no doubt, before we could have got a footing on the ridge.

Once up there, the weak point was revealed: there was no line of retreat for the Boers, except over open country, where we could have slated them handsomely as they went. I think, all the same, that they should have held this fine ridge all along its length, and eventually withdrawn to a secondary position in rear, which they could have held for any length of time. This secondary position, we found, they were actually occupying in strength, but they neglected the primary position, and thus lost an opportunity, to my mind, of checking our advance for, possibly, another day, and doing us a lot of harm besides. However, the enemy's mistakes are always our gain.

Our two companies advanced in column of sections, in widely extended order, with considerable distances between the sections, as we expected to meet a heavy flanking fire going across the valley. As it happened, however, only a dropping fire was opened on us, and we reached the farm unscathed, scattered through it, and stretched away up the hill beyond. A moment's glance sufficed to show that this hill was of no advantage to us, and so we pushed on round it to the left, down the cleft, across the road and up the other side. Nothing was to be seen from here but the gently rising hill, with some rocks on our left front, so we lay down and waited for further orders, as our original instructions to occupy the ridge had been completed.

On our right rear we could see the C.I.V.'s still

coming over the ridge and disappearing over the rising ground to the right, and, from their movements, we could judge that they were coming under a hot fire as they crossed the heights and came out on the open ground. From what we saw afterwards, this view appeared correct, as the enemy, failing to occupy the ridge itself, had retired to a strong position among rocks quite 1,500 yards to the right front, where, at his leisure and in perfect safety himself, he could slate our troops as they advanced over the open.

Hearing all this firing on our right, while in front of us was absolute peace and quietness, we became rather suspicious, and searched the ground in front with our glasses; but, as is usually the case, no signs of any enemy could be seen. The longer this stillness continued the more suspicious it appeared; and we advanced cautiously when, shortly afterwards, half of D company arrived with an order to move on and occupy the rocky ridge to our left front. Another company was coming to support us, and some guns were following: another Brigade was coming up in rear, so, apparently, a general advance was being made. Still full of suspicious feelings intensified by the stillness and inaction, we moved on, but deployed into a wider front, so as to occupy as much of the ridge as possible when we got there. The half of D company under Lieut. Ashworth was on the right, then came E company under Captain Aldridge, while F under Captain Gilbert was on the left: each being in column of half companies and well extended. There were about 80 or 100 yards between the two lines, which were now advancing over an open grassy plateau, that rose gently to our front, where frowned the black rocks, our objective.

Slowly we went on, and a few shots dropped over, coming, seemingly, from our right; later some more spirted up the dust at our feet, and we quickened our pace slightly as we approached the rocky fringe which was our destination. About 30 yards on our side of the edge, there was a fringe of loose rocks and boulders, and, as we reached the first of these and mounted the gradual slope which led upwards to the top, we were enabled to look over the summit of the rocks, and our heads thus became visible to the enemy beyond, who were evidently waiting for this. Suddenly there was the most terrific outburst of rifle fire from our front, and a perfect hailstorm of bullets rattled, whistled and shrieked over our heads ; luckily we were still too low down, or else the Boers were just a moment too soon in delivering their fire, as but few men were touched : instantly the officers yelled to their men to get under cover, and down all hands dropped into perfect safety. Then up we crept on hands and knees to the top, which was fringed with enormous rocks, furnishing the most excellent cover: and through the interstices of these we could open fire on the enemy ; not that we actually saw any enemy (during the whole of that eventful day I did not see one single Boer), but we found out where they were. In front of us, and on the other side of a deep valley covered with rocks, was another rocky ridge, exactly similar to that upon which we were lying ; and from this the enemy's bullets were still shrieking and whistling over our heads, fired, doubtless, from chinks and crevices between rocks similar to those we were now using.

About 800 yards was the range, and we pushed up every rifle into the firing line, made head cover for ourselves, and kept up a furious fire for some little time. The second line coming up behind us, composed of the rear half companies, had some casualties, Lieut. Morphett being shot in the thigh, and one or two of the men being wounded.

Private Bowles of F company was shot on the foot, through boot and all, by a dropping bullet; he was much astonished and spun round and round several times.

Soon afterwards B and C companies, under Major Panton and Capt. Wroughton, came up to reinforce us, and they also were spread out behind rocks and told to keep up a continual fire. Probably owing to the fact that they could see nothing, the enemy gradually reduced their rifle fire until it almost ceased; but they now opened on us with a couple of pom-poms, fortunately for us not beginning until after we had reached the rocks and had established ourselves under cover. Almost at the same time, a heavy shell fire was commenced at us, but soon discontinued, as we afforded the enemy's gunners no object to shoot at. This shell fire was from our left front; we could not locate the gun, but wherever it was, it remained there, and in action, all the afternoon, although we were not afterwards troubled by it. The pom-poms came from the far right, where we could just distinguish the rocky tops of some elevated ground, and had they been closer would no doubt have done considerable damage, as they were quite on our right flank.

As though all this shell and rifle and pom-pom fire was not enough, we were now treated to a shell from the rear, which struck close to a man of B company and covered him with dust and dirt. Taking a man with me, I ran down into a safe spot, and we both waved our helmets vigorously for some minutes, when apparently we were observed from the battery which was firing at us, as no more shells came over our way.

The intensity of our firing had now somewhat dropped, as had that of the enemy, neither of us giving the other much to fire at; but the Boers were very watchful, and you could not look over your rock without one or two shots whizzing past immediately.

There was nothing more to be done but to sit and wait ; it was impossible to advance further, even if we had had orders to do so.

About five o'clock there was a tremendous outburst of firing, but not all in our direction ; and then we saw, to our left rear, a battalion of Guards, (Coldstreamers they were) coming up towards the rocks. They went through precisely the same experience as we had, and after a while commenced company volleys at the opposite side of the ravine, where the Boers were concealed, and continued for some time to pour in consistent volley firing. Meantime the Boer fire dropped to almost nothing, but every now and then, whenever there was a longer interval than usual between the volleys of the Guards, the rattle and whizz of the Mausers developed suddenly into a furious hailstorm, and as quickly died away again, showing that the Boers had some system of control of fire.

General Bruce Hamilton came up to where I was and had a look at the position, and I pointed out to him the direction from which the pom-pom fire had come; he looked at the hills through his telescope, and said he saw some of the Boers' horses collected at the base of a rock, and would send a gun up to us to have a shot at them. The gun came up shortly afterwards, but it was then too late to see any distance, and the shells fell short.

All the afternoon, a most interesting artillery duel had been going on between the 82nd Battery and the enemy's gun to which I have alluded, as being in position to our left front : our battery came into action near the cleft in the hill through which the road past Botha's Farm runs, and for some hours shelled the Boer position on all sides. The Boers answered the fire pluckily, and shelled the battery consistently for some time: we had a

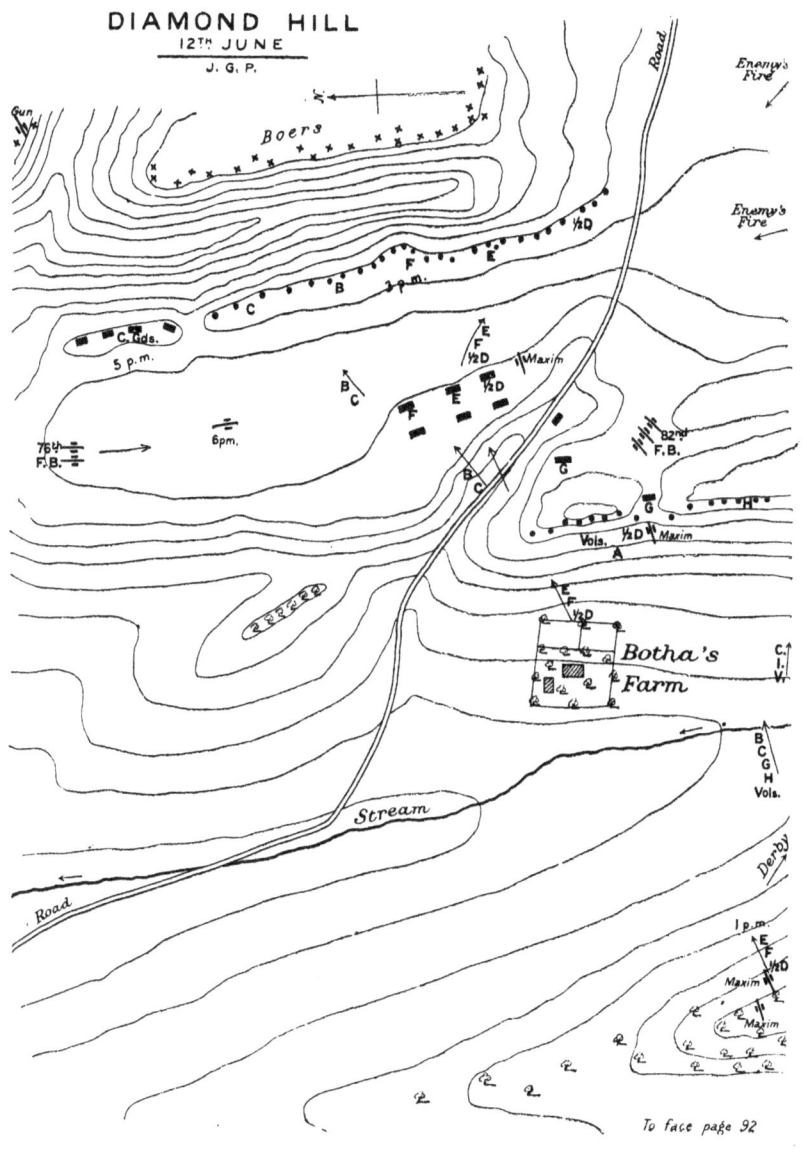

good view of the whole action, and it seemed marvellous that our guns could be worked at all in the face of the clouds of shrapnel which were hurtling through the air, all round the battery; but although they lost heavily in men and horses, they kept their guns going until it was too dark to see any longer.

Just as it was getting dusk, orders were received to withdraw from the position after dark, but to leave three companies on picket, and to send the remainder to the camp, which was being formed at Botha's Farm, behind the hill. B, C and E companies were therefore left on picket, and F company and the half of D returned to camp.

The remainder of the battalion had stayed in reserve behind the hill near the farm, G company being in advance somewhat and on the left of the 82nd Battery, and the others behind the hill, near the Farm.

Sad to relate, Captain Maguire was shot through the head whilst ascending the hill near the farm: he was not even in sight of the enemy, and must have been killed by a dropping bullet fired at extreme range. Poor Maguire, always so cheery and full of spirits; it was his first and only action, and he was the only man of ours killed in the two days fighting.*

---

*Our Casualties on the 12th of June were :—
KILLED.
    Captain C. Maguire.
WOUNDED.
    2nd Lieut. G. Morphett.
    Cr. Sergeant F. Akehurst, B Company.
    Lce. Corporal A. Tester, G ,, (died of wounds)
    Private R. Davis   G ,,
    ,,   W. Miller   D ,,
    ,,   C. Divall   F ,,
    ,,   J. Bowles   F ,,
    ,,   A. Dennett   F ,,
    ,,   F. Needham   B ,
    ,,   F. Guntley   D ,,
    ,,   G. Wadham   Vol. ,,

Lord Roberts wired to the War Office on the 12th of June as follows:

"After surrendering the city (Pretoria) Botha retired to a place about 15 miles east on the Middleburg road: he had a small force at first, but during the last few days the numbers increased, and his being so near the town kept up excitement in the country, prevented burghers from laying down their arms, and interfered with the collection of supplies.

"It became necessary to attack them. This I did yesterday.

"He held a very strong position (practically unassailable in front) which enabled him to place the main portion of his troops on his flanks, which he knew from former experience were his vulnerable parts.

"I sent French, with Porter's and Dickson's Cavalry Brigades and Hutton's Mounted Infantry round by our left: Ian Hamilton with Broadwood's and Gordon's Cavalry Brigades, Ridley's Mounted Infantry, and Bruce Hamilton's Infantry Brigade round by our right.

"Both columns met with great opposition, but about three in the afternoon I saw two of Hamilton's Infantry battalions advancing to what appeared to be the key of the enemy's defence on their left flank. This was almost gained before dark and I ordered the force to bivouac on the ground they had won."

CHAPTER X.

TO SPRINGS.

Boers retreat during the night—Elandsrivier station—Through the Boer positions—To Pretoria—Off again—Irene—Bad state of clothing and boots—Difficulty of repairing the latter—To Springs—Clothing and stores obtained from Johannesburg.

During the night the Boers vacated their position absolutely, so on the 13th June we made an early start, and the Brigade moved round to the southeast in a circular direction and then headed east to Elandsrivier station. On the way we passed some low hills on the south which had been held the day before by the enemy, and we saw the place, at the foot of the hills, where their horses had been standing, apparently for many hours. These were the horses which had been seen by the General, but which it was too dark for our shells to reach. The ground was also strewn with Mauser cartridge papers and boxes, showing that they must have refilled their bandoliers at this place before starting. Their final position at Diamond Hill was plainly visible, due north of this spot, the intervening ground being flat and open veldt; and it was, possibly, very wise of them to have retreated during the night, and not exposed themselves to the risk of being caught with open country in their rear and no cover for miles.

Elandsrivier is a small roadside station, with no town or houses near. The Boers had done all the damage they could, smashed the water-tank and pump, broken into the booking-office, looked into the safe with the aid of a hammer and cold chisel, and written a notice for us on a sheet of paper which we found pinned to the wall.

It was written in pencil and ran as follows :

"Sorry not to have found here the price of a ticket to St Helena.

DE VAN DER MERWE,
Lieut.-Colonel Commanding the Potchefstroom Infantry.
Elandsrivier, 12th June, 1900."

Possibly Colonel De Van der Merwe has, ere this, been provided with a free passage to the island he mentions!

The Camerons rejoined us on the 14th, having been detained with their baggage and the convoy all this time, and having to their great sorrow missed all the fighting.

On the next day, the 15th of June, the Brigade moved off towards Pretoria, passing on the road the Diamond Mine, and entering the defile which had formed part of the main Boer position on the 12th. This defile had been, seemingly, held in great force by the enemy, and it was somewhere on the right of the defile that they had had their gun in position: the defile, which was the main road to Pretoria, wound in and out, the track threading its way among the hills for some considerable distance.

About half way through we passed a farm with a large dam, and here there were numerous indications of the recent presence of a large body of Boers with their wagons, as the ground was covered for some space with hoofmarks, remains of fires, cartridge papers, etc. This laager had been immediately in rear of the final Boer position, which we passed, black and frowning, on our left; from the front it was steep and impassable and covered with huge rocks; on top, the hill sloped to the rear, and the descent on the enemy's side was easy, so that the position presented many points in favour of the Boers.

On either side of the defile, or pass, at this point were huge ravines covered with black rocks, running up into the hills: one of these ravines on our left was recognised as being the one which had lain between us and the enemy, and just beyond it was the hill which we had occupied.

We were now just clearing the defile, and the position revealed itself to us in all its massive strength : on the right it ran back for miles, a huge wall of rock, black and glistening, and rising almost sheer out of the plain, but with a low glacis of grassy veldt in front ; on the left the position was more in the nature of a range of grass covered hills, with some broken ground and a few isolated kopjes in front. This was the ground that we had manœuvred over on the two previous days, and, having now passed through the Boer position in two places, we were quite at a loss to understand why they did not make a better stand, and we thought ourselves very fortunate in having escaped with the moderate loss that we had experienced.

The road to Pretoria wound off to the right, and passed for some miles at the base of this precipitous range of rocks, which continued to run in a northerly direction towards Pretoria.

We camped at night at the foot of these hills, at a farm called Schwartz Kopje ; from here the range became lower and lower until it merged into the hills round Pretoria.

Around us were many farms, and some country houses belonging to Pretoria people, whilst a few miles to the north lay the railway line, and a large distillery at a spot called Eerstefabrieken.

Lord Roberts wired to the War Office on the 14th of June as follows :—

" As I telegraphed yesterday from our outposts 15 miles east of Pretoria, the Boers evacuated their position during the night of the 12th. They had paid so much attention to strengthening their flanks that their centre was weakly held, and as soon as this became evident on the 12th I directed Ian Hamilton to attack.

" He moved against Diamond Hill with the Sussex, Derby and City Imperial Volunteers, supported on his left by the Guards' Brigade under Inigo Jones.

" It was grand seeing the way our men advanced

over difficult ground and under heavy fire. The casualties were, I am thankful to say, less than 100—a very small number considering the natural strength of the position that had to be carried. Our seizure of Diamond Hill caused the Boers to feel that they were practically surrounded, and this resulted in their hasty retirement. They were being followed yesterday by some of our mounted troops.

"Hamilton speaks in high terms of the three battalions above mentioned, and of the admirable manner in which the 82nd Field Battery covered the advance, the good work performed by De Lisle's Mounted Infantry, and the valuable assistance afforded by the Guards' Brigade."

Next day we made our second entry into Pretoria, this time from the East. The place was full of troops, the Guards' Brigade, 19th Brigade, and others being camped close to us on the east of the town. On Sunday, the 17th, and the next day, we remained in camp, but spent a good deal of time roaming over the town, and buying bread and whatever else we could find to eat. Although the first day was Sunday, the Canteen people found out that the worthy shopkeepers of Pretoria were not averse to turning an honest penny, and were mostly inside their shops, like spiders in their webs, waiting for business—but only, of course, through the back door. The Canteen laid in a good stock, although at famine prices, but in the afternoon the District Commissioner ordered the shops to be opened, so that the troops could buy what they wanted. This thoughtful act was productive of much benefit to the rank and file.

Too much rest, however, has always been an unknown quantity to the 21st Brigade, so the next morning we trekked again, and, going through part of the town, we were all pleased to find that Lord Roberts had come out in the early morning to see us go by. The band struck up the march past, and we all looked our best and strode onward as though we had only just landed. There is one point about Lord Roberts which every man on that column realised, and that is the power of the veteran Commander-in-Chief to see more in a glance than most men in a prolonged stare. There were few men in the battalion who did not catch the Field-Marshal's piercing eye as we went past, and each felt that his innermost thoughts were being ferreted out. General Kelly was by his chief's side, and looked very pleased to see his old regiment, and to hear the familiar old tune.

We reached Irene in good time, and found there Captain Mackenzie and about a hundred men, mostly lame ducks: they had been left at Irene when we were there last in order to escort a battery by rail to Vereeniging, and had now returned, having completed this duty.

Unfortunately for them they had missed all the fighting of the 11th and 12th round Diamond Hill, but their turn was to come in good time. A large number of soldiers of all regiments, released prisoners, were at Irene employed in repairing the railway line. The Boers had blown up the bridge some time previously, but it was an easy matter to make a diversion, and the traffic was not stopped for long.

From Irene, Captain Wroughton and myself were sent on by the General by train to Johannesburg, with orders to buy canteen stores and some clothing for the men, and to rejoin at Springs in two days time. As regards clothing, the men were pretty well in rags, and their boots were in tatters. The khaki serge, with which the reserve men had been provided, was shoddy of the worst quality, and wore out with the greatest rapidity: the City Imperial Volunteers, who were all dressed, or rather undressed, in it, were a piteous sight: in fact they were so badly off that many of them had bought themselves tweed and moleskin trousers in Pretoria, to cover their nakedness.

The khaki drill lasts much longer, and has the advantage of being washable : besides, it keeps the dust out much better than the serge, or rather shoddy, and it possesses the further advantage of being all of one colour : it was a common sight to see men in serge with coats and sleeves, or pockets, of quite different shades, while, as for trousers, they were all the colours of the rainbow. Khaki drill is, of course, not so warm as the shoddy, but the addition of cardigan jackets and drawers enables men to suit themselves as to warmth. We had never received the warm coats issued to many regiments ; we could not have carried them if we had, as we were so short of transport; but De Wet had collared all our clothing, boots and mails at Rhenoster. By the way, the British soldier, no matter how generous he may be to an enemy, will never forgive De Wet for destroying all the mails on that occasion, as the harm that was done and the uneasiness that was caused to thousands of friends at home was inflicted on the unfortunate writers of the letters, not on the soldiers to whom they were addressed.

As regards boots, we were in a terribly bad way; the incessant marching and want of grease, which we had no means of carrying, and the absence of any means of executing slight repairs had played the deuce with them. Our shoemakers were always at work in camp, whenever there was a halt for a day; but leather and other materials were not easily procurable, and we should have needed at least twenty-five men to cope with the work in the time available : nor is any provision made for carrying tools and leather in the wagons. On every march quite a number of men, who had no boots, had to be carried on wagons, and I have often seen men walking along with no boots at all, merely their putties twisted round their feet. Nothing could be done, either, to improve matters : boots were not to be had, although in every town a demand was at once made for all the boots in the shops. Those produced were either Bond-street shoes, or else miners' boots, which are not intended for walking in, as a number of our officers and men, who tried them, found to their cost.

It seems such a farce to establish shoemakers' shops in peace time, when there are hundreds of civilian cobblers to be had, and then, immediately a regiment goes on service and the shop would be of some benefit, to close it.

Another ridiculous anomaly, which will hardly be believed, is that in the Artillery, the drivers, *who never walk*, carry two pairs of ankle boots, one on their feet and one on their saddles; but, in the Infantry, *who never ride*, only one pair of boots is allowed, those on their feet !

The advance on Pretoria had been so rapidly executed that the railway was occupied, day and night, in bringing up food for the troops, and had absolutely no room for stores, clothing, boots, or even, for some time, for the mails.

On the 20th of June the battalion left Irene, and marched about 14 miles to Vlakfontein, bivouacing near the head quarters of the East Rand Exploration Company : the evening was enlivened by the biggest veldt fire experienced, as yet, during the campaign. With a strong wind blowing, it came down on the Brigade camp at such a pace, that although steps were taken to burn a fire guard along the hill above the camp, when the fire was about a mile and a half away, yet the zone was completed only just in time ; indeed several carts had to be hurriedly removed to places of security.

Next day the march was continued through the usual undulating country ; on the way a vast pan, or depression in the ground more or less full of water, was passed : it was fully a mile across, and, although at the time nearly dried up, it gave us an idea (for it was the first that we had come across in the course of our wanderings) of what these enormous natural reservoirs must be in the rainy season.

On the right flank, large numbers of tall chimneys and mining shafts could be seen about eight miles off, which proved to belong to the coal mines of Boksburg and Brakpan. These must be most prosperous centres in times of peace, but just then only one or two gave signs of being at work, and probably they were only pumping to keep the water within limits.

This 21st of June was eventful from the fact that it brought the first rain which the battalion had experienced since leaving Glen ; and as all our notable events were heavily scored and immense successes, so was this thunderstorm. Rain and hail came down in torrents, followed by a fall of snow, which was more interesting than pleasant ; and the unfortunate battalion, which on this day was on baggage and rear guard, reached its camp at Springs wet and wretched after a tramp of about fourteen miles.

Fortunately the weather cleared up, and this, with a plentiful supply of coal procured from the railway station, completely altered the complexion of affairs; and, as is usual with soldiers (particularly on service), in half an hour all trouble was forgotten.

The Royal Canadian Regiment of Infantry was in garrison at Springs : they formed part of General Smith-Dorrien's Brigade, which was on the line of communications between Pretoria, Johannesburg and the Vaal ; they had fixed themselves up in the large engine shed at the railway station, and were quite settled down, with bugle calls and other camp comforts.

Springs is purely a railway station, there being no town or village, or anything of that kind ; in course of time this little station will find itself on the direct line, via Middleburg, to Delagoa Bay, as the branch line, which already exists, to the coal mines at Springs is undoubtedly on the direct road between Johannesburg and the main line at Middelburg ; this new line will save a considerable journey round by Pretoria, and will enhance the importance of Johannesburg, bringing it into direct communication with the sea.

Captain Wroughton and I, when we left the battalion at Irene, had a long journey to Johannesburg : we started at half past six in the evening and, although the usual run by train is about two hours, the distance being only 24 miles, yet we did not get into the Park station until 1.30 a.m. Later in the day we went round to the larger shops, and bought stores and tobacco for the Brigade canteen to the value of about £1,500. We were lucky to be able to buy about £350 worth of English tobacco, at such a price as enabled it to be sold retail at 8s. a pound, the usual price in the shops in Johannesburg being 12s. a pound ; but we had been told of a Bonded Customs store in Johannesburg, in which was a large quantity of tobacco belonging to Boer dealers, whose property had been confiscated ; this was being sold by our Government to the British troops, so we decided to purchase a large quantity.

We then went round to the wholesale clothing merchants to try and buy shirts, trousers and socks for the men of the Brigade, and were fortunate in finding a large quantity in a store owned by Lazarus and Jacobson ; we took all the shirts they had and all their stock of socks, and that of another large firm close by. The trousers were very fancy articles : they were mostly of moleskin and corduroy, cut in the approved coster pattern " saucy over the trotters," and we took all that we could find large enough to fit our men. We visited several other large warehouses, but could find no more of the articles we wanted. At the railway goods station we had some trouble with the stationmaster, who was a new hand. He was a sergeant in an Infantry regiment, who, of course, tried to introduce red tape into the matter, and kept back the cases, two whole truck loads of them, saying that they were officers' mess stores and that we must pay freight first; all this trouble with the train starting in half an hour, and the Brigade leaving Springs, the other end of the line, the next morning. However, this stationmaster listened to reason eventually, and we got away at last, only two hours late, and arrived at Springs during the night. Early the next morning the stores were transferred to ox wagons, and went on with the Brigade.

CHAPTER XI.

TO REITZ.

Heidelberg—The ladies' flag—Surrenders—Useless rifles—A duck hunt—Grass fires—Villiersdorp—Frankfort—Reitz—A Boer farm.

We left Springs on the 22nd of June, and had a march of about ten miles before we reached our next camp, Grootfontein. This we found to be about eight miles from Heidelberg, which we reached fairly early the next day, the Cavalry and the Mounted Infantry having gone on in advance and having come into contact with several strong parties of the enemy.

Just outside the town we were met by some ladies in a carriage, who had come out to meet the British troops, and who had brought a most gorgeous banner, all worked in silk by hand, with a portrait of the Queen on one side and the Union Jack on the other, together with an inscription, embroidered in white silk, "Presented to the Royal Sussex Regiment by the Ladies of Heidelberg, 23rd June, 1900."

Of course, the name of the regiment was left blank at the time the banner was presented, but the ladies stitched the name in that afternoon. It seems that they had been working hard, embroidering this flag in secret, for several months, and had determined to present it to the first British regiment to enter the town after the Boers had been driven out; and as luck would have it, it was our turn to lead the Brigade that day.

The ladies explained all this while the regiment halted by the roadside, and then the colonel thanked them in the name of the regiment, saying we would always keep the banner in the regiment in remembrance of the loyalty of the ladies of Heidelberg. Then the band struck up and we marched off to camp, the Sergeant-Major carrying the flag at the head of the battalion, and we all cheering the ladies as we passed them. They were greatly pleased at this, and stood and watched us go by, smiling and waving their hands; while we, all in rags and tatters, with dirty, hairy faces and worn out boots, grinned amiably in return.

We remained four days at Heidelberg, most of us being accommodated in the railway goods sheds, and in some tents which we found there; the Derbyshire were in some small empty houses, and the Camerons in tents, the C.I.V.'s being put up in the engine shed. There was now leisure to issue the clothing which I had bought in Johannesburg, and which was sadly needed; and we had time to wash ourselves and our clothes, and to clean up a bit—not before it was needed.

Extract from Divisional Orders, 25th June, 1900.

"A telegram has been received from the F.-M.C. in C. heartily congratulating Hamilton's force on the occupation by them of the important town of Heidelberg and on the dispersal of the enemy from its vicinity. In this telegram the F.-M. desires Lieut.-Gen. Ian Hamilton to remain quiet in Heidelberg until his broken collar bone is set, when he will rejoin his force. Meanwhile Lieut.-Gen, Sir Archibald Hunter is ordered to take over temporary command, and Gen. Hamilton, much as he regrets his enforced separation from his troops, cannot refrain from congratulating them in passing under the orders of so distinguished a leader as his friend Gen. Hunter."

The Brigade Canteen opened at the railway station, and in three days sold out the whole of the enormous stock brought from Johannesburg; the profits of this canteen up to the date of leaving Heidelberg worked out to £186 15s. 9d., which was divided among the battalions of the Brigade and the battery, the former receiving £44 16s. 4d. each, and the latter £7 10s. 5d.

Heidelberg is the prettiest little town that we have seen in these colonies, and the most English; there is quite a large population, and a large colony of Hindustanis working on the railway, which is an important line, as it connects Johannesburg with Natal. The bridges and culverts had been destroyed by the Boers before leaving, so that trains could not run up to the town just yet from the west, but had to wait outside, some miles away.

Quite a large number of Boers had come in to surrender their arms and to take the oath of allegiance, but I am afraid that this was, in many cases, merely an empty form ; in this town, as in others, many of the rifles brought in were old and valueless. The older rifles, which were of all kinds and patterns (Westley Richards, Enfields, Martinis and many bearing no maker's name, merely the seller's), must have been splendid and costly weapons in their day. There were many quaint old shot guns, besides several of the earlier patterns of breech loading rifles, such as Whitworths, Spencers and Remingtons, many of which were rusty, damaged and out of order.

Every man over 16 and under 60 in the colony had been compelled to purchase a Mauser rifle from the Boer Government at a cost of £3. 7s. 6d., so that if he did not return it to us when he surrendered, he must have either disposed of it or hidden it for use on some future occasion, by himself or his friends.

General FitzRoy Hart, who had commanded the Brigade in which we served when at Aldershot, marched in with his Brigade of Irish troops the day after we arrived at Heidelberg, and encamped on the opposite side of the hill to us. We were greatly interested at seeing them proceed to pitch *tents*, when we poor wretches had been sleeping out on the veldt for months, and had every prospect of continuing to do so for some time to come—a prospect, I may as well say at once, which was realised to the full, as we did not receive tents until the 13th of November.

On the 26th of June the Brigade marched out of Heidelberg and trekked away south, accompanied by an enormous convoy of about 180 wagons of supplies, which retarded our progress considerably. We camped that evening at Bierlaagte, a pleasant little farm belonging to an English company and managed by an Englishman, where there was a large dam in the centre of a big depression in the hills, which afforded plenty of water to the transport animals. There were a few duck on this water, but what with Major Cardew on one side and Capt. Gilbert on another, and a crowd of men throwing stones on the other two sides, those duck had an unhappy time, and had to bow to the inevitable. There were other amusements on this occasion besides duck shooting ; we were just seeking our bivouacs when we got orders to turn out and protect the camp against another enemy, which was approaching rapidly from the south east. This was an enormous grass fire, which was roaring and flaming and throwing out immense clouds of smoke about a mile away. Driven by a strong breeze, the fire, which extended over a wide front, was travelling towards us at an alarming rate ; the whole Brigade turned out, formed line just beyond the limits of the camp, and lit small fires in hundreds. By judicious fanning and with the aid of the in-draught, these small fires soon joined hands and roared away to meet their friend in front. When the two fires *did* meet there was a most tempestuous greeting, and then they both disappeared and all was over. Our manœuvre was most successful, and we slept peacefully, without any fear of being burnt in our beds.

It is astonishing what an amount of damage these grass fires can do when they flash over a camp :

rifles are charred, belts and clothes scorched, harness destroyed, rations ruined, and animals severely burned; and all by a wretched little flicker of flame running across the grass.

Frequently these fires are caused by carelessness, and, as a rule, the mounted scouts in our front got the credit of starting them; but the result to the country was terrible at this time, July. There wasn't a patch of grass, from Reitz to Winburg, for miles on each side of the road, and the wretched transport animals suffered terribly from the want of grazing.

Villiersdorp was reached at seven in the evening on the 29th of June, after a tiring march of 17 miles, during which the battalion was convoy escort to the 180 wagons, which contained our supplies for 14 days.

This escort duty is a wearisome business, as the ox wagons are always the last to start; and although they travel at a good pace—quite as fast as infantry want to march—yet even one drift is disastrous to thoughts of getting into camp reasonably early. As a rule, the wagons move four or even eight abreast on open country; but once a drift is reached, single file is very often the only means of crossing, and this means a long wait for the escort. If the drift is a bad one, and double teams of bullocks have to be used to get each wagon across, the loss of time is very great.

Villiersdorp is a tiny little town on the banks of the Vaal, situated in a hollow of the ground, where it is not seen until one is quite close upon it. There are a few stone houses and a shop, but the town is, as yet, quite in its infancy, although like Topsy, it will grow in time. Anyhow the designers of the place have left lots of room, as the town is well laid out, with wide streets and plenty of elbow room. I sincerely trust that the very first job that the Town Council of Villiersdorp set about, will be the construction, over the drift, of a first class, man's size, doubled bottomed and copper fastened *bridge* of the most expensive quality, so that future generations of tired foot soldiers may not have to lug heavy wagons up and down banks.

On arrival we camped on the Transvaal side of the stream, as it was late; but the ox wagons started crossing at daybreak, so that by mid-day nearly all of them were over. They were followed by the Brigade baggage, and at three o'clock in the afternoon the troops moved across the Vaal once more, and led off to our camp, six miles out. The last time we crossed the Vaal was on our entry into the Transvaal on the 26th of May; now, just over a month later, we recrossed it and moved into a part of the Orange Free State, or Orange River Colony, as it should be called, which had not hitherto been traversed by our troops.

Frankfort was reached next day, the 1st of July, and here we remained a couple of days to rest the transport animals. It is a larger town than Villiersdorp, but not nearly so important as Heidelberg, and apparently does a trade with the surrounding farmers in wool and hides—as is the way with most of the small towns in this colony, whose *raison d'être* is apparently exchange and barter.

The farmers bring in the wool, mealies and hides, and the dealers take them over at a price—not too high, you may depend—and serve out clothes, agricultural implements and other things in exchange. The dealer ships off his lot of wool down to the railway, and eventually to the large firms at the coast, who send him consignments of stores in exchange, and so the game goes on merrily. The ox wagons which take the hides and wool down to the railway bring back stores, building materials and so on; thus there are no empty wagons wasting their time trekking about the country. Most of the shops in a town have the inscription—

"Wolkoper, Allgemene Handlaar"—which may be interpreted as "Wool-broker, General Dealer,"—and most articles required on a farm may be purchased there. On market day farm produce, bullocks, cows and other animals are sold or exchanged : every town, however small, has its market square, and its bell, and its day when the farmers come in and sell their stuff and talk politics and drink too much whisky.—The C.I.V.'s left the Brigade on the 4th of July and proceeded with a convoy to Heilbron ; they never rejoined the Brigade again.

Leaving Frankfort on the 4th of July, the battalion had a terribly bad time with the convoy, as we were on guard over it on that day, and there was one of the worst sandy drifts in South Africa to be crossed, three miles out of Frankfort. If there is one kind of drift which is worse than another it is the sandy one ; wet drifts are no trouble, except that the mules stop in the middle to drink and take their own time in starting again : rocky ones can be cleared : muddy ones can be repaired : steep ones can be cut down, but for sandy drifts there is no cure except brute force to haul the wagons out of the sticky, clinging sand.

Although to the next camp we had only eight or nine miles to go, and we started at eleven in the morning, yet we did not get into our bivouacs at Rietfontein until exactly twelve hours later, and then it had been freezing since seven o'clock that evening. However, that good old soldier Pearce, the Quartermaster, who had got in fairly early, had started fires and boiled water for the men's tea, although he had to take all the wood off the biscuit boxes for fuel. We thought at the time that that day's work was pretty well a record, but it was to be beaten hollow by one or two days which we experienced afterwards.

The next was also a long day's work, but good

going over the veldt, although there was lots of it, as we tramped a good twenty miles before settling down for the night. Scarcity of water was the reason of this long march: we had halted for a couple of hours at mid-day, and went on again with the intention of reaching water, so we had to stick to it and trek away until we did come to water. Major Shaw, the Brigade Major, did a fair amount of galloping that day, looking for water, and no doubt his pony, if he is still alive, has not forgotten the 5th of July.

However, the next day compensated us for our hard work, as we had a short march of merely ten or eleven miles, which, with a halt at mid-day for a couple of hours, brought us into camp about four o'clock. There is no doubt that, where troops are marching with a big convoy, it is a wise thing to give the infantry a rest of a couple of hours in the middle of the day, as it enables the convoy to close up, to water and feed, and to get a short rest too. Transport animals travel all the better after being watered and after having had a short rest, and it is a sound policy to do this, as the column travels all the faster afterwards. The Boers, when they are trekking, water their animals much more frequently than we do, and they often made the remark to me that we were killing our bullocks by not giving them a rest. On all marches the pace of the column undoubtedly depends on the rate at which the slowest wagon travels, and matters should, therefore, be arranged with regard to that fact. Apart from considerations of safety, it is not sound to see the troops trekking away into camp with the convoy sprawling along the road, and with the rear guard clustering behind the last wagon.

Another short march fetched us into Reitz, at mid-day on the 7th of July: half the battalion and two guns were sent to occupy a farmhouse at the foot of a hill, about a mile and a half away from the town—but such a farm house! The doors and windows were gone, the ceilings and floors had been wrenched away, part of the corrugated iron roof was gone, and several of the rafters had been cut off short with saws, so that the rest of the roof was in rather a dicky condition. This mass of ruins rejoiced afterwards in the select name of "Joe Muggins' Farm."

All Boer farms are more or less similar, and the buildings and outhouses are practically identical in their shape and general appearance. First of all there must be one or more dams which contain the water supply for the cattle, and which are usually constituted so as to drain a considerable area of watershed. A few trees are sometimes planted to bind the embankment, but as a rule the burgher does not bother about improving his property by arboriculture, but contents himself by growing an orchard of peaches and apricots, and by planting a number of eucalyptus trees round his homestead. This is indispensable in every well-conducted farm.

The buildings themselves are very ramshackle in design, the fact being that the farmer on his first arrival builds himself a hut, which, as he becomes a prosperous man, and his family increases with years, he adds to whenever an opportunity occurs. There is always, however, a bit of neglected garden in front of the house, with a step or two of stone leading up to the verandah or *stoep*. As a rule, small rooms exist on the sides of the verandah, whilst the *sitzkamer* or drawing-room opens on to it. This is a sealed-pattern room, and very funny to look into, as all are alike, varying only in the quantity of furniture crammed into it by the wealthy farmer. An American organ with perhaps a piano, of course hopelessly out of tune, is flanked by the regulation two arm chairs and six straight backed ditto, all carefully hung around with antimacassars.

On the walls are crayon enlargements of photos of the master of the house and his *vrouw*, supported by lithographs of various crowned heads, and enlivened by coloured pictures from the Christmas numbers. The floor is covered with a carpet and a few skins, and a few odd tables rest in fixed positions, supporting some china ornaments and other little knick-knacks. The family Bible, containing the records of births, deaths and marriages, occupies a prominent position in the room.

The dining-room is close by, and is really the living room of the family, and, like the *sitzkamer*, is conspicuous by its want of ventilation. At meal times, the men of the family sit down first and are waited on by the ladies of the family, and by Kaffir servants in various stages of undress. After the biltong and stormbacks are finished, the women folk are permitted to see what they can find left to satisfy their appetites. Another prominent room in every Boer house is the guest chamber. Here everything is spick and span, and the furniture is complete in every detail, including a washing basin and a bath; but of course no self-respecting Boer would dream of spoiling his record by wasting such a lot of water. The kitchen usually contains an American stove, and has a brick oven built outside one end of the room. Of course, all baking has to be done on the farm, and lucky has been the soldier who has reached a farm before his comrades, and has been enabled to buy his loaf of bread.

Outside in the compound, various animals of the usual farmyard type, with a few guinea fowl, a peacock and perhaps an ostrich or two, roam at large. A large wagon shed with a loft above, a woolshed and one or two smaller storehouses comprise all the outbuildings. The ploughs and other agricultural implements, which by the way are universally of American manufacture, lie about everywhere.

At Reitz we remained from the 7th to the

13th of July, being occupied during the first two days in constructing some temporary defences on both sides of the town, which was commanded by large hills of some considerable elevation; these were held by our battalion, and upon them earthworks were constructed in prominent positions. The town is a small one of little importance, consisting of only a few houses : there were hardly any residents left on our arrival, and nearly all the houses had been emptied of their furniture, so our Head-Quarters companies were enabled to occupy them as billets.

The Highland Brigade, who had left the neighbourhood of Frankfort the same day as we did, and who had marched parallel to us, but at some considerable distance away, did not halt at Reitz, but continued on through the town on their way to Bethlehem.

The convoy wagons were emptied of their supplies, which were stored in various buildings, and a column, consisting of the Derbyshire and some Mounted Infantry, went off, under command of Col. Cunningham, to Heilbron. The Derbyshire have not been seen since in the 21st Brigade, as they shortly afterwards formed part of a Brigade of which Colonel Cunningham was given the command; as they are to remain in South Africa and as we are commencing a long tour of foreign service in India, goodness knows when we shall see this fine old regiment again.

At the Farm where A, E, F and G companies were stationed, we had a company and a half on picket daily ; their posts were rendered more defensible, and huts were built with corrugated iron roofs for the pickets to sleep in at night, as it was still very cold in the early morning. Veldt fires were constantly blazing all round us, and one night, at eleven o'clock, E company had to turn out to save our two guns, which were established on the hill above us, from being burned out. It took E the best part of an hour to put out the dangerous part of this fire, and it had to be done by beating out the flames with blankets.

Continuous firing early one morning from one of the pickets turned us all out in alarm : the regimental staff galloped off to see what the enemy's strength was, and in what direction his attack was coming : the battery hurriedly harnessed their horses and got ready to move up the hill, when a message came down to the General to say that it was a false alarm. It turned out that the picket had seen a herd of buck quietly grazing, and thinking some venison would be a good thing for dinner in place of the usual trek ox, had first let off a volley at 800 yards and had then continued with independent firing for some little time !

A considerable number of burghers came in every day and surrendered their arms, taking the oath of allegiance also; but, as before, many of the guns and rifles sent in were worthless : several were of very weird patterns, with all sorts of curious backsights :· one had flaps, sighted to a number of distances, fitted along the barrel from the breech to the muzzle ; another had a hinged backsight leaf which ran in grooves from one end of the barrel to the other.

CHAPTER XII.

TO MEYER'S KOP.

Leeuwspruit—Bethlehem—De Wet surrounded—Ridley goes to Slabbert's Nek—De Wet already through—Meyer's Kop—Rifle Positions—Inefficiency of shrapnel—Necessity of adapting tactics to those of the enemy—A looted store.

We marched out of Reitz on the 13th of July, and camped at Hartebeeste Hoek about dusk, experiencing an icy cold night with a very heavy frost: the companies on picket suffered severely, as there was no wood to be got in the neighbourhood. Our march the next day to Leeuwspruit, just outside Bethlehem, was very trying indeed: there was a strong wind blowing from our front, and clouds of dust gathered up from the burnt up veldt stung our faces and filled our eyes and mouths. There was not a patch of grass anywhere, nothing but black ground for miles: the battery on this occasion, with unusual want of thought, persisted in marching on the windward side, every now and then raising up great clouds of dust, which came rolling over to us like black smoke from a huge fire. It is difficult and trying for horses, which walk faster than men, to keep in rear of a battalion of infantry, and for this reason a careful battery commander tries to get on the flank of infantry ; but when the wind is blowing from that flank, it is very uncomfortable for the foot soldiers.

We halted a day and a half at Leeuwspruit, and left that place at three o'clock in the afternoon on the 16th of July for Bethlehem, reaching the town at dusk and halting for orders on the outskirts. The Camerons received orders to remain at Bethlehem with the G. O. C., the Headquarters of the Brigade, the Supplies and the Field Hospital ; but we were directed to fill up our wagons with several days' rations, and to proceed, with Major Simpson's battery, the 81st, to a farm called Sevastopol, lying somewhat to the south west. We waited a couple of hours while our wagons went off to draw rations, which were all over the place—biscuit in one camp, tea and sugar in the town—and eventually we got away, at 8.30 p.m., in pitch darkness. We led out through the town, looking still and ghostly in the dark, and up a steep and terribly sandy road, which tried our overloaded wagons to the utmost, until at last we reached the open veldt, where the road was hard, and clear from rocks and sand. On the top of this hill we had a long wait, while the wagons were closed up : we lay down and tried to keep warm, but the cold was too intense, and finally the whole battalion had to stand up and move about to keep their blood circulating. So we went on, halting every now and then to allow the lagging wagons to close up, until at last at the top of a sudden drop into a valley our advanced guard was challenged by a picket, whom we found to belong to Ridley's Mounted Infantry, camped about a mile further on.

It seems that news had been received that De Wet, who was almost surrounded by Hunter's and Rundle's Divisions and was shut up inside the cordon of hills enclosing the Caledon Valley (access to which was only to be obtained by certain passes which were watched by several Brigades), was suspected of an intention to break out; and we had been packed off in a hurry to guard Ridley's baggage and rations, while he dashed off towards Slabbert's Nek, one of these passes, to intercept De Wet in case he tried to break out in that direction.

At half past two in the morning we formed up in the valley, posted pickets and got some sleep; but at half-past five we were on the move again. Ridley had gone off at daybreak, taking his baggage with him, so we started and marched about four miles, and then halted by the roadside near Meyer's Kop, for further orders. In the distance, another four miles on, rose the hills surrounding the Caledon Valley : we could just distinguish the break in the range leading to the pass or Nek, which was somewhat inside the fringe of low-lying hills. Four miles to the south could be seen the camp and tents of General Paget's Brigade, with which signalling communication was opened. A signal station was also established on the top of Meyer's Kop, and communication opened with Conical Hill, a sugar loaf peak about five miles south of Bethlehem. Orders were received in the afternoon from General Hunter, who was then in Bethlehem, directing us to remain at Meyer's Kop for the present ; so the Colonel selected a site for a camp, and we settled down in a valley close under this kopje, bivouacing on a dirty piece of blackened, burnt up ground, which was the cleanest that could be found.

The force under Lieut.-Colonel Donne's command consisted of our battalion, the 81st Battery, a few local irregulars of Prince Alfred's Guards, and, later, some of the Lovat Scouts.

We heard afterwards that De Wet had succeeded in breaking out of Slabbert's Nek before we arrived, passing within a mile of where we were then camped, and had gone off with 1,200 men and no wagons, only Cape carts, in the direction of the railway. All our available Mounted Infantry, under General Ridley, had hurried after him, and General Broadwood, with his cavalry, had snatched up the Derbyshire regiment to look after his baggage and had hastened off in the same direction. The futility of chasing mounted men with a force dependent for their supplies on wagons escorted by infantry was soon apparent, and, as is now a matter of history, De Wet succeeded in making good his escape, and led our troops a dance which lasted for months, and covered the greater part of the Orange River Colony.

Our energies were now concentrated on keeping the remainder of the Boer commandos inside the Caledon Valley, exit from which could only be obtained from the passes at Ficksburg, Slabbert's Nek, Retief's Nek, Naauwpoort Nek and Golden Gate; these were watched—at Ficksburg by Rundle, who was advancing up the Caledon Valley towards Fouriesburg; by Paget's Brigade and ourselves at Slabbert's Nek; by Hector Macdonald's Highland Brigade at Retief's Nek; and by Bruce Hamilton, who with the remains of his Brigade was advancing towards Naauwpoort Nek; but, as regards Golden Gate, which was not passable for wagons, it would appear that this pass was not watched by any of our troops.

Meyer's Kop was a rock of extraordinary shape. Imagine a huge sugar loaf, which had been cut in half horizontally, so that the lower half formed a great truncated cone, and then stick this up in the centre of a level plain, and you have a fair idea of what this kopje, at whose base we bivouacked for six days, looked like. There was a certain amount of débris and many huge rocks scattered around the base of the kopje; its sides were quite perpendicular except on the north, where there was a winding path by which access might be had to the summit. The top was almost flat, one enormous table-top of rock, about 80 yards across and full of huge pot holes, which in ages gone by had been washed out by the action of water.

There were numerous other kopjes similar to this one in the neighbourhood, and it is easy to conceive how, at one time, all the surrounding country had been at the bottom of the sea, and how it had risen gradually, the pinnacles of rock like Meyer's Kop, all scored and washed clean by the rushing water, appearing first out of the sea. At one corner of the rock, on the top, were piles and piles of cartridge cases, Mauser, Lee-Metford and Martini, lying in little heaps in places which showed us how each Boer marksman had taken up his position, concealed behind most excellent cover, whence to shoot down from his point of vantage our soldiers as they advanced across the open plain beneath or showed themselves over the rising ground, at points of which every Boer of course knew the range. To these men, each snug in his little nook among the rocks, our rifle fire would have no terrors, as our bullets would whizz harmlessly over their heads, even if aimed in their direction—an unlikely event, for the chances would be hundreds to one that the Boers would never be spotted as long as they used cordite.

Shell fire also would cause no trepidation to a Boer well posted behind cover; but I doubt if he would have been so happy, or would even have remained so long behind his cover, had he been exposed to the old fashioned shell fire from mortars, where the projectiles, fired at a high angle with a varying charge of powder, sailed slowly and gracefully, humming to themselves, through the air, their track marked by a thin stream of blue smoke from the burning fuse; and then, dropping quietly immediately in rear of the enemy's parapet or into his trenches, burst into hundreds of fragments and spread devastation around.

Something of that kind is what has been wanted in the class of warfare which we have been carrying on lately with the Afridis and the Boers, *i.e.* against a much scattered enemy, invisibly and securely posted behind rocks, and armed with the latest development in small bore rifles.

Shrapnel is all very well when used against an enemy in a formation like quarter-column, and its moral effect is at all times good; but its killing powers against a thin line of skirmishers, say ten paces apart, advancing across a plain or posted on a ridge are limited to the width of front to which its 256 bullets will, on the explosion of the bursting charge, extend, and are about equal to the damage which might be done by, perhaps, two rifles. The trajectory of a shell is too flat to cause any harm to a Boer or an Afridi behind a rock.

At Meyer's Kop the rocks on the east had received a vigorous shelling on one occasion from our guns, and it interested some of us to potter about, looking at the marks on the rocks and ground that showed where the shells had struck, picking up shrapnel bullets and fragments of iron, trying to estimate the number of shells fired, and examining the ground to see where the enemy's sharpshooters had been lying.

On this particular occasion (I don't know when it occurred or what troops of ours had been engaged), the ground on the slope of, and below the eastern side of the kopje, was covered, over a large area, with shrapnel bullets and bits of shell; and the large prominent boulders, some of them as big as haystacks, bore marks where shells had struck in numbers; *but*, away up on a corner of the kopje, fifty yards off, were at least 500 cartridge cases, showing where some three or four men had lain in perfect security and had kept up a harassing fire in spite of our shrieking shell, and the whistling but inoffensive bullets from our bursting shrapnel.

They had played the Boer game, which the introduction of smokeless cordite had rendered so easy; they had studiously avoided all the prominent objects behind which one would naturally expect to find an enemy, and had selected other places on the flanks, from which to pour in, unobserved, their annoying and ceaseless fire, whilst our advancing troops blazed away, and continued to blaze away, at the top of the hills, at green bushes, and at any stone walls in the neighbourhood, instead of impartially searching with their fire the slopes of all the hills in their front, or watching the spirts of dust thrown up by the Boer bullets and trying to discover from these indications the direction whence the fire was coming and the probable location of the marksman.

These are all points which, unfortunately, can only be learned when bullets are flying around, but a very little instruction in this goes a tremendously long way; and when skirmishing is again introduced, as it must inevitably be, into the curriculum of instruction we give our infantry soldiers in peace time, no doubt more attention will be paid to the question of adapting your system of warfare to meet that of your enemy. The invading force which enters an enemy's country is, to my mind, entirely at the mercy of and eventually forced to adopt, any system of warfare which may be thrust upon it by the owners of the country; thus, a widely scattered enemy must be met by our thin clouds of skirmishers: changes of position rapidly carried out by an enemy entirely mounted must be checkmated by our strong bodies of mounted infantry: the withdrawal, when pressed by us, of the enemy to a previously selected position must be met by our timely flanking movements: the invitation by the enemy to a frontal attack over a suspiciously open piece of country must be met by an attack delivered somewhere else.

In fact, whatever the enemy obviously wishes us to do, must not be done, lest we be drawn into a trap; and above all nothing must ever be taken for granted. I am fully aware that these axioms are as old as the hills, and that every soldier is supposed to absorb them with his military milk in his infancy as a recruit; but I am afraid that he does not assimilate enough of this particular kind of diet.

Many are the instances, some of them microscopic, some of them serious, which I have seen of the neglect of the golden rule—take nothing for granted; and I might also add to this rule another, namely—never despise your enemy—to which the attention of all amateur soldiers might be drawn when they next race off in the direction of any campaign which may be threatening.

This queer Meyer's Kop made an excellent helio station from which signalling communication was easily maintained to the north and south; and it was also a first-rate observation post, from which the surrounding country for miles round could be seen. One of the officers was usually on watch up there from daylight to dark, and it was really a very pleasant way of spending three or four hours on a fine day. Sometimes we could see what we thought were Boers riding about on the sky line, and we used to especially watch the entrance to Slabbert's Nek, in the hopes of seeing some of the enemy moving about. Once or twice we went out with a few men and some wagons to procure forage from the farm of an Englishman named Passmore, a horsebreeder and trainer, and a jockey well known at Johannesburg, who had a run near us, but who had had to bolt when the Boers arrived in the neighbourhood. This man had opened a small store on his property, but when we arrived we found that it had been carefully looted. I never saw such confusion as there was; nearly everything had been torn down or off the shelves and thrown promiscuously on to the floor; things looked as though a whole troop of monkeys had been allowed a free hand for half an hour or so. Only once have I seen anything approaching such a state of matters, and that was years ago, when Captain Farrell's pet monkey was accidentally shut up in his master's quarters for a couple of hours; and the havoc that monkey, who was of an enquiring turn of mind, played with writing table, dressing table, chest of drawers, and tin uniform cases may be better imagined than described.

Passmore's store however had been visited, it was suspected, by Kaffirs and not by Boers. It was a curious circumstance, noticed by one of our officers with a Sherlock Holmes disposition, that all the tins, of which there were a number containing mustard, medicines, pepper, linseed, ginger and other things, had a small opening, roughly made, evidently to enable the contents to be examined. Now, no white man would have gone to the trouble of doing this, even if he couldn't have read the label, which was plain enough in every case.

G and H Companies were sent in with wagons, on the 20th of July, to Bethlehem, to draw another supply of rations and to get the mails, sixty-three bags of which were waiting for us. They returned the next day in the afternoon, together with the Bedfordshire regiment, who camped alongside of us, but left the next evening to join Paget's Brigade, which was only a few miles away.

The Bedfords, who had been equipped earlier in the campaign than we had, when things were more plentiful, were very well provided as regards transport. They had plenty of wagons, Scotch carts, ammunition carts and water carts, while we were still limited to the one water cart with which we originally started, and the two old Scotch carts, procured at a farm, which we utilised to carry some of our reserve ammunition. The four ammunition and other carts we had brought from home had been left at Glen for want of mules to draw them.

CHAPTER XIII.

RETIEF'S NEK.

A bad night—Start for Retief's Nek—Description of ground—Orders to attack—Leading companies take wrong direction—Remaining companies advance against Nek—They close up to the Boer position—Further advance impossible—Death of Sir Walter Barttelot—Orders to retire at dusk—Difficulty of bringing in wounded—A good Samaritan.

It was dark on Sunday evening, the 22nd of July, when the Bedfords started from Meyer's Kop; and directly they had gone the wind rose and the rain came down in torrents, splashing up the black soil, turning the camp into a morass, and penetrating through everything—blankets, waterproof sheets, canvas sheeting. The wind blew our blankets about and the rain drenched everything for many hours without ceasing, all fires were quenched by the downpour, and we sat and cursed and were wretched. One or two of us were fortunate enough to get hold of some corrugated iron, and I remember getting an hour or two's broken sleep by crawling, all wet and muddy, under a long sheet of this iron, which I had stretched over my blankets.

To add to our troubles, one of the companies on picket fired a few shots in the middle of all our discomfort, but, as the firing did not continue, no further steps were taken: however, about half-past two, the Volunteer company burst out into heavy firing which they continued for some time. As they were on picket quite close to us, the Adjutant ran up to see what was the matter, and found that they were firing at some lights some distance in front of them: so the firing soon stopped, and we huddled under our dripping blankets until three o'clock, when we were routed out and told to pack our kits and load the wagons. Overnight the Colonel had had confidential orders to move before daybreak towards Retief's Nek, where we were to meet General Hunter and receive further orders; so by four o'clock we were on the move. The night was pitch dark, but luckily the rain had stopped : the whole camp and the ground round it was a sea of mud, and it was with the greatest difficulty that we could start the wagons, already fully loaded with rations and mails, to which had been added the men's blankets, now trebled in weight owing to the absorption of rain : in consequence of the compression, the water was soon running out of the bottoms of the wagons, which will give an idea how wet the blankets had been when loaded.

As it was, after squelching and slipping along in slimy mud, we had to wait at the top of the hill for the wagons to be hauled up to drier ground; by that time it was dawn, and we were able to proceed at a better pace across country towards Retief's Nek.

There was one nasty drift on the way, muddy and slippery, which caused considerable delay to our small column; but after this we trekked along for some hours over grassy veldt, until we came in sight of Retief's Nek, when the Colonel rode on to communicate with General Hunter, and the battalion halted under the lee of a huge mass of rock, rising sheer out of the plain. This was about eleven o'clock, so we seized the opportunity to eat some biscuit and what cooked food we happened to have in our haversacks, and to rest ; for after our dreadful night and long tramp, we were fairly well tired.

After some little while, the Colonel came back, summoned the officers, and told us the orders he had received from General Hector Macdonald, who was in charge of the operations; we then went some little distance aside, and the position was shown to us and the orders explained.

In front, the ground, level and grassy, stretched away for about a mile and a half to a low conical hill, which appeared to be of slaty rock, and the top of which shone and glistened in the sun like white marble; a little to the rear of this, and seemingly connected with it by a narrow nek, rose another hill, very similar in appearance, but dark and lowering. Separated from these hills on our right by a gap, perhaps 600 or 700 yards wide, rose a spur with a knoll half way up, a little less in height than the kopje (which we had now named Marble Kop), and from this knoll the spur rose abruptly to a great height, broken and jagged, the slopes covered with huge black rocks: this cliff bore round to our right for perhaps a mile or more, very steep and precipitous, until it was abreast of where we were standing, when the range of mountains swung away to our right and was lost in the distance. Still to the front, but a little to our right, rose a narrow grassy kopje, with a couple of houses at its foot. This kopje was separated from the great range of hills by a narrow, funnel shaped passage which seemed to be about 600 yards wide at the entrance; but whether this narrow kopje, which ran straight back, eventually joined the broken and jagged cliffs in the distance, or whether it was an isolated hill and the passage ran round behind it, could not be decided from the spot upon which we were then.

Marble Kop was the position the battalion were to attack, and it was to be supported in its advance by the battery, which would take up a position on a hill which we could not then see, but which was immediately in front of Marble Kop, and some considerable distance away from it: no nearer position could be found for the guns.

On the left of Marble Kop rose abruptly to a point a lofty range of hills, looking quite inaccessible, and bearing round to our left in a great sweep. Between this point and Marble Kop was another gap of some considerable width, which was the pass of Retief's Nek; and down at the bottom of this pass and hidden in a fold of ground, the road ran from where the guns were posted straight into and beyond the pass.

Our orders from General Macdonald were to attack Marble Kop, and on arrival there to open an enfilading fire on a trench which the enemy was reported to have dug across the pass: there were to be no supports for us, and there was no information as to the position of the enemy, or his strength, or whether Marble Kop was occupied by him: a deadly stillness was in the air, and the strongest telescope did not reveal the presence of the enemy at any point which was visible.

The companies now proceeded to move off in the following order:—G company under Captain Mackenzie, then H under Captain Wisden; after them A under Major O'Grady, followed by B with Major Panton in command, and C under Captain Wroughton; E under Captain Aldridge bringing up the rear. The remaining companies were on various duties; D under Lieut. Ashworth was escorting the guns and took no part in the action, F under Captain Gilbert, and the Volunteer company under Sir Walter Barttelot, were baggage and rear guard respectively: they came up shortly after we had advanced, when the wagons had been parked by Major Scaife, who was baggage master—these two companies then proceeding to join in the attack.

The leading company, G, was directed to advance towards Marble Kop, proceeding in a circuitous direction, and skirting the base of the narrow kopje, then in front and lying at our feet. This kopje G should have left on the right. The companies were to advance in column of sections, each extended to ten paces, and with large intervals between each line; all officers and supernumeraries were to be in among the men in line, so as not to render themselves too conspicuous. The companies were soon fairly launched and moving off across the grassy veldt in great parallel lines, about a hundred or more yards apart, and stretching well away to the right and left, so as not to afford to the enemy a more extensive objective than was necessary. The leading company was a long way off, and the men were appearing smaller and smaller as they got further away to the front, when it was noticed that the column, instead of skirting the narrow kopje in front and leaving it on their *right*, had misunderstood these instructions and were entering the funnel shaped passage, thus leaving the narrow kopje on their *left*.

There was then no time or means of recalling them without considerable delay, owing to the distance, fully a mile, which they had already traversed, so it was considered advisable to allow them to continue their advance in the direction which they had chosen; the point of attack had been distinctly pointed out to every one concerned, and if, as often happens in these widely extended movements, certain contingencies had arisen which necessitated the direction of the attack being changed, yet no further instruction could be given by the commanding officer, and the execution of the attack must, perforce, be left to the discretion of each company commander.

Under the extended order system as carried out during this war, the company commander becomes a far more important personage than he has been during the last twenty years, with an immensely free hand, within certain limits, directly active operations commence.

The machine guns under Captain Green had gone along with H company, and had by this time, with the three leading companies, gone quite out of sight into the funnel shaped passage; C company, which was the fifth in order of succession, was just inside the entrance, and E was following in rear;

the ammunition cart and water cart and the rest of the first line were coming on behind. This was the situation about one o'clock, and I was walking up the narrow kopje, intending to watch the progress of events from its summit, when suddenly from inside the passage on the right, into which the companies had gone, came, like a clap of thunder, a most fearful outburst of firing, which continued for some time without intermission, and which echoed and re-echoed among the ravines and rocky hills, until one could hardly hear one's own voice.

From the top of the kopje nothing could be seen, either of our men or the enemy, and the infernal pandemonium still continued in the valley below; but to the incessant ping-boom, ping-boom of the Mauser, unmistakeable from its propinquity, was now added the ping, ping, ping of the Lee Metford, and the continuous stutter of the Maxim, as this highly strung machine, shaking and quivering with nervous energy, stammered out whole belts full of ammunition without ceasing. Undoubtedly, Captain Green had got hold of a soft thing and was taking the utmost advantage of it, and squeezing the last ounce out of the Maxim, which fired as it had never fired before and probably never will again. The water in the casing fizzed and spluttered, but more was handy; the empty belts littered the ground, but the ammunition cart was not far off, and so the vastly important work of spattering with bullets the hillside opposite, which a moment before had been as still as the grave, was continued without intermission. The companies in front had dropped into cover behind some huge rocks which fringed both sides of the valley, immediately on the first shots being fired; and they had ever since continued to fire at their invisible foe, who were lining the hillside and the jagged crest line not 800 yards away.

Captain Mackenzie had, at the outset, exposed himself somewhat recklessly, and had been knocked over in the open with a bullet in his ankle; his subaltern, Lieut. Hopkins, seeing this, shouted to a couple of men to accompany him, and dashed out without a moment's thought towards his captain, in the face of a murderous fire which covered the ground around them with a cloud of dust spirts. Together with the two men, who turned out to be Corporal Hoad and Lance-Corporal Neville, Lieut. Hopkins raised Captain Mackenzie and bore him, groaning and sweating with agony from his broken ankle, to safety.

For this gallant act these three, the young officer and the two Corporals (both young soldiers), were recommended for the Victoria Cross, the highest distinction to which a soldier can aspire. However, in lieu of this, Lieut. Hopkins was offered a company in the Manchester regiment, and the two Corporals were each awarded the Distinguished Conduct Medal.

Nothing could be done to withdraw the companies in front, and the Maxim had also to remain; but orders were sent to B, C, and E companies to move to their left to the other side of the kopje. This they soon did, and the attack was launched again at Marble Kop, but on this occasion from the direction in which it had been originally intended to advance. As matters turned out, however, it was perhaps as well that the mistake had been made and the advance commenced in the wrong direction, as our three companies, although useless to the battalion in continuing the advance, were still of inestimable value where they were lying, as they held a good number of the enemy in check and prevented them from leaving their cover and proceeding to other positions, from which they could, perhaps, have done more damage. While our three companies kept up a dropping fire and while the Maxim rattled out its scattered shots at intervals, no Boer would dare to leave his cover; and so matters remained *in statu quo* in this valley until dusk.

Meanwhile, our battery had commenced shelling vigorously the slopes of the hills on the right of Marble Kop, and B and C companies, with E following, were moving over to the open ground directly in front of it; from here they advanced in succession by half-companies and stretched away out into the veldt, E company being meanwhile held in reserve.

We sat and watched the companies diminishing in the distance, and, when the leading half-company was about a thousand yards from us and about the same distance from the foot of Marble Kop, we saw rifle fire opened on them from their right front. They continued their advance like a parade ground movement, halting, lying down to fire and then rising and going on again, the lines in rear conforming to the movements of those in front, and the men on the right of all the lines delivering their fire against their hidden enemy among the hills on the right front. Gradually the lines in rear decreased their distances, closing up to the front and reinforcing and thickening the firing line : this manœuvre adds more rifles to the firing line and enables more fire to be brought to bear on the enemy, but at the same time it increases the vulnerability of the foremost line, rendering more men liable to be hit owing to their proximity to each other, so, possibly, the advantages may or may not outweigh the disadvantages. In this particular case, however, where the enemy were behind perfect cover, the disadvantages of thickening the firing line predominated, and the enemy's bullets fell pretty thickly amongst our men.

It appeared at this stage of the proceedings, that Marble Kop was unoccupied, and that the bulk of the firing was coming from a concealed party of sharpshooters at long range, stationed somewhere on the right front, upon whom the shrapnel of our guns seemed to have little or no effect: however our men, although hampered by having to fire half right, continued to pour in a constant fire at ranges of from 600 to 800 yards, and perhaps longer.

About this time, also, F company and the Volunteer Company appeared, coming up from the rear in similar formation (half company columns) to that adopted by us: seeing that the firing line wanted a wider front instead of a thicker formation, F company was directed by signal to continue moving to the front, but to gradually edge off to the left, so as eventually to come up on the left of the present firing line, composed of B company.

So F company trudged off and carried out this manœuvre beautifully, coming up into line with B company and lying down and opening fire about half an hour later: meantime the Volunteer company had received similar orders to move further off and to prolong the line to the left of F company; this movement had used up all the companies at our disposal, except E, who were now moved off to the left also, but were still to remain as a reserve in rear of the centre, in view of possible contingencies which might arise. There were one or two wounded being brought in, so a dressing station was established under some cover, formed by a few large rocks and a tree or two; and the doctor, who had remained in the valley on the right attending to one or two men of G company who had been hit, was sent for. The first line transport with the ammunition carts, water cart and the medical officer's cart had, for some inexplicable reason, remained in this valley, although the majority of the battalion had been moved in another direction; they did not come near us all the afternoon, men having to be sent over to get ammunition, which, at a later stage of the fight, was running short rapidly.

For the second time that day I sat down and searched the hills thoroughly with a telescope; not a sign of an enemy did I see, and yet the jets and puffs of dust thrown up amongst the men spread all over the veldt up to a thousand yards in front distinctly showed that the firing was from the right front. Away on our right, the spur, which has been alluded to as being separated from Marble Kop by a gap about six hundred yards wide, was being steadily shelled by our battery all along its length, and on its face where it joined the big jagged cliffs and trended off to the right; but it was now seen that this spur continued round to the left also, and forked out into another lofty range of hills, which swung round with a semi-circular sweep, enclosing a valley into which various underfeatures and knolls led out from the spur and from the lofty range itself. The conclusion I came to at the time was that the Boers were in position on these knolls and underfeatures, rising in tiers, one above another, and that the majority of the firing was directed on our men through and over the gap between the spur and Marble Kop; this supposition was supported by information given by the stretcher bearers, who were now coming in pretty frequently with wounded men from the firing line, so I signalled information to this effect to the officer commanding the battery; the distance, however, was too great, and the enemy were too well posted for shrapnel to do any harm: moreover, the gunners, from their long distance in the rear and because of the intervening end of the spur, could not see any of the underfeatures, behind which the enemy were situated.

The advance was continued until the right of the firing line, B company, was about 600 yards from the foot of Marble Kop; they could go no further with any advantage, and were fully occupied, as was C company, in keeping down the fire from their right front. Beyond them F company was pushing forwards towards the left of Marble Kop where the pass opened out, and were moving down into a fold of the ground, which hid them from my sight; slightly behind them and on their left was the Volunteer company, slowly pushing on, firing and advancing, and lying down to fire again, and continuing this with the greatest coolness and steadiness.

I was watching them through my telescope for some little time, noticing Sir Walter Barttelot running forward and the half-company following him, and I thought how unmistakeable a leader he looked, with no equipment and no rifle, standing and pointing with his stick to places which men should occupy. Sir Walter did not know the meaning of fear or nervousness, and the pluck and marvellous endurance he displayed during the campaign was a constant wonder to all of us, and put to shame many a soldier of half his age.

Soon the Volunteer company disappeared, like F company, in the fold of the ground, and I hoped that they would succeed in pushing on into the pass and round by the left of Marble Kop, and so create a diversion in the state of affairs. One or two wounded men being brought in from these companies proved what I suspected—that the huge, black, conical hill, rising on the left of the pass, was also occupied by the enemy's marksmen, who were behind the rocks and ledges of the steep slopes. This being so, things looked bad for our chance of being able to push round the left side of Marble Kop, which was, like its front, a slippery mass of smooth volcanic rock rising to a sharp pinnacle, and without an atom of cover. Nothing was to be gained by rushing this rock and swarming up its slippery sides (which we could easily have done), because, once there and necessarily crowded, we should have been exposed without the least protection to an overwhelming fire from the hills on the right and left of the Kop, while we could have done little good by our rifle fire, which would, of course, have to be directed up hill.

However, half of E company, waiting patiently in reserve, was sent out in support of F and the Volunteers, in case they should succeed in gaining a footing, and I went out myself a little way to find out if I could see what was beyond the fold in the ground into which these two companies had disappeared. Soon I met a stretcher borne along with difficulty by two men of F company, Privates Stewart and Biles, and upon it I was shocked to see Sir Walter Barttelot; he was unconscious and breathing heavily, and had been shot through the body by a bullet fired from the lofty hill on our left front. Sadly the men continued on their way to the dressing station, where Dr. Edwards immediately attended to him; but the case was hopeless from the first, and he breathed his last, still unconscious, soon after arrival.

From the men I learned that Captain Gilbert with most of his Company had brilliantly dashed into a Kaffir kraal under a severe fire from the left, and were there doing their best to subdue the enemy's scathing fire; several men had been wounded, Lieut. Anderson had been dangerously shot in the neck, and more stretchers were wanted. On the way back, therefore, volunteers were called for from E company to go out with stretchers, and right gallantly they came forward, plenty of them; they went out under the steady shower of bullets, right up to the firing line, and brought back most of the wounded who could not walk.

About four o'clock, a message was received from the Colonel that, if it was impossible, without supports as we were, to carry the Nek, a retirement should be made, and a reply was sent that the Nek could certainly be carried, as the men were only waiting for the order to rush Marble Kop; but that the advantage thus gained would be valueless, as no troops could remain on the smooth pinnacle, with no cover and commanded on both sides.

Orders were therefore sent to each company commander to retire as quickly as possible as soon as it was dusk. All this time the firing in the valley on the right had been going on, and at intervals the Maxim spluttered out a handful of rounds and kept the enemy from quitting, and, possibly, from taking up other positions from which they could have added their quota of fire to that already being showered on us.

The stretchers were still coming in, and some of the men of E company had once more volunteered to make another journey, although this work was much more dangerous than lying behind an ant heap in the firing line, and the men deserve all the credit that it is possible to give them for their pluck and coolness. Four volunteers, when asked for, were also easily forthcoming to carry to the four Company commanders the orders to retire; one of these men, Hurrell, of E, had only just returned with a stretcher, but off he went again, and, I am thankful to say, safely returned.

There were now a number of poor fellows lying on the grass, and the doctor and Corporal Knapp and Private Gill were busy doing the best for them that circumstances would allow; several others, who were only slightly wounded and were able to walk, were sent off to camp, and the stretchers were sent back to the firing line in anticipation of the retirement at dusk.

Although we had been in action since mid-day and it was now nearly five o'clock, not an ambulance had arrived; but at last ours was seen slowly

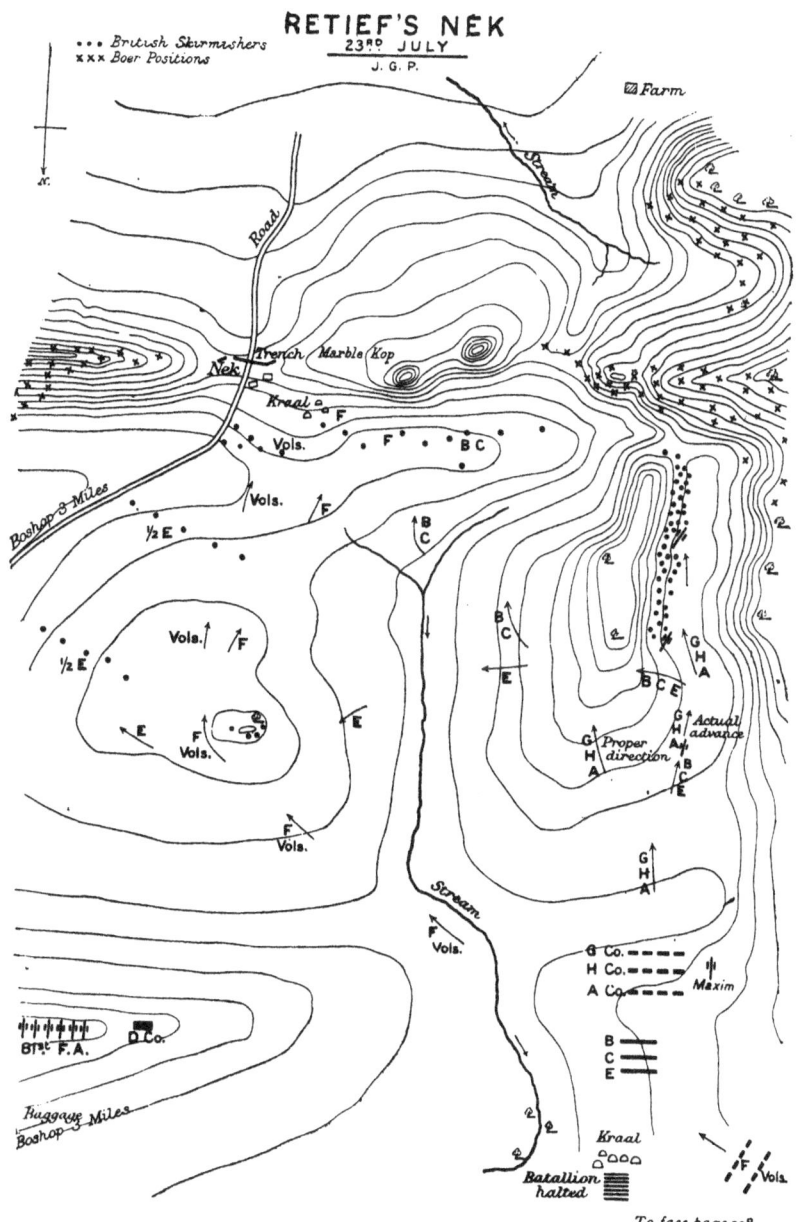

approaching from the valley on our right where it had remained : the labour of removing the groaning, wounded men—one of whom had been shot in the body, another in the thigh, another in the chest—in the clumsy old ambulance, which carried only two at a time, was commenced by the doctor.

It was now getting dusk, and a desultory fire was still being kept up by the enemy, when suddenly this increased in intensity and became a continuous clatter of musketry. The whole veldt between us and Marble Kop became spattered with puffs of dust thrown up by the Mauser bullets, some of the shots even reaching to the dressing station, which, unfortunately, had no Red Cross flag raised, although the Boers must have seen the ambulance wagon standing by with its white tilt and large flag flying.

The reason of this sudden outburst of musketry was the retirement of our men, who were running back smartly to be clear of the heavy fire : several little clumps of men were lagging somewhat in rear, carrying their wounded with them, and the Boers kept up a furious fire directed on these small parties. Several men were hit in this way, and the remainder were furious at the conduct of the Boers ; but their firing was perhaps excusable, as, in the dusk, I doubt whether they could distinguish the stretcher parties at that long distance.

In contravention of the old-fashioned idea that all retirements should be conducted slowly, and that it is a disgrace to move out of a slow walk, is the common-sense feeling that, if troops are to withdraw under a heavy fire, the quicker they carry out the movement the earlier they will be beyond range, and the fewer casualties will occur : troops who have served in India on any of the numerous hill expeditions which take place in that country soon learn to act upon this plan.

It was almost dark when the companies began to arrive at the dressing station, and, as the bullets were still flying about, we formed up in a hollow a little further back and waited for the remainder to come in : a good many men, and almost all the officers, were still in rear bringing along their wounded. Some of the companies, notably F and the Volunteers, had a long way to come, and the former had to wait till quite dark before they could rush out of the cover afforded by the kraal and successfully carry in those who had been badly hit. Lieut. Anderson had been very dangerously wounded in the throat, and the men had some difficulty in moving him : his wound had been bound up under a dreadful storm of bullets by a young soldier called Say of F company. Several other men were especially noted in their care for wounded comrades and their total disregard of danger : a large number of others showed the possession of bravery in a marked degree by securing and issuing ammunition, carrying orders, and assisting in other ways, under a heavy and continuous fire.

*Our casualities were severe, there being one

---

*Our casualties during the day were as follows :

KILLED.

Capt. Sir W. G. Barttelot,   Private C. Buck, B Company
    Volunteer Company   ,,   J. Mills, B   ,,
Private E. Bennett, G

WOUNDED.

Capt. E. L. Mackenzie   Private E. Coldwell, F Company
2nd Lieut. J. C. W. Anderson   ,, W. Croft, F   ,,
,, H. G. Montgomerie   ,, H. Smith, F   ,,
,, G. E. Leachman   ,, A. Holder, F   ,,   d
Clr.-Sergt. A. Nye, F Company   ,, H. Weeks, F   ,,
Lce.-Corp. J. Butt, H   ,,   ,, A. Thomas, C   ,,
,, A. King, F   ,,   d   ,, F. Baker, C   ,,
,, F. Manser, C   ,,   ,, M. Jeal.   C   ,,
Private A. Clarke, B   ,,   ,, W. Brown, C   ,,
,, A. Perry, B   ,,   ,, A. Winchester, C   ,,
,, E. Brown, B   ,,   ,, G. Duke, C   ,,
,, J. Leadbetter, B   ,,   ,, P. Griffiths, H.   ,,
,, L. Paddon, B   ,,   ,, W. Boniface, G.   ,,
,, J. Hall, B   ,,   ,, J. Hiscock, Vol.   ,,   d
,, J. Nicholls, B   ,,   ,, M. Weller,   ,,   ,,
,, J. Hyde, B   ,,   ,, P. Pilcher,   ,,   ,,
,, A. Baker F   ,,   ,, E. Gouldsmith. Vol.,,
,, G. Parsons, F   ,,   ,, R. Burtenshaw, E   ,,

    d Died of wounds.

officer killed and four wounded, whilst three men were killed and thirty-two wounded.

The three companies in the valley on our right retired about the same time as we did, and we proceeded to camp, which lay behind the position occupied by the battery and by D company, their escort: it must have been nearly seven o'clock when we reached our bivouacs and the wagons were brought up and unloaded of their wet and sopping blankets. However, we were too dead tired (having worn our blankets and heavy equipment for fifteen hours) and exhausted for want of sleep and food to think much of discomfort; and first we had to look after our wounded. Volunteers were soon forthcoming, and we managed to procure some tents, without any pegs, which we at last succeeded in pitching : the wounded arrived, the majority being able to walk, but some being brought in on stretchers, and a few, two at a time, on the single wretched ambulance which was all we had; and they were stowed away and made as comfortable as we could manage in the tents.

A real genuine Good Samaritan of a modern type appeared in the shape of an acting Chaplain, Mr. Leary, a Colonial born and bred, who did right good service in looking after our men—whom he had never seen before. He went to and fro with the ambulance, and, after one or two trips, got the men taken on a couple of miles further and put in the Field Hospital, which was at Boshop Farm. He is a right good man, just the one for a soldiers' padré, and he ought to be a Bishop: I hope he will be one before long.

We managed to rake up some Bovril, and gave the wounded that and some tea: the padré took out a bucketful of soup to give to the men still waiting at the dressing station to be removed. Our doctor, a civilian named Edwards, and also a

Colonial, from New South Wales, worked like a horse: his labour and the padré's that night only began when ours was finished.

The following orders relating to the action were published a day or two afterwards:—

Extract from Battalion Orders, 24th July, 1900.

"It is with the deepest regret that Lieut.-Col. Donne records the death in action yesterday of Sir Walter Barttelot, Bart., Commanding the Volunteer Company. Sir Walter Barttelot served throughout the long and arduous marches of the battalion, showing an example of fortitude and devotion to duty unsurpassed in the annals of the regiment, and which had deservedly won him the love of his comrades of all ranks. Sir Walter Barttelot passed unharmed through the actions of Welkom, Zand River, Doornkop, the Capture of Pretoria and the battle of Diamond Hill, in all of which he led his volunteers to the attack. In the desperate assault yesterday on the Boer position at Retief's Nek, he fell gallantly at the head of his company, to be mourned both by the regiment and the county of Sussex as one of the bravest soldiers and truest of men that have given their lives for Queen and country."

Extract from Battalion Orders, 26th July, 1900.

"Lieut.-Gen. Sir A. Hunter, K.C.B., referred as follows to the conduct of the battalion in the action of Retief's Nek on 23rd July.

"'Your men worked splendidly in the attack. They could not have done more. I wish you to convey to them, please, my high admiration of the dauntless way in which they advanced under such a fire.

"'Nothing could have been finer, and I deeply deplore the heavy losses incurred.'

"Lieut.-Col. Donne feels proud to publish these remarks from such a distinguished General as

Sir A. Hunter, with whom he has often had the honour of serving before.

"Although the attack could not be pressed home, owing to darkness and the cross-fire of the enemy, yet the losses of the battalion were not in vain, and the boldness of the attack on the right justly contributed to the success next morning of the turning movement on the left, which resulted in the rout of the Boers.

"The names of those who have fallen in this, as well as in all other actions, will be recorded at no distant date on a monument to be probably erected in the County Cathedral at home, or in such conspicuous place as may be deemed worthy to commemorate their deeds of valour on these South African battlefields." *

Sir Walter Barttelot was buried the next day under a huge eucalyptus growing by itself in a field to the east of Boshop Farm: two of the men who had been killed were buried there, too; their names were Bennet and Buck.

A slab of timber was erected over Sir Walter's grave, upon which an inscription had been cut by one of the Volunteer company.

---

* They are inscribed upon the Memorial at Brighton.—ED.

CHAPTER XIV.

TO THE BOER LAAGER.

Bearer Companies—Retief's Nek—Artillery driving—Naauwpoort Nek—White flags—Golden Gate—Orders to take over surrender of five commandos—To Raats' Farm—The Boer laager—Surrender of arms and horses—Organisation of prisoners—The Commandants—Basuto visitors—Destruction of ammunition.

During all the time we were between Bethlehem and Retief's Nek we had been away from the Bearer Company and the Field Hospital, and had only one ambulance with us to perform the necessary duties of both of these units. When leaving Bethlehem, our doctor, who was then a civilian of the New South Wales Hospital, tried to get an ambulance to accompany the regiment and the battery, then *en route* to Meyers Kop; but he met with considerable opposition to his request from the Bearer Company authorities, who apparently did not mind a whole battalion and a battery going off without transport for the sick or possible wounded, but hated having to give up one of their ambulances. The doctor had, eventually, to go to General Hunter and get an order from him before he could secure the wagon which was required.

The idea of separating or breaking up the unit was so distasteful that the request for a wagon was, at the time, compared to that of a battery commander being asked to break up the organization of his battery by sending one gun away with troops.

The comparison between a battery of the Royal Field Artillery and the miserable collection of half-a-dozen old ambulance wagons was too delicious for words, and will, no doubt, be appreciated by our gallant gunners! There is no branch of the army in which such a sacred regard for the everlasting red tape is evidenced in the field as in the Hospitals and Bearer Companies: " At all costs keep your wagons empty," should be their motto, which will be supported by many a footsore soldier, with ragged clothes and worn-out boots, who has been refused even a temporary ride in these vehicles.

At the time when we were in such trouble with our boots, and had to wear miners' highlows and anything that could be picked up in the shops, many a man might have been saved days and days in hospital by a lift in a wagon at the critical time: of course, the Bearer Company say at once, "We are not here to carry men with bad boots, our duty is to take wounded men from the scene of action to the Field Hospital," and decline to receive him: the Field Hospital say "We cannot take you unless you are handed over by the Bearer Company": the baggage master shouts at once, "Come off that blank wagon, don't you know you musn't ride on transport wagons?" and so the wretched man gets left behind by all.

There are two sides to every question, however, and all soldiers know that once a schemer obtains the slightest privilege from the hospital or the doctor, his example is immediately followed by crowds of imitators.

The practical advantages of the Bearer Company in the field are not very apparent, and the general who ordered the Field Hospital and the Bearer Company in his brigade to be amalgamated was a sensible man.

On the 25th of July at five o'clock in the morning we moved across to join the Highland Brigade camp, which was at Boshop Farm, a couple of miles away. Most of the Highlanders were out on the hills on the left of the pass, and only the Seaforth Highlanders were in camp: they also left about eight o'clock as there was an action going on. It seems that the Highland Light Infantry had attacked the hills on the left of Retief's Nek the day before, while we were making our attack on the pass; but the enemy were in great force, and resisted to the utmost the advance of the regiment, who, however, suceeded in getting a footing on the end of a ridge. In the early morning the pickets pushed on and occupied a prominent knoll, from which, as soon as it was light, a further advance was made along the ridge, which eventually led on to the range of hills on the left of the pass ; once this was reached, all opposition ceased, and the Boers fled.

In the afternoon we moved to a new camp at the Nek itself: there was an enormous convoy to go before us, so we did not get into camp until dark: the Highland Brigade and ourselves, not to mention the convoy, were all jumbled together in the jaws of the pass. However in the morning the Highlanders and the convoy and most of the other troops went back again, and moved round by Boshop Farm towards Naauwport Nek, whilst we were ordered to remain with a battery and some Yeomanry and guard the pass. After the usual pickets had been posted, we moved to a new camp, somewhat better sheltered from the bitter cold winds ; and here we remained in peace a couple of days.

A very fine example of what our artillery can do in the way of driving was seen during our short march from Boshop Farm to Retief's Nek, the day after the battle. Two guns of Major Simpson's battery, the 81st, were with the rear guard, and had moved to the summit of a hill, which they vacated at dusk, then proceeding to camp; the guns were under a young subaltern, and took a bee line from the hill to the camp in the distance. The hill was very steep, and near the foot of the slope, which they went down with all breaks on, was an outcrop of smooth rock, about fifteen or eighteen feet wide, running round the hill like a belt, and as steep as the roof of a house. Perfectly unconcerned, the young officer rode at this slippery place, and, without an instant's hesitation, shoved his horse across it, the intelligent animal sinking on his haunches and sliding to the other end on his iron-shod hoofs.

Steadily, the drivers followed in succession, the horses repeating the example of their leader and sliding down with taut traces, the gunners clutching on to the drag ropes in rear, slipping and cursing and falling in a heap at the foot of the slope, the heavy weight of the limber driving it forward and tearing the ropes out of their hands. And so they all got down without mishap and continued on their way to camp.

The ground behind the pass was very open for a considerable distance, the hills enclosing a grassy fertile valley, with a farm at the upper end and a spruit running across to the south: the farm was deserted, although all the furniture and a good deal of wheat and oats had been left.

On the left of the pass and sheltered in several ravines, which ran deep into the hills, the horses of the Boers had been kept waiting, apparently about a day, while the owners were busy with their Mausers amongst the hills; from the marks there must have been several hundred men employed in defending Retief's Nek alone. On the second day of our halt, a lame Boer with his rifle and bandolier crept up openly to a picket at the farm and surrendered himself; it seems that he had been fighting against us on the Nek, but had slipped among the rocks when retiring and had sprained his ankle.

Orders were received to move off towards Naauwpoort Nek, so we left on the 27th of July and marched round past Boshop Farm, which was still used as a hospital (there being one or two cases which could not be moved to Bethlehem as the others had been), and along a very bad road for some twelve miles to a place called Hebron. The Bedfords, who had been at Slabbert's Nek, followed us up the same day and told us about the fight at Slabbert's Nek, where they had had to storm the position, meeting with some opposition, but eventually carrying the hill without much loss to themselves. They had then remained to secure the pass, as we did at Retief's Nek, and had camped on a hill, making with great labour a road up the heights for the guns and the wagons. This had just been finished when orders were received to join us and proceed to Naauwpoort Nek; so the unfortunate Bedfords had to drag their wagons and guns down again late in the evening, and march most of the night, so as to arrive at Retief's Nek before we started; altogether, they had an uncomfortable time for a few days.

Continuing our march next day, we passed on the left Little Spitz Kop, which we afterwards heard had been cleared in gallant style by the Camerons who had passed that way some days previously, and were now busy watching Naauwpoort Nek. We also passed the spot where the Highland Brigade had bivouacked the day before, opposite the Nek; but our little column still pushed on, over several bad drifts, until dusk, when we camped at Groendraai, having trekked fully 15 miles.

On the road we passed a deserted *winkel*, full of mealies and sheepskins, which had been broken into by some of those who had preceded us. A *winkel* is a small roadside store, with a stock, mostly suitable for Kaffirs, of clothes, cheap jewellery and rubbish generally, which the owner of the *winkel* disposes of in exchange for wool, sheepskins, mealies and other things: we met the manager of this place the next day coming back to look after his property.

Next day, the 27th of July, we trekked off
again, and about mid-day joined General Bruce
Hamilton, with whom were the Camerons; the Highlanders had been clearing the hills with which we
were surrounded, and even then we could hear firing
occasionally. After a while our battalion was sent
out to clear and occupy a large, flat-topped kopje,
which rose straight out of an extensive valley. This
kopje turned out to be unoccupied, and, leaving
B company on picket there, the battalion moved
on to camp.

The next day was a peaceful one; there was,
however, a good deal of excitement about, which
we could not fathom : several flags of truce were
sent out by the General in various directions, and
every one was wondering what it all meant. The
battalion went out also, and C company, under
Captain Wroughton, was despatched to climb to
the top of, and picket, a perfectly awful hill, a
long distance away, and a fearful climb.

It took them a long time even to reach the foot
of the hill, and longer still to climb up the steep
slope ; we watched them through our glasses, tiny
specks moving slowly, very slowly, up and up, and
then disappearing over the sky line. As soon as
they had reached the summit, A and D companies,
under Major O'Grady and Lieut. Ashworth, Major
Scaife being again baggage master, proceeded
along the valley, protected on the right by Captain
Wroughton's presence up the hill, and on the left
by B company, still on picket on the kopje we had
occupied the previous night. A and D moved straight
out about two-and-a-half miles to their front,
where there was an isolated, conical-shaped kopje
with a flat, straight spur running off to its right and
joining it to the hills further on. To this flat spur
the two companies were directed to proceed, and to
remain there until ordered to withdraw.

From their high elevation, both of our parties

could see, in the valley beyond, but at a very great distance, numbers of Boer wagons trekking in all directions, evidently in a disorganised kind of way : they were, of course, quite out of range, even of our cow gun, which had accompanied the Camerons from Bethlehem, and was now in camp.

In the afternoon, we withdrew our pickets and proceeded to camp, which we did not reach until the late afternoon, the pickets having taken a long time to withdraw. We found the camp had been moved about a mile to a new site on the far side of the drift; the wagons and the convoy had amused themselves during the day by crossing this drift, which was fairly good but terribly steep on the ascending side, necessitating double teams of oxen. Earlier in the day, before we started, we had sent our empty wagons across the drift to a place opposite our camp, and just on the other side of the spruit: we had carried our bundles of blankets and other baggage across by hand, and loaded them on the wagons, so our wretchedly weak and overworked mules had a rest that day.

The next morning, the 31st of July, we marched off again towards Golden Gate: the Mounted Infantry, who were in front, carried white flags, which were also borne by those on our flanks, and it seemed as though an armistice had been declared. However, no information was given to us, so we trekked on steadily until the afternoon, when the General, who had ridden on in front some miles, sent back word to the Colonel to say that he wanted to see Major du Moulin.

So I rode off, followed by the usual chaffing remarks about canteen jam and other things, and found the General about 4 miles ahead at Klerksvlei, with his staff and escort. There, he gave me orders to ride on to Raats' Farm, about 4 miles further on, and to receive the surrender of five commandos. This was news indeed, so accompanied by Lieut. Bellamy, who was then assistant to the Provost Marshall, with a few of his mounted Police, an orderly with a white flag, and one or two other officers, I hurried off at once, as the sun was beginning to drop towards the horizon, and there was an immense amount of work to be done, and very little time to do it in.

The General had told me some of the particulars of the surrender, which was entirely unconditional, with the reservation, granted by General Hunter, that private property should be respected, and that each burgher should be allowed a horse to ride to his destination, wherever that might be; and he instructed me to take over the arms and ammunition at once and to remove the horses for the night.

We rode on for some three or four miles over grassy veldt, huge ranges of hills on the right and left closing in on us as we advanced further; they appeared to meet in front of us, and, in fact, did close together to within 600 or 800 yards, forming the redoubtable Golden Gate. Across the mouth of this pass ran a deep spruit with steep banks; this was Klerks Spruit, and it was crossed by a terribly steep and bad drift, almost impassable for ox wagons, and entirely so for mule wagons, which would have had to be unloaded.

After almost meeting, the ranges of hills bore away again from each other, enclosing broken and hilly ground, which formed the outskirts of the mountains shutting in the famous Caledon Valley, at the northern entrance to which we now found ourselves; just beyond the drift was a farm, a substantial, well-to-do farm of considerable area, with a large orchard and several outhouses. This was Klerksvlei, owned by Mr. Solomon Raats, and it was around this farm in all directions, as far as one could see in the fast fading light, that the Boers were encamped : the whole neighbourhood was covered with men, horses, wagons and bullocks.

It was with a distinctly weird feeling that I rode into the heart of the enemy's laager and drew up on a slight rise of ground, just outside the farm : a small party of Mounted Infantry had followed us, and these now closed up behind and dismounted.

I sent for the five commandants, who soon appeared, each surrounded by a small crowd of retainers; and to them I gave instructions that each commando was to be formed up immediately, in order that the arms and bandoliers might be collected and that the horses might be counted.

There were several officers present, who had accompanied me, either on duty or as spectators with the General's permission, so that I was enabled to provide an officer to attend to the surrender of the arms and other matters of each commando. This was a business which took some considerable time, as each commando mustered about 300 to 350 men, and the rifles and bandoliers had to be brought up one by one and stacked in wagons. After all had been given in, the horses and ponies, a wretched lot of crocks, were handed over to men of the Mounted Infantry and led to the other side of the drift, where Major Lean's corps of Mount Infantry, the well-known 5th M.I., took over charge and formed a cordon round them.

Nearly the whole of the rifles with which the Boers were armed were Mausers : there was an occasional Lee-Metford, captured from our troops in Natal, usually, and perhaps a Martini or two. The ammunition was carried in bandoliers of every imaginable shape and pattern, mostly home made ; but some of the burghers preferred cartridge bags of leather or canvas. Many revolvers had been surrendered, but these were mostly weapons taken from prisoners, such as R.A. drivers or A.S.C. men, and were as a rule out of order.

It was considerably after dark that evening before the horses had been got away, and there remained several wagons piled up with rifles; there were bullocks in plenty, so these wagons were soon on the move across the drift and into the Mounted Infantry camp under a guard. The commandants informed us that there were many Boers out in the hills to whom information had been sent of the surrender, and who would come in the following morning and give up their rifles. Meantime, there was nothing further to be done that night, so a guard was mounted on the farm, where Lieut. Bellamy and myself were remaining; and the other officers and the Mounted Infantry went back to camp, taking to the General a brief report from me of what had been done.

Old Mr. Raats was very civil, providing a room and preparing supper for us and looking after our horses; there were quite a number of Boers staying at the farm also, among them being six or seven of the biggest men that I had ever seen; they were very tall, enormously broad shouldered and stout in proportion, and quite filled the dining room at the farm when they all came in at once.

The Boer laager was not all composed of fighting men by any means; there were large numbers of non-combatants—women, children and Kaffirs, hangers-on who attended to the feeding of the commandos or drove sheep and cattle, and other nondescripts who did not belong to any commando, but who accompanied the Boers, all the same. Then there were a number of what they called "trek Boers;" these were Boers with their families, cattle, wagons, horses and all their belongings, who had quitted their farms and were moving or trekking with the commandos; these men had some splendid wagons and teams of magnificent oxen with them.

There were many Boers who spoke perfect

English, and among them in particular two wearing the Red Cross badge; these two stated that they belonged to the Identity Department of the Red Cross Society, and produced papers in proof of this. One of them, Mr. Nelson, informed me that their duties were to remain with the commando to which they were attached, and to keep a list of any men killed or wounded, forwarding a copy to Pretoria when an occasion offered.

This system appears to have been the only means by which any record was kept of the casualties among the Boers, but the killed and wounded were so few that no doubt it worked well enough.

There was a parson, or predikant, also accompanying the commandos. He was, of course, not a fighting man, but was very loyal to his own folk, and, when we asked him what he would have done if any fighting had taken place, he replied that under ordinary circumstances he helped to look after the commissariat arrangements, but that if we had attacked the camp he would have taken a rifle at once and assisted as well as he could to defend his country. We assured him that his sentiments did him credit.

For several hours that night the Boers collected in groups round their camp fires, singing hymns, and it was late before everything was quiet, and we were able to sleep. Mr. Raats had provided us with the guest chamber of his house, and this room was fully furnished in the most elaborate style, including even a bath. Our first step had been to throw up the narrow window and ventilate the room as much as possible; we should have preferred to sleep in the open, but as we had no kit except what we stood up in, this was not advisable.

Soon after daybreak the next morning the collecting of rifles was proceeded with: numbers of Boers came crowding in from the hills around, eager to surrender their arms and ammunition, and in a few hours we had accumulated a large heap on the ground. The ammunition we filled into bags and loaded on wagons, but the rifles were placed in a great pile and burned, as we had no means of carrying such a large number: they were rendered quite useless, as the barrels were made soft by the heat, and all the foresights, backsights and other attachments were melted off.

The Boers told us that they had left nine or ten wagons, mostly loaded with rifle ammunition, on the road about 3 miles off; the bullocks had been taken away by the Harrismith commando, and the wagons were left there with a few Boers in charge; they also said the road was terrible, and that it would take a long time to bring in the wagons, even if bullocks were sent out for this purpose.

A report to this effect being made to the General, the Engineer officer, Lieut. Evans, was sent out to destroy the wagons. This was done during the day by blowing them up; unfortunately, owing to some Kaffir putting a bag of powder in close proximity to the fuse, a premature explosion took place, and the old sergeant of the R.E. section, Sergeant Munn, was somewhat seriously injured, while Lieut. Evans himself was cut about a good deal.

During the morning the officers whom the General had detailed to assist me reported their arrival: they were, Captain Wroughton of our battalion; and Captain Tufnell, Lieut. Lambton and Lieut. Key, all from the Mounted Infantry; these, with Lieut. Bellamy, gave us one British officer to each of the five commandos: but, as Lieut. Bellamy had to return to his proper duty as assistant Provost Marshal, Lieut. Bond was applied for in relief of him.

As soon as the officers arrived we were able to get the Boers into some sort of organization. Each commando had its Boer commandant, who had under him his adjutant and secretary, both of whom usually spoke English; and the remainder of the Boers were distributed under the orders of a certain number of Field Cornets, corresponding to our section commanders, who knew all about the men, and had rolls of them and other information.

The commandants themselves knew nothing about their men, their names or other details, but left all that to the Field Cornets.

The five officers were posted to the commandos as follows :—

To Du Plooy's Commando .... Lieut. Bond, vice Lieut. Bellamy.
,, Potgieter's ,, ... Capt. Wroughton.
,, Joubert's ,, ... Lieut. Lambton.
,, Crowther's ,, ... Lieut. Key.
,, Jonker's ,, ... Captain Tuffnell.

Having thus a certain nucleus of organization to go upon, the officers went off, each to his own commando, to make themselves acquainted with their commandants and to ascertain the quantity of rations available, besides obtaining other information, such as the numbers of men, horses, wagons, Cape carts and bullocks, in each commando.

Of these commandos, that of Potgieter was the most important and the strongest in numbers, and the best looked after by the commandant and his Field Cornets; nearly all the burghers came from the Smithfield District, while those in the other commandos came from the districts of Bethulie, Thaba N'Chu and Winburg.

Jonker was not really a commandant, but, being the oldest Field Cornet, he was selected by us to organise and look after the burghers of the Harrismith commando, composed of those who had elected to surrender instead of going off with Olivier.

Commandant Du Plooy was the most respectable and reliable, as far as one could observe in the fortnight the Boers were under our charge; but all the commandants were men of standing and position, accustomed to be treated, as could be seen, with a good deal of deference by the burghers; they appeared to be all honourable men, and were most courteous in their address and manner of speaking on all occasions.

Commandant Joubert was a truculent old gentleman, who apparently failed to thoroughly grasp his position, and, while not exactly objecting to any orders which were given him, he showed his disapproval in other ways, and usually had a good deal to say on any matter that came forward.

General Bruce Hamilton rode over that morning and had an interview with the five commandants, and ascertained that they thoroughly understood the conditions upon which their surrender was accepted; these were, that each burgher was to be allowed a horse to ride to his destination, and that all private property was to be respected. The Boers had a great fear of being compelled to walk, and would have done anything sooner than go on foot, a thing to which they have never been accustomed. They were amazed at our infantry marching as they did every mile of the road, and frankly admitted that the Boers could have done nothing of the sort.

Lieut. Bellamy was busy all that day enquiring into the cases of the trek Boers and such other non-combatants as were willing to take the oath of allegiance to Her Majesty, or of neutrality, and to go quietly back to their farms: to these passes were issued and the people allowed to go off at once. This reduced the crowd of wagons very considerably, as nearly all of these burghers had one, if not more, wagons, and usually one or two vans or covered carts in which the womenfolk travelled, if they were well-to-do people.

Several of them had droves of cattle and flocks of sheep also. The remainder of the wagons, which were almost entirely those that had been captured from our convoys on different occasions, were loaded with the burghers' kits and with their rations of meal and some coffee. They said they had been out of tea and sugar for a long time, that the coffee was merely roasted beans and mealies, and that tobacco was almost unknown. However they had plenty of cattle, which largely made up for the absence of other food; as the Boer is a great meat eater, and, unlike other civilised people, can exist on meat alone for a considerable period.

There was one field gun amongst the wagons: this had belonged to U Battery, R.H.A., and had been captured by the Boers at Sanna's Post; several artillery ammunition wagons were also found, which, with some of the wagons which were loaded with gun and rifle ammunition, were all sent away to the General's camp.

The hills and ravines around Raats' farm were full of cattle and mules grazing, so we sent a number of the Boers to bring them in and to inspan them into the wagons and Cape carts, as it was now necessary to shift our camp to a better site where the commandos could be separated somewhat. There was plenty of space about a couple of miles outside the Golden Gate, and in the afternoon each officer moved his commando and encamped it in a new spot.

Here the wagons, carts and horses were drawn up with some regularity, and the officers were enabled to check the numbers previously given in by the commandants, which were found to be substantially correct in every case.

Another important matter was the equalising of such rations as were in the possession of the Boers: stock was therefore taken by each officer, and Captain Wroughton arranged about the sharing of what flour and other stuff there was, and saw that the fat oxen were collected and put into a drove in charge of some of the burghers, until they were required for slaughtering.

During this day the battalion had been moved to the same spot upon which the laager was encamped: several pickets were furnished round the prisoners, and sentries placed on the roads leading in and out of the pass.

All the burghers paraded with their horses the next morning, so that those which were fit for use by the mounted troops might be taken, and others given in their place. An Artillery officer came down to select these horses, and from the way he went about the business, carefully examining each animal all round and passing his critical hand over fetlocks and back sinews, it was plain that he did not realise that he had about 1,200 horses to look through that morning. However, our time was precious, and we had plenty to do without meddling in other people's affairs, so the Artillery major was left to run his own show; it came to a climax a few hours afterwards, as we received orders to move before he had selected more than a few horses.

From that time on we were beset with people who either wanted another horse, or thought they saw their way to getting a better one. None of us had any peace; there was always someone who wished to exchange his horse for a better one, and on going down to the lines we were pretty certain to see several strangers "looking round," as they called it—but we soon knew what that meant. The Boer laager seemed to be considered a fair field for anyone to exploit, one officer going so far as to send his men down to take some of the Boers' blankets away from them!

A party of Basutos from across the border, which was only three or four miles away, came over to pay their respects to the General; they were a chief and his interpreter and a retinue of sorts. A more motley crew has never been seen; they were all mounted on ponies; the chief was an enormously fat young man, bursting out of a slate coloured tweed suit, and wearing a black pot hat; the interpreter was similarly rigged out in a suit of dittoes; but the retinue were equipped mostly with a simple tuft of feathers in their hair. Some of them had blankets, but, the day being close, they carried them strapped on to their saddles. Whilst the chief was making his salaams to the General the crowd of retainers strolled about, and eventually became such a nuisance that after the interview was concluded, the whole gang were requested to withdraw to their own territory.

The ammunition which could not be carried with us for want of the necessary transport was handed over to the Mounted Infantry and to our battalion to be destroyed. This was no easy matter, but some was burned and exploded, some buried, and a quantity thrown into the pools of water in the spruit.

Major Lean was very successful with five or six wagon loads of powder and ammunition which were given him to destroy; the powder was strewn broadcast over the ground, but the boxes of ammunition and the wheels and other woodwork of the wagons were piled, sandwich fashion, into a huge heap and set fire to just before leaving the camp. As the boxes burned the cartridges were exploded, and a terrific noise, like a general engagement or the last stage of the attack as practised at General's inspection, echoed and re-echoed among the hills for several hours. No doubt, a good many cartridges escaped destruction, but it was impossible in the time available to destroy the ammunition more thoroughly.

Amongst the Mauser ammunition which was given up in the bandoliers, there were many clips containing cartridges whose bullets were covered with bright green fat ; this gave rise to the statement that the Boers had wilfully used poisoned bullets. This theory was regularly harped upon by some war correspondents in their letters, but a more disgraceful insinuation against our enemies never existed, nor one more erroneous from a musketry point of view.

It is quite plain to any unbiassed person that any grease which might be upon the bullet when it is placed in the chamber of the rifle would be completely wiped off during the passage of the tightly-fitting projectile through the barrel, from which it emerges as clean as when made, and bearing the marks of the grooving. Enquiries among the better class Boers regarding this rumour elicited the fact that many of them were in the habit of dipping the cartridges in fat prepared from bucks which they had killed, with a view to lubicating the chamber and barrel of the rifle : the buck fat, after exposure to the air, turned green ; the Boers were much amused at the ridiculous conclusion at which these correspondents had arrived.

CHAPTER XV.

TO WINBURG.

Escorting the prisoners—Authority of the Commandants—Strength of the commandos— Biddulph's Berg—Senekal—Sardines—Winburg —Release of old men and boys—Remainder of prisoners entrained.

The battalion camped on the 31st of July at Klerksvlei, but next day moved about three miles further on with a view of forming a guard to the prisoners, whose laager had then been established at Korfshoek. The march was commenced on the 2nd of August, when the laager with the battalion as escort, together with the Mounted Infantry and the guns, returned to Klerksvlei, proceeding the next day to Weltevreden, a long weary march of 15 miles. There was a halt of a couple of hours on the road after we had gone about 5 or 6 miles, as we met the Highland Brigade on their way to Harrismith. Some Mounted Infantry were also encountered on the look-out for horses: and we smiled as we saw them select some that had been handed over to us as useless the day before. However, we said nothing. We got off again at last and marched back on the road by which we had come from Naauwpoort Nek. We halted once for a couple of hours to enable the wagons to cross a drift, and took the opportunity to have some food, and to water and graze our animals. At this spot, with a strongish breeze blowing, one of our companies, lying on the grass, seized the occasion to start a grass fire, which spread like a flash and necessitated our moving; endeavours were made to turn the course of the fire or to put it out, but without avail, so we had to inspan and trek pretty smartly. On our road we passed the site of our former bivouacs, and marched on for another few miles before camping at Weltevreden. Next day we were afoot at eight o'clock, but halted a good many times during the day, principally at drifts, of which there were several, and also on two occasions to allow the Eighth Division, under General Rundle, to pass us on their way to Harrismith. The troops of the Eighth Division were much interested at the sight of the Boer prisoners riding along, a huge column of 1,500 men; and I think the burghers themselves were also impressed at the sight of the numerous troops we passed on our way, first the Highland Brigade and then the Eighth Division.

We bivouacked that night below Little Spitz Kop, a wretched place for a camp—bad water out of a dirty sluit, and the whole neighbourhood as black as your hat as the result of a grass fire.

The 5th of August was a terribly long day; we started at seven o'clock and trekked along steadily for mile after mile, halting at mid-day for a couple of hours to refresh man and beast, and eventually reaching Bethlehem at six in the evening, just after dark.

Stringent orders had been issued by General Hunter with regard to the safety of the prisoners, and these were read to commandants and explained by them to their burghers; the prisoners, however, were quite resigned to their fate, and I myself was sure that none would be missing when we arrived at our destination; and in this I was quite correct, as afterwards was proved. The burghers were at all times quite under the thumb of their commandants, whom they looked up to with unswerving fidelity and supported with implicit obedience; thus when they were informed that the commandant himself would be held responsible in the event of any man of his commando deserting, there was little doubt in my mind as to their compliance.

The battalion furnished a cordon of sentries round the Boer camp that night; they were relieved next day by the Bedford regiment, whom we found in camp next to us. There was a halt for the troops that day, but there was not much rest for us in the Boer laager, as there was a good deal of organising to do which there had been no opportunity of carrying out before. Seeing that the five officers under me were all very busy, the General decided to attach five more for duty, and they came and reported themselves during the day. This was a great addition to our administrative staff, as it enabled two officers to be apportioned to each commando, one of whom paraded and rode with the mounted men on the march daily, whilst the other rode with the wagons and superintended everything connected with them: by this means we were enabled to get things done with some regularity and precision, especially as Captain Tufnell volunteered to look after the whole of the wagons and Cape carts when in camp and on the march, while Captain Wroughton undertook the duties of Quartermaster and superintended the ration question: of these two tiresome jobs, I am not sure which was the most worrying.

The five officers who joined us were Lieut. Willett, of our regiment, 2nd Lieuts. Greenwell and Veasey of the Bedfords, 2nd Lieut. Lord Murray of the Camerons, and Lieut. Henderson of the City Imperial Volunteers. The services of Sergeant Flynn and Drummer Briggs were also lent to us to facilitate issuing orders and carrying messages.

The first thing to do was to have a proper roll call of the commandos; we had had no opportunity before then of doing this, although the adjutants of each commando had prepared rolls of their men, so a careful muster was taken by the officers, the numbers of the prisoners proving to be as follows:—

Commandant Jonker	....	239 burghers.
,,	Crowther	....	379 ,,
,,	Joubert	....	190 ,,
,,	Du Plooy	....	227 ,,
,,	Potgieter	....	512 ,,

To these had to be added four men who were sent down by the Provost Marshal, and seven had to be deducted, who were admitted to hospital in the town, making a net total of 1,544.

After the roll call was concluded the burghers were directed to give up all property belonging to the Free State or to the British Government, and this order resulted in a most miscellaneous collection of articles being made, comprising tents, waterproof sheets, entrenching tools, bayonets, military clothing of all kinds which had been looted from the Derby Militia, and from the trains which had been held up and wrecked by De Wet ; saddlery and telescopes taken from the Yeomanry who surrendered at Lindley; and hundreds of smaller articles, Gladstone bags, tin uniform cases, water bottles, haversacks, ration baskets, signalling panniers, books, canteens and equipment, which had all at one time belonged to the Derby Militia.

There was very little property belonging to the Orange Free State, with the exception of a few tents and some waterproof sheets ; we were careful not to receive anything which might be considered as the private property of the burghers, and the whole day long numbers of these simple minded men came to us, bringing all sorts of articles, and asking if they could retain them.

In any case each Boer was allowed to keep a blanket for himself and one for his horse, a waterbottle and a waterproof sheet; and we did not interfere with the clothing they were wearing, much of which was our khaki serge, with many overcoats and khaki warm coats.

Some of the wagons, which were covered in and suitable for the purpose, were sent over to the hospital to assist in carrying the sick and wounded.

During the afternoon the commandants were received by General Hunter at his quarters in the town, where they drank coffee, and, with the assistance of an interpreter, made the polite and cautious remarks usual on such occasions.

A few horses were exchanged for some in the Mounted Infantry, but all those which were of the slightest use had already been taken. At night our custom was for all horses, after watering, to be taken to the Mounted Infantry lines, where they were fastened together in huge rings, under a guard, the Boers going back to their lines and coming at daybreak again to receive their animals. Any possibility of our friends taking French leave during the night was thus precluded.

The commandants were warned and directed to inform their men that any insubordination would be severely punished, the offender being placed under a guard and compelled to walk instead of riding; and the commandants were held personally responsible that none of their men attempted to escape.

During our subsequent march to the railway, prisoners were constantly being received in twos and threes from the Provost Marshal, and a large number, some seventy-five, of the remainder of those who had surrendered to General Hunter at Fouriesburg, were handed over to us on one occasion.

The morning of the 7th of August saw us out of Bethlehem for the second time and tramping along the well-known road to Meyer's Kop, over which some of us had already marched three times.

Bethlehem looked better by daylight than it did when we left it in the dark on the 16th of July; it is a large town and, as is usual, well laid out with a fine church in the middle, but it would be a good deal prettier if the indolent Boers could be persuaded to plant a few more trees. It is a curious trait in the Boer character that, notwithstanding their Dutch origin, they do not appear to care in the least for flowers, or trees, or gardening of any kind.

In the teeth of an icy cold wind, which raised clouds of dust, we tramped along, past Sevastopol, and our old friend, Meyer's Kop, to Bester's Farm, a few miles beyond the latter place, and continued our march the next day and the next in similar fashion, halting at each mid-day for a couple of hours.

On the road we passed the redoubtable Biddulph's Berg, which had been some time previously the scene of a severe action, where a battalion of Guards was heavily engaged and suffered from a very large number of casualities, over 150, I believe. They had a terrible experience in this action which has happily seldom occurred in warfare before ; the grass was very long and dry, and there was a breeze blowing from the rear, where a number of people were watching the fight ; these individuals were seen to drop matches on to the dry grass, and the consequent fire was soon beyond their power to extinguish. Rapidly the flames grew and spread to the right and left, and rushed, fanned by the breeze, straight down upon the unfortunate Guardsmen, extended and carrying on the attack upon the enemy in front: there was no escape, and the roaring flames swept like a rolling torrent down upon the soldiers, scattering them in all directions and scorching them severely: worse than this, the wounded, of whom there were a considerable number lying in the long grass, were badly burned and suffered terrible agony : it was a truly dreadful experience.

On the 9th of August we reached Senekal, crossed the drift, and camped just beyond the town; the opportunity was here taken to buy what food could be purchased, for the Brigade Canteen; but there was little to be had, and that was at famine prices.

Captain Wisden, however, struck what shopmen call a "line" of sardines, in which he invested largely for the Officers' mess, and which proved to be the worst possible kind of fish that had ever been put in a tin. How the wretched animal had existed when it was alive was a marvel, as it consisted, seemingly, of one huge backbone and little else; but no doubt the bad oil, into which it was put when it was tinned, brought about a speedy death and released the poor creature from its sufferings! Captain Wisden will never hear the end of this, and all our officers will in future beware of that particular brand of sardines.

Senekal is a small and neat town at the foot of a huge kopje, and was occupied, when we passed through, by the other half battalion of the Bedfords: it is the scene of one of the mishaps to the Yeomanry when Major D'Albiac was killed and a number of others killed, wounded, and taken prisoners; through great negligence they had not searched or occupied the kopje, which frowns over the little town at a distance of a few hundred yards, and from here the Boers suddenly opened fire on the men walking about down below, and shot Major D'Albiac, a well-known man, who had been in the Royal Horse Artillery, as he rushed out of the hotel.

The next three days were occupied in moving towards Winburg, two marches of 11 miles each, and the last of fifteen, into the town, which we reached about three o'clock in the afternoon. Each day we had halted for a mid-day rest, but the journey, although through open country, was not a pleasant one owing to the wind and the dust ; the camping grounds also were filthy, as they had been used so frequently during the last few months, no water being procurable elsewhere : they were surrounded by dead mules, horses and bullocks : carcases littered each side of the road as well, between one camp and another.

So we were pleased to reach Winburg and to camp on the plain beyond the railway station, with the possibility of a few days' rest, and the chance of buying some bread—a commodity we had not seen in any quantity since leaving Pretoria in the middle of June. I foresaw, however, a good deal of work for myself and the ten officers with the Boer laager, as the burghers were to be handed over and despatched by train to Cape Town : they had not been told this or given any hint of their destination, and even now we were careful to say nothing further than that they were going off in the train; but, of course, the more intelligent of them quickly grasped the facts and fully imagined that they were bound for St. Helena : they had not, apparently, heard of Ceylon.

For the next three days there was very little rest in the Boer laager for any of us : the very afternoon of our arrival round came Major Maclaughlin and another officer of the Remount Department, who demanded all the horses and ponies : Captain Camilleri, one of the Transport Officers, also turned up and said he wanted all the Cape carts and most of the wagons : Major Cardew said all the saddles and harness were to go to the Ordnance Stores, and Major Orr, of the 18th Royal Irish, the Railway Staff Officer, had his little say, too, about the probable departure of the Boers, which was to take place as soon as trains could be made up.

We did not attempt to do much that afternoon, as the whole camp was overrun with visitors from the town and idlers of all kinds who came to stare at the Boers and ask us questions, which we had no time to answer. The first thing was to get off the horses and ponies, which were sent in batches to some cattle kraals near by; the animals belonging to the Commandants and Field Cornets, which had not been taken from them or exchanged during the journey, were collected together and sent separately to the same place, and by a little after dark we had got rid of all the horses and ponies, some 1,200 in number.

Next morning, the 13th of August, we were early at our work, and got all the saddles and harness together and laid out in rows, and collected any more Government property, tents and other things, which had been used on the march.

The drinking water was a long distance away, and the Boers were much amused at our forming some of them into water parties and marching them off, under a guard, to fetch water for their messes; they tramped off in fours, calling to each other and laughing, just like so many children.

After breakfast there was a muster parade of each commando, when the officers in charge called the rolls and ascertained that all their men were actually present: this was a long business and took some hours. The rest of the day was occupied in moving all the wagons and Cape carts to the outskirts of the camp, and closing in the commandos a good deal, so as to form a smaller circle for the sentries to guard; for, all this time, and in fact ever since leaving Bethlehem, the Boer laager had been surrounded by a cordon of sentries by day and night.

The following morning, such wagons, oxen and Cape carts as were of any use, were removed by the transport people, and the saddles and harness, about four wagon loads, taken away to the Ordnance stores: the burghers did not like this part of the performance as they had all written their names on the saddles, with what object goodness only knows, and were not at all pleased when some of them were called upon to come and load the saddles on to the wagons.

In the course of this day passes were given to the families, several of whom were still with us, and they were permitted to go to their farms with their wagons and oxen; the old men and the boys were also mustered, and a selection made of those to whom passes might be issued with the privilege of going to their farms and remaining there. A large number turned up, most of the men being old and feeble, and some of the boys being very young, so that we made a careful selection, rejecting all those whose appearance gave the impression that they were able to carry and use a rifle, and issuing passes to the remainder.

Altogether, there were no less than 105 permitted to go away, and they were sent off that afternoon: some of the boys and older men, who belonged to the Bethulie District, and who had no wagons, were provided with railway passes to enable them to get to their homes speedily.

Had it been known that the disturbance and guerilla warfare in the Orange River Colony would continue for so long after the dispersal of what might be called the Boer army, it is probable that not a single man, woman or child would have been permitted to go back to their farms; which, although their occupants had taken the oath of allegiance to the Queen, became centres whence horses, wagons and supplies of all kinds, besides information as to our movements, were furnished to the nomadic bands of insurgents who roamed the country.

That afternoon we succeeded in despatching Potgieter's commando, 477 strong, by train to Cape Town; the burghers fell in, with their blankets and rations, and marched down to the train (which had steamed up close to the camp), with all the regularity of soldiers ; they were to travel under a guard of militia, who were ready waiting, and to whom we handed the Boers over as they got into the trucks.

They all seemed happy enough, laughing and chatting, and many of them waved their hands to us as the train steamed off.

The next morning another batch, over 800 strong, was sent off, and the remainder followed an hour later, bringing our connection with the Boer laager to a close.

CHAPTER XVI.

UP AND DOWN.

Bloemfontein—Men and officers waiting there—Kroonstad—The Brigade re-fitted—Wasted comforts—Shopping for the canteen—Famine prices—Traders' profits—Ventersburg road—Half battalion to Winburg—Winburg attacked—Capture of Commandant Olivier—Bloemfontein—Ladybrand—Leeuw River Mills.

I went down in the train with the last batch of prisoners as far as Bloemfontein, as the General wished me to go to the Ordnance stores, and see what could be done about bringing up clothing, boots and other stores for the men, who were now in rags again and very badly off for boots. Several officers from the Brigade had been sent down at various times for this purpose, and I, with these officers and what stuff we could get, was to meet the Brigade at Kroonstad on the 20th of August.

Leaving Winburg about mid-day, the train reached our destination about half-past six, and there we quitted it, seeing the last of our friends, the Boer prisoners: they were lively enough and, all the way down, had looked with interest at the Militia battalions guarding the line and the bridges, and at the various entrenchments thrown up by them, and at the fortifications of biscuit boxes and barbed wire at each place. At Brandfort they met plenty of friends and evident sympathisers, who had apparently been allowed on the platform to see them, but at Bloemfontein the train stopped outside the station, and then ran through without stopping at the platform.

I stayed a couple of days in Bloemfontein and found all the other officers there; they had succeeded in getting all the ordnance stores they wanted and were ready to return, but could not get permission to do so; however, a visit to the D. A. A. G. soon settled that, and the next trouble was to get all the trucks, which had been loaded at the Ordnance siding, attached to a train and despatched.

The Assistant Director of Railways, Captain Nathan, R.E., was an old friend of mine, and arranged to have the trucks put on to a train on the 18th of August, by which we also arranged to leave. There was a most serious congestion of traffic at that time; rows and rows of trucks were waiting, and had been waiting for some time, for an opportunity to be despatched up country; there were no less than fourteen trains of remounts passing forward, and these, of course, had to receive precedence over others; the mails also had been waiting for days. There was the greatest strictness observed as to who travelled and why, and the contents of each truck were carefully examined to see that no private stores were loaded on it, and even the carriages were examined, just before the trains started, by the Railway Staff Officers. I had tried to get some Canteen stores shipped; four cases of tobacco, which were urgently wanted by the men, I had even brought down to the station, and I succeeded in smuggling one on to a truck. There was plenty of room in the guard's van and lots of space upon several trucks upon which troops were travelling, but the guard was a surly Dutchman, an uncivil brute, who started the train as the three cases were actually being loaded; so they had to be dropped on to the line and left behind, to be eventually sent up by ox wagon, which cost the Brigade Canteen no less than £5.

The streets of Bloemfontein were a curious sight in the daytime, crowded with soldiers of every imaginable regiment, and full of staff officers, whose red tabs on their collars had procured for them the designation of "rooineks," or red necks, which is the sneering nickname the Boers have had for years for British soldiers. I saw more than one man of the Royal Sussex, who seemed in no anxiety to rejoin ; several others had got hold of jobs which kept them away from the hard work and danger of marching and fighting, and put extra pay in their pockets.

The rest camp was crowded with soldiers, all perfectly well and fit for duty, and waiting to go up country and rejoin their regiments ; many of them had been waiting for weeks ; there were officers, too, in dozens, and all had the same tale to tell— they had been stopped at Bloemfontein on their way up country, and had been ordered to remain and do garrison duty indefinitely.

It is a severe blot on the administration of the Line of Communications that such a state of matters should be allowed to exist ; that regiments at the front should have been kept short-handed of both officers and men, while numbers of both ranks were loafing about the streets of Bloemfontein, or spending hours picking up weeds and placing white stones in rows in the Rest Camp. Not only did this happen in Bloemfontein, but the larger towns, such as Winburg and Kroonstad, were all full of unattached soldiers whose regiments were at the front. If these men were required for purposes of defence, it seems curious that a battalion or a half battalion could not have been detailed instead of an incongruous mob.

Towards the close of the campaign our battalion must have had several hundred men scattered about in various places : many of them were employed in hospitals and at offices and in all sorts of ways, but directly any attempt was made to get them back, many men were reported as " unfit to march." The conclusion I came to was, that these men must either have been discharged before being fully recovered, or else their detention at other than their proper duty was being winked at by certain officers for their own convenience.

Leaving Bloemfontein at six o'clock in the evening, our train had run only about 15 miles before a truck succeeded in getting off the rails; this was caused by a bale of blankets falling from a wagon on to the line and getting under the guard rail of the axle and grease box, which lifted the wheels and shoved them to one side: however, by the aid of two iron slides carried on the engine for the purpose, we were soon up again on the line and on our way to Kroonstad, which we reached the day before the Brigade was due. There was still a good deal to be done in getting the stores carted up to camp, but, with some trouble, this was managed by the next morning, when the Brigade arrived. The stores were unpacked, and the men were soon issued with some clean shirts, socks and boots, while some cases of comforts, sent out by people at home, were eagerly opened and their contents distributed. The articles which were most appreciated were drawers, shirts, socks, handkerchiefs and writing sets, which were all really useful; but, unfortunately, the contents of many bales and boxes consisted largely of Tam o'Shanters and knitted garments, which the men had no means of carrying, except on their backs; and they had quite enough on them as it was with rifle, equipment, 100 rounds of ammunition, blanket and two days' rations. After a man had once been issued with a soft cap and a cardigan jacket, he did not want another; and the quantity of these articles, in proportion to other things, sent out by the kind and thoughtful donors at home was unfortunately large.

Among the bales of ordnance stores were many containing warm khaki overcoats of the Indian pattern, but as our transport was so limited we had to return these useful garments, having no means of carrying them.

As the Brigade was likely to proceed on the trek again, it never having been known to rest more than two or three days at a time, the opportunity was taken to fill up the Brigade Canteen wagons with stores, and a small party went shopping with a traction engine and three trucks and bought all they could get ; as usual the shopkeepers, some English, some German, declined to part with any quantity of their stock, which they were, of course, hanging on to in the hope of prices rising, and I had to obtain an order from the District Commissioner to compel them to sell, though at enormous prices—eighteenpence for a tin of milk or a pot of jam, and other things in proportion.

As luck would have it, I succeeded, at my next visit to the town, in discovering the exact profit which these firms had made out of the Brigade Canteen over this transaction, and as all this talk about stores and prices serves to show how an English soldier is treated by his affectionate countrymen on his arrival in a beleaguered town, this must be my excuse for harping so long on one string.

There was an enterprising man who had arrived from Bloemfontein with several wagons full of stores, which he sold equally to the few merchants in Kroonstad. On the very day and at the time delivery was being made, I turned up with my traction engine and trucks and my order from the District Commissioner, and purchased most of these stores, nearly all the cases being handed over at the storehouse of the enterprising man. The prices I was charged by the various storekeepers were those fixed as the selling prices in the shops ; the prices the traders paid to the enterprising man I was afterwards fortunate enough to drop upon, and I found that in every case the profits were enormous, averaging over 36 per cent., and ranging from 75 per cent. for sardines to 20 per cent. for jam and milk.

Since our last stay in the town Kroonstad had developed strong breezes, which fetched up clouds of dust and hordes of flies from the Remount Depôt, and poured them both unceasingly into our camp. The 21st of August was a particularly dusty day, and we were not so very sorry, therefore, when in the evening orders were received for us to be off again : some of us, this time, went by train, as one half battalion was to proceed by rail and the other by road, marching with all the wagons and carts of the Brigade, to Geneva Siding, about 15 miles down the line.

The first party to move was the right half battalion, composed of B, C, D and E companies, under myself : they paraded at eleven o'clock in the evening and marched to the station, and waited there for some time, after loading the first line transport and some guns—the 76th Battery of the Field Artillery ; we eventually made a start about three o'clock in the morning. On arrival at Geneva I found there the General and the Camerons, who had proceeded by an earlier train, and was then directed to proceed to Ventersburg Road in the same train, and to remain there until the arrival of the General. So we steamed off again, enjoying, as we knew the other half battalion would also do, the new experience of sitting in a train and being dragged to our destination.

On our way down we passed Holfontein, where were some troops guarding the bridge, and, a few miles further on, we reached the spot where, some weeks previously, a train had been held up at night by the Boers, an officer and a few men who were in the train being taken prisoners and the train looted and burned. The officer was bringing up some stores for the General, which, of course, were looted ; but a few of the Boers paid for their recklessness, as they found some liquor, got drunk, and were easily captured, about eight or a dozen of them, by the Mounted Infantry from Ventersburg Road, who rode out on hearing the explosions of dynamite.

They were too late, however, to save the train, which was burning fiercely; many wagons of biscuits, beef and other supplies were burned clean out, only the iron frames of the wagons and thousands of blackened and empty tins being left on the line. Some of the wagons, thrown off the line, and tons of empty tins, showed us, as we passed, where the incident had occurred.

We reached Ventersburg Road about seven o'clock, and found some troops there under command of Lieut.-Colonel White, R.A.; the permanent garrison was composed of the Malta Company of Mounted Infantry, under Captain Pine-Coffin, who had come out with us on the "Pavonia," and a company of the Buffs Militia, under Captain O'Grady, a cousin of our Major of the same name. We camped outside the station, and bye-and-bye the General arrived, with the Camerons, followed about six o'clock by our Head Quarters and the other half battalion.

Ventersburg Road, a little roadside station, boasted only a couple of sheds besides the usual station buildings, water tank and goods shed; everything, however, was strongly entrenched and defended; a huge Supply Depôt had been established, and the boxes and the bags were utilised to form protection for the garrison, an interesting sight being a machine gun mounted on a pyramid of sacks of oats. The Supply subordinates had made themselves comfortable inside houses built of biscuit and beef boxes and roofed with tarpaulins, but the valuable sacks of oats, bags of mealies, sacks of sugar and other stores were pitched about anywhere, and were rotting and mouldering away on all sides; four bags of costly sugar were utilised to form steps up to a water tank, and were, of course, ruined with wet and mud; the enormous goods shed, which would have held the whole stock of the more valuable Supply stores then going to waste in the open, was full of bales of wool belonging to Boer farmers, of which the greatest care was apparently being taken by the railway authorities, while valuable food supplies were being ruined. The responsible man was a Corporal of the Army Service Corps, who was some time afterwards placed under arrest for selling rum and stores to the Boer residents and sympathisers in Ventersburg; they had run out of supplies, and thus replenished their larder. On our next visit, some time later, we brought with us the Brigade Supply officer, Lieut. Lloyd, whose energy was only equalled by his capability; and he very soon had things put shipshape, the wool bales fired out of the shed, and everything done Bristol fashion, as they say at sea.

The water supply of Ventersburg Road was its chief drawback: the Boers had damaged the water tank and the pumping engine, and had blown up the windmill pump, throwing it across the platform, where it remained for weeks; the only other source of supply for water was a spruit, about 2 miles away, to which water carts had to be despatched daily, and where all animals had to be taken to water.

The ground in the neighbourhood was level for a considerable distance to the west and east, rising somewhat to the north and dropping to the south. In the distance on the east were some hills about 7 miles away, and beyond them about 2 miles lay Ventersburg town, a hotbed of Boers and their friends, and a place of assembly for all the rebels in the surrounding country; it was only equalled by Bothaville, another town on the west side of the railway, and about sixty miles off.

On the afternoon of the day we arrived, I accompanied the General on a reconnaisance, carried out by all the mounted troops available towards Ventersburg town; we rode out to the hills outside the town, and the General went on with a small escort, returning in about an hour: there was a nasty piece of country between the hills and the town, which, however, the Mounted Infantry assured me, could easily be turned from either flank.

Our Head Quarters and A, F, G, H, and the Volunteer companies left Ventersburg Road station at six o'clock in the evening on the 25th of August by special train, arriving at Winburg a little after three o'clock ; they detrained at once, and received orders to move at five o'clock with the Cameron Highlanders, the 39th Field Battery, and the 5th Mounted Infantry to relieve Colonel Ridley and the Queenstown Volunteers, about 120 men, who for three days had been surrounded at Helpmakaar Farm, some twelve miles to the north-east of Winburg. On arrival there it was found that the Boers, after summoning the garrison to surrender at seven o'clock that morning, had made off; so the force, together with the beleagured garrison, returned to Winburg, arriving there about seven in the evening, and bivouacking to the east of the railway station.

About five o'clock the next morning the camp was alarmed by rifle shots, and it soon became evident that an attack was being made upon the town: so the garrison all stood to arms. The half battalion of the Bedfords, who were at the station ready entrained to return to Ventersburg Road, were moved out in the train to a point north of the town nearest to a kopje upon which the main attack seemed to be directed by the enemy ; two companies of the Camerons went up the hills, to the south-east of the town, to support the picket there, and A and F companies of our battalion went to the south-west of the town ; these companies were sniped from some bushes on a small detached kopje to the south of the town, but one man only was hit on the heel of his boot; a few shells were also fired at the pickets east of the town by a gun, or a couple of guns, of the enemy's posted to the north-east. Two guns of our battery came into action between our bivouacs and the railway station, and dispersed some Boers who were gathered on the top of the detached kopje; and the firing then ceased as suddenly as it had begun.

Some Mounted Infantry were shortly afterwards seen coming in from the north escorting twenty-four prisoners, who were found to include Commandant Olivier and his three sons. These four had, unknowingly and unarmed, walked straight into the hands of three or four of our Mounted Infantry, who had bluffed them by pretending that the rest of their regiment was close at hand. The Commandant was in a furious rage when he realised how neatly he had been trapped.

It appeared that the Boers concerned in the advance upon the town were under Commandant Fourie and included also Commandant Haasbruck; the latter with his commando was to have made a simultaneous attack upon the south end of the town, but, matters at the north part of the picket line being brought to a head sooner than was anticipated, his attack was too late to be of any use. The Boers, it was ascertained, had tapped the telegraph wire, and intercepted an order to General Bruce Hamilton, to withdraw his troops to Ventersburg Road; so, when three trains containing Yeomanry, which had come in during the night of the 26th, steamed out again in the early morning of the 27th, the Boers mistook these for trains containing General Bruce Hamilton's force, and attacked the town, expecting it to be held by only the usual small garrison.

The column proceeded at noon on the 31st of August by train to Bloemfontein, where they arrived at eight o'clock in the evening, proceeding to the Rest Camp for the night, which they spent under canvas for the first time during the campaign. The next day orders were received to march at seven o'clock, the same troops as before being required to make a forced march to Ladybrand to relieve the garrison there, who had been shut up for three or four days; so the force marched to the Waterworks, a good 20 miles, passing the scene of the disaster at Sanna's Post. Next day the column marched to Thaba N'Chu, a long 19 miles, and camped to the west of the town; they moved next day at five in the evening, and, after a bad march at night, reached camp at Andriesfontein at two o'clock in the morning. After resting until three in the afternoon, the column proceeded to Zonderzorg, about 13 miles, marching again the next day at seven o'clock in the morning towards Ladybrand, where the Boers were found in position at Plat Kop on the left of the road.

But they retired discreetly before the fire of the 39th Field Battery and one of our pom-poms, and signal messages were received about 11 a.m. from Colonel White that he had reached Ladybrand with his Mounted Infantry; so the infantry column was then halted, and eventually returned to camp.

On the 6th of September the column marched at three in the afternoon to Leeuw River Mills. On parade, before marching off, the General addressed the troops, thanking them for the way they had supported him in the trying work of the past few days, during which they had borne fatigue and hardship without complaint, showing that they had set out determined, cost what it might, to do their best to relieve their comrades, beleaguered in Ladybrand. He ended by saying that they had travelled upwards of a thousand miles with him up to then, and that he hoped soon all would get a prolonged rest, when he would try and get tents for them; but he felt sure that, if circumstances demanded that they should still go on, they would continue to give him the support that they had all along cheerily given him, as long as their Queen required them.

On the 12th of September, a move northwards was made, the column halting at Brand's Drift Farm, and continuing next day as far as Zamen Konst, where they were joined by the right half battalion and the remainder of the Brigade. The left half battalion, since leaving Thaba N'Chu on the 2nd of September, had been under the command of Major O'Grady, Lieut.-Colonel Donne having remained at Thaba N'Chu in command of the troops at that station.

CHAPTER XVII.

TO LINDLEY.

Right half battalion to Ventersburg town—Back to the railway—Rain—Boers blow up the line and burn train—The armoured train upon the scene—To Bloemfontein—Off again—To the waterworks—An invasion of Kaffirs—Thaba N'Chu—Zamenskornst—Meeting with the left half battallion—An abortive round-up—Senekal—Lindley—Picket attacked.

On the 25th of August, when the left half battalion left Ventersburg Road, I was directed by the General to proceed to Ventersburg town with a miniature column consisting of our right half battalion, B, C, D, and E companies: one company of the Derbyshire who had joined the Brigade at Bethlehem, and had remained with us ever since in the hope of some day rejoining their regiment: four guns of the 76th Field Battery, under Captain Moloney, and some of the Malta company of Mounted Infantry, under Lieut. Attfield, together with our baggage and seven days' rations.

Full of spirits at the prospect of getting a look-in at a fight on our own, we marched off at two in the afternoon towards the range of hills in the distance: having seen the ground before, it was easy to take the ever necessary precautions of picketting the hills on the right and left of the road by mounted men sent on in front, so as to cover our guns and baggage from the fire of an overzealous enemy; when we had passed safely, these pickets dropped down and formed our little rear guard, and so we reached the town about seven o'clock and reported to Colonel White. We camped in and around the school house, which a thoughtful staff officer had got ready for our reception, sticking lighted candles all round the large schoolrooms.

Colonel White was going out in the direction of the enemy the next day with all the troops in the town, so we had to take over the pickets and hold the town until his return. Disappointed at losing our chance of a fight, we consoled ourselves next day by moving into various empty houses, as it was possible we might have to remain in Ventersburg. The town was a small one, but was used as a halting place and rendezvous by the Boers, who found many sympathisers among the residents. It was well situated and easily protected, and would have made pleasant quarters for a half battalion as a permanent garrison; it would have afforded the Boers one town less in which to assemble and hatch plots and make descents on the railway line at Holfontein, only 12 miles away.

We were fated, however, to move again, and at eight o'clock next day, the 27th of August, my small column returned to Ventersburg Road: in the distance to the north, we espied a huge cloud of mounted men, wagons and Cape carts, with whom we opened communication by helio, finding them to be Colonel Le Gallais' force, bound for the town we had just left.

On reaching the railway station about mid-day we found that General Bruce Hamilton and the remainder of our Brigade had gone, and that most of the other troops had also moved. Next day, Colonel Le Gallais' force, and also Colonel White's, arrived and camped near the railway station, so that Ventersburg Road was pretty well crowded, and with all the horses, mules and bullocks was rapidly becoming anything but sanitary.

We had a very unpleasant time on the 29th of August; all the afternoon it rained steadily, and by night the place was a swamp and our camp a wretched sight; as many men as could be stowed away in sheds and under verandahs at the station were sent there, and the rest of us lay in our dripping bivouacs and put up with the drenching rain and soaking water under us as best we could. Fortunately, the rain stopped in the early morning, but our camp was a sight : in the middle of a lake about two feet deep was the bivouac of two men, my servant and my groom, who had rigged up overnight an excellent shelter of fencing wire and blankets, under which they were secure from rain, but not from the flowing stream which soon surrounded them ; numbers of mules and bullocks died during the night, and their swollen carcases poisoned the air for some days, until they were dragged off to their cemetery, where they were laid out in rows, and reminded us, every time the wind blew, of the unfortunate ending to their existence.

During these days and the next four or five, a constant succession of trains laden with remounts for the cavalry and Mounted Infantry, and occasionally with enormous loads of supplies, passed up north, day and night.

Orders were received for all details of the 21st Brigade to proceed to Bloemfontein, but White's and Le Gallais' troops had to go first, with their horses and their transport of Cape carts : this took three days to complete, and we were to follow when sufficient trains should arrive.

On Saturday night just after midnight, or rather on Sunday morning, I was awakened by hearing three dull explosions, evidently at some distance ; and in a few minutes, Lieut. Bellamy came running up to say he thought the line had been blown up. As this might have been merely the preliminary to an attack on the railway station, with its great piles of stores, four patrols, each consisting of a section under an officer, were sent out at once in the direction of the explosions, with orders to communicate with the two pickets which we furnished to the north and north-west, and then to move round in a circular direction and to return to camp ; when they came back other patrols were sent out and kept going until dawn. Soon, reports began to come in : Lieut. Ashworth, who was on picket well out to the north, reported that a train had passed him going north; that he had heard the slow panting of the engine going up the incline at Holfontein, about 5 miles off, followed by the explosions and a few rifle shots, after which all was still; but that the glare in the sky showed that the train had been set on fire.

This glare increased in intensity, and soon the fireman of the engine arrived, followed in a while by the guard and another railway employé, a passenger, who were brought in by the pickets, and told us the whole story. It seems that on the train reaching the top of the bank, there was an explosion of dynamite in front of the engine, upon which the driver applied the vacuum brake; he then tried to run back, but, after climbing the hill, he had no steam left to blow off the vacuum and so release the brakes, and then, hearing another explosion in rear, he and the fireman jumped and ran, the former going north and the latter south. The guard and the passenger told a similar story, and added that the Boers fired a few shots at the engine and the guard's van, from a distance of about 300 yards to the right of the line, apparently with the intention of driving off the trainmen, in which they succeeded; and they then set the train on fire. It was full of medical and Ordnance stores and forage.

Very fortunately, Captain Nanton, R.E., the Deputy-Assistant Director of Railways in this district, happened to be in the station with his armoured train, and dashed off as soon as the reports reached us, after entraining some of the Derbyshire as escort.

This armoured train, which usually lived at Kroonstad, but occasionally rushed up and down the line, was a queer looking object; the engine was in the middle, sheathed all over in boiler plating; at one end was a box car, also covered in plating, with a Maxim gun in it and a crew of men to work it; there were loopholes for the machine gun and for rifle fire. There was another car behind the engine, upon which were mounted two Naval quick-firing 12-prs., firing a huge brass cartridge.

This weird-looking train puffed away rapidly, as Captain Nanton was anxious to try and save some of the wagons, if possible, from the wrecked train, and the platelayers from down the line, having come in on their trolley, went off also. At early dawn, Captain Pine-Coffin with all his available Mounted Infantry went out, and sent in reports later to say that he was following on the tracks of about twenty mounted Boers, who had ridden from the train in the direction of Ventersburg town, which Colonel White's force had left only a couple of days before. Pine-Coffin followed up these tracks until they separated, and led off in many different directions, when, further pursuit being hopeless, and the enemy having at least six hours start, he returned to camp.

Later in the day, Captain Nanton returned with his armoured train, dragging one truck full of half-burned rubbish, and the engine of the defunct train, which was covered with a nice assortment of bullet holes, but was unharmed, though technically "dead," as the fires were out.

The stories of the fireman and the guard were correct, the line having been blown up in two places, and practically the whole train destroyed by fire, only one wagon being saved: the burning wagons had been dragged into a convenient siding and the line repaired, so that the trains which had accumulated at Ventersburg Road were enabled to go off in turn, but only up till dusk, as, after this, it was not considered advisable to run trains during the dark hours of the night.

Some details of our regiment and some of

the Camerons (nearly a company), turned up on the 2nd of September and were attached to us, and next day our trains arrived, and, after shipping off the battery, the section of the R.E., the hospital wagons and the Derbyshire men, we followed in the last train. The whole of the baggage wagons and the ox wagons proceeded by road to Bloemfontein, under charge of Captain Wroughton and Lieut. Pearce.

Our train reached Smaldeal a little after six o'clock in the evening : there we had to remain all night, but there was plenty of coal about, so we made ourselves comfortable, sleeping by the side of the train.

General Allen was at Smaldeal with a small garrison at the station, which is the junction with the line running to Winburg.

At daybreak, five o'clock the next morning, we continued our journey, passing on the veldt our wagons trekking along. We stopped an hour at Brandfort to cook our breakfast, after which we went on, passing Glen, our original starting place several months before, and reaching Bloemfontein about the middle of the day.

Having wired to say we were coming, we were expected, and the A.D.R. and the R.S.O., and various other officials with half-a-dozen letters after their names, were waiting for us, and, best of all, had provided wagons ; so there was no delay in loading up our baggage, ammunition and rations, as there had been on the first visit to Blomfontein of our battalion.

Now, we thought, at last we shall have a few days' peace in the comfortable tents of the Rest Camp, and we all made plans how we were to spend our days ; many of the men were allowed passes that very afternoon to go into the town, and it was as well they went when they had the chance, as that night we were off again !

At half-past seven that evening, I received orders for our half battalion, the battery and the hospital wagons to move as soon as possible to the Waterworks, about 22 miles. Nothing was said about transport, so I had to race off and find General Kelly-Kenny, who told me to apply to Colonel Long (at the other end of the town) for wagons. The General also said that it was possible the Waterworks might be attacked at dawn, and our assistance might be required, so that the sooner we got there the better. The men of the Camerons were to go with us, but not the details of the Derbyshire, who were to remain.

After seeing Colonel Long and being passed on by him to the Divisional Transport officer, I managed to get authority to procure wagons from the Rest Camp; so I went off there, and asked for all they could spare and a water cart, which, after some demur as to the number of wagons, they promised to send up. About half-past ten these arrived at the Rest Camp where we were quartered, and after loading up we started; luckily, there were plenty of wagons, so we were able to relieve the men of the blankets they carried on their backs, and also to load the wagons lightly—the mules had a long march before them and had already done a full day's work.

There was a good moon, so we trekked along steadily until three o'clock in the morning; when the moon disappeared, and we halted where we were, posted pickets and got out our blankets, and had a couple of hours' sleep. Up again at dawn, we loaded our wagons with the blankets and moved off by half-past five; we reached a suitable spot near Bushman's Kop about eight o'clock, when we halted a couple of hours for breakfast, but were off again by ten o'clock, eventually reaching the Waterworks, in very good style, after a long tramp of 22 miles, at half-past one in the afternoon.

The next day's march was a short one of merely 8 miles to a pan, filled with very dirty water, which was all we had. Things looked lively that night, as the pickets brought in a Boer prisoner, who turned out to be one of our own wagon drivers; he had gone out of the lines to a farm, without permission, and probably to give information. Naturally he protested his innocence, but he was put in charge of a sentry, and warned that on the first bullet being fired into camp by the enemy, he would be shot dead by the sentry; luckily for him, the night was a peaceful one, although our camp was invaded—not however by the enemy. Soon after midnight we heard a sentry calling out repeatedly in a mild sort of way " Guard, turn out!", and then we saw that he was one of the picket sentries, who had found himself suddenly overwhelmed by an advancing mass of Kaffirs, jabbering, chattering, and understanding no known language, but steadily moving on with their bundles.

In vain the sentry tried to stem the rushing tide of natives, but he might as well have tried to stop a house, so he retreated backwards, feebly yelling for assistance, and on arrival in camp the Kaffirs were stopped.

However, at cock crow the infernal jabber and chatter commenced again; they were Basutos, who had been working on the railway and were now going home, all with plenty of money to spend on wives and cows, which they told us was their intention.

Twice during the night mounted men had arrived with orders, the upshot of it all being that we were to march as far as Israelspoort, about 6 miles further on, and to remain there, holding that position, until General Hunter and his escort, who were coming up behind, should have passed; the baggage, however, was to go on into Thaba N'Chu.

Israelspoort was the place where Ian Hamilton's column had their first taste of fighting in April; a *poort* is a spot where the road passes over a neck or saddle in a ridge, and this particular one was commanded by huge kopjes on either hand. These were occupied by Mounted Infantry pickets, whom we relieved; and we sent on our baggage and waited for General Hunter, who arrived just after mid-day, and, after chatting a while, went on; we followed later, reaching Thaba N'Chu and camping at the eastern end of the town about two o'clock in the afternoon.

The town is a small one, situated in a recess among high hills which shut it in, but at some distance, on three sides; like Ventersburg and Bothaville, the surrounding district is a turbulent one, and there have always been restless Boers in the neighbourhood, who have frequently threatened the Waterworks and Bloemfontein.

Our Colonel had been left in command of the town, while the other half battalion marched to the relief of Ladybrand; the troops under him were not numerous, consisting only of half a battalion of the Bedfords, a battery and some Mounted Infantry.

Our wagons and a huge convoy arrived on the 10th of September, and with them, in addition to Captain Wroughton and Lieutenant Pearce, came Lieut. Montgomerie, who had been shot in the leg at Retief's Nek, but had since recovered, and now rejoined for duty. On the next day all the wagons, except our proportion, went off by road to join the Brigade, and we also received orders to march, at half-past nine that night, at which hour the moon was expected to show up.

It was a lovely night and the march was only a short one of about eight miles, but it took us four hours, all the same, as we had to wait occasionally to allow the lagging convoy to close up. Starting again at half-past nine in the morning we marched until mid-day, when we halted for an hour and a half, and eventually reached camp at Zamenskornst about three p.m. after a tramp of 17 miles.

All the troops which had marched to the relief of Ladybrand were camped on the opposite side of the spruit, including our other half battalion, who, of course, came and laughed at us for having missed all the hard marching they had had into Ladybrand. There was a wide, sandy spruit between the two camps, and the ox convoy started at early dawn, about three o'clock, to cross this: after them went our mule wagons and the battery and all the details, telegraph people and so on, so that the battalion, which furnished the rear guard, did not have to move until half-past seven.

The mounted troops comprised men of the Mounted Infantry of several Corps—Brabant's Horse, Rimington's Scouts, Kitchener's Horse— and there were also representatives of many other regiments, both regular and irregular, as General Hunter and his staff accompanied us, with interpreters and servants, guides, escort and men in charge of their baggage wagons.

At the entrance to camp at Allendale, about 12 miles away, there was another sandy drift, which tried the bullocks very much : two paths had been made, but of course it is unnecessary to state that whenever the drivers *could* manage to cross their tracks and create a block or a collision, they invariably did so to the great delight of the baggage master, for whom, sometimes, the English language was not sufficiently copious, and who had to fall back on Hindustani.

However after much delay the last wagon was got across, and the rear guard passed on into camp, which was not far off. We all turned in early, as at midnight we were to start again : it appears that the enemy were among the hills, which formed an excellent position at Doornberg, lying in the centre of a triangle formed by the three towns of Winburg, Ventersburg and Senekal, and was easily accessible from either, both from our point of view and from that of the enemy. Winburg was occupied by our troops, but the other two towns had not been consistently held throughout the campaign, and the enemy were able, therefore, to use these towns to some extent as bases.

The operation upon which we were now engaged was an extensive "round up," to use a Bush phrase, which exactly expresses what we were about to do. There were columns, each preceded by clouds of mounted troops, coming from the north, the east and the south, and we were in great hopes that at last we had got the enemy properly cornered, as it did not seem possible for him to escape anywhere, the country being open rolling veldt all round the position which he was occupying at Doornberg.

Having, therefore, a rough idea of the plans upon which we were working, we were prepared for some long marches, and we were not disappointed. Leaving Allendale at midnight, on a moonlight and starry night, we marched off to the north : as bad luck would have it, we were following a battery, which is an annoying thing on a night march, when, as everyone knows, each unit has to keep touch with the troops in front so as not to lose distance.

All troops open out on the march to a certain extent, which is greater than that fixed in the drill books, but which actual experience in marching shows is quite necessary ; when, therefore, the head of a column of all arms on the march is halted for the usual ten minutes every hour, those in rear do not stop dead in their tracks as they should, but continue closing up until they have resumed their proper parade ground intervals.

This was exemplified on this occasion, when we tramped for two hours and fifty minutes without a halt, the early part of the march being a constant succession of checks, caused by the frequent "backing and filling" of the battery in front of us. Nothing is more annoying on the march than these checks, which throw you out of your stride and bring you up all standing, and nothing is more easily avoided by the common sense adoption of wider and more elastic intervals between units and companies.

About eight o'clock the column halted, as we were all staggering for want of sleep; so we had breakfast and slept and rested until half past two in the afternoon, when we continued on our way to Klein Saxony, about 2 miles short of Winburg.

With a couple of companies of the Composite Battalion, which had been formed of all the details attached to the Brigade, and some Yeomanry and two guns, I was detailed to look after the rear; and this small army of mine did not reach camp until half-past seven. We had a long rest, however, as we did not start the next day until the afternoon, at half-past one, when we proceeded on our way, skirting Winburg on the east and then marching in a straight line to Marais Farm, where we had once before camped, when with the Boer laager.

On the 17th of September, the Brigade moved off again, early in the morning, towards Doornberg, camping at Rooikraal, about 13 miles distant—a very pleasant camp, with plenty of grass and good water, which we enjoyed after all the miles and miles of burnt up veldt we had trekked across since leaving Frankfort. The following morning we thought that the great closing in movement was actually taking place around the huge dark mass of flat topped mountain which we could see, lowering in the distance, on the other side of a smiling grassy valley, as we moved off at six o'clock, marching some 10 miles. We then halted under the lee of a razor-backed ridge, being careful not to show ourselves over the sky-line, and a few pickets and look-out men were posted. We could see, or thought we could see, an occasional mounted man on the hills opposite, but they must have been our own men; for we heard later that the Boers had escaped during the night out of the net which had been so carefully drawn round them, and had trekked off to the east.

It was said at the time that their escape was due to the laxity of a certain Brigade, operating from the east, who either did not move at all, or else moved too late, to shut in the Boers at the only loophole by which they could have cleared off. Finding a drift practically unguarded, or rather held by a ridiculously small force, without the support of the Brigade which it should have had, the Boers pushed through during the night successfully, and were miles away when dawn broke.

Disappointed, we camped at the spruit near by, and marched the following morning towards Senekal, camping about 11 miles from that town, on the same spot upon which we had camped on the 10th of August, when with the Boer laager. This was a disgusting camp, with remains of our dead animals strewn about, and water like pea soup, drawn from a succession of mud holes. During the march we had passed a Krupp ammunition wagon which the Boers had abandoned; the wheels of it being the only part made of wood had been burned by our Mounted Infantry, who were following up on the enemy's tracks.

Senekal was reached the next morning, the 20th of September, just as General Rundle's Division, the Eighth, was leaving; we camped to the east of the town and remained there for two days, making a long trek, however, of 14 miles on the 23rd towards Lindley. Our bivouac the next day was at Kruisfontein, which we reached after a march of about 12 miles; this place was a couple of miles south of Wit Kop, a huge, isolated flat topped kopje rising out of the plain and dominating the surrounding country. Towards this kopje we marched the following day and camped at its foot, the two companies remaining there until the next day, when the Brigade moved at six o'clock into Lindley, camping to the north of the town about a mile out on the Heilbron road and beyond the drift.

For two days we remained at Lindley, but the morning of the 28th saw us on the road again, marching towards Heilbron, one half of our battalion being baggage guard to the usual gigantic convoy and the other half being rear guard.

About two o'clock the advanced guard and the main body halted and camped, the convoy and the baggage guard closed up and we all settled down: and then we heard that we were all to return to Lindley the following day, as General Hunter had received orders to garrison most of the towns in his district, which comprised the north eastern portion of the Orange River Colony, and that a beginning was to be made by leaving the 21st Brigade at Lindley.

So the next morning, the 29th of September, back we went to Lindley, arriving about 11.15 a.m. The rear guard had marched back during the night, escorting the baggage of Colonel Le Gallais' troops, and experiencing great trouble with their wagons, three of which we found derelict on the road; we succeeded in tinkering up two of them and bringing them along with us.

General Hunter and Colonel Le Gallais left the same afternoon, and our Brigade took up its quarters on the east of the town, and threw out pickets on the hills surrounding the hollow in which Lindley is situated. In the afternoon about four o'clock, when A company, then on picket to the south west, was about to be relieved by B and E companies, who were then on their way out, a good deal of firing was heard from that direction, and I was sent up by the General to see what was the matter and to deal with it. Two guns and a pom-pom went out also, and on reaching the hill it appeared that one of the sentries of A company had been shot dead by some Boers who had ridden up within a few hundred yards, fired at him, and then ridden off to take up a position behind a rocky kopje (about 2,200 yards from one picket and 1,500 from the other), from which they kept up an annoying fire. Our men had occupied some trenches and sangars which had been made by our predecessors, Paget's Brigade, I believe, some time previously, and which were all of inferior construction and badly situated. Two of our men were in consequence soon hit, but the remainder kept up a continuous rifle fire on the enemy, invisible behind their kopje.

The guns and the pom-pom soon came into action against this rocky hill, and after a few shells the enemy's fire ceased.

The General had now come up, and the Boers, seeing a little group on the top of the hill, opened fire on us from a spur to our right front, which ran down to meet the rocky kopje alluded to above, and which apparently afforded the snipers a means of retreat secure from observation.

At 2,000 yards B company replied to this fire, and the Boers, moving further away, every now and then sent a few shots in our direction, which, however, failed to reach us, and struck the ground in front.

It was getting dusk, and the enemy were using black powder, so we were able to locate them, and kept them moving by our fire delivered at 2,500, and then at 3,000 yards, beyond which the Lee-Metford is not sighted.

And so this little incident closed, but unfortunately it had caused us three casualties.*

Some time afterwards we discovered the reason of this attack; it appeared that the Boers had seen the column of Colonel Le Gallais and General Hunter's escort moving away from the town that afternoon, and had jumped to the conclusion that nearly all the troops had left Lindley; so they came on boldly, as they did on the occasion of our first departure from the town in May—but to be disappointed this time.

The Brigade now settled down in Lindley, the pickets entrenched their posts, and everything was done according to Cocker. A large convoy of those wretched ox wagons, after storing in the town all the rations they had been carrying, went off to Kroonstad with an escort supplied by the Camerons and the Bedfords; the sick and wounded were sent away by this convoy, and all the mule wagons which could be spared, the whole being in charge of Captain Wroughton.

However, in a couple of days the escort returned, bringing with them a five-inch gun, under Captain Massie, R.A., and we learned then that they had met General Hector Macdonald's Highland Brigade at Kaalfontein Bridge, about 20 miles out, and that he had taken on the convoy and sent the escort back with the cow gun and some mails for our Brigade.

A visit was also paid to Groonvlei, a farm about five miles to the north along the Heilbron road, with an escort, and several wagon loads of wood were brought in, there being none in the town.

---

*KILLED.
Private G. Latter, A Company.

WOUNDED.
Lce.-Corp. A. White, A. Company.
Private H. Beeney, A Company.

Finding an empty house which was suitable for the purpose, a Soldiers' Club was started, under the management of Mr. Leary, the active and energetic padré who will always be remembered in our battalion for the way he looked after our casualties at Retief's Nek. Things were made as comfortable as possible, and tea and such eatables as could be got (except biscuit, which was studiously avoided) were sold in the evenings. Open air concerts of a rough and ready kind were regularly held on three evenings a week, cricket, football and hockey matches, and games such as quoits were played as often as could be arranged with the few materials at hand, and preparations made to lighten the tedium of what promised to be a long stay in Lindley.

CHAPTER XVIII.

THE RAILWAY NEEDS REPAIR.

Wit Kop—Half the battalion goes on tour—Kaffir Kop—Clearing the country—Necessity for it—Mobile columns required—Kaalfontein Bridge—Rearguard attacked at Doornkop—The line blown up—A repairing expedition.

Everything was quiet in Lindley for a few days, and then, on the 3rd of October, the General sent for me at half-past nine at night and told me that he had ordered two companies of ours, under me, to proceed at five o'clock the next morning to Wit Kop, where, apparently, some of our mounted troops were in difficulties, having been engaged with the Boers most of the day.

The General also told me in confidence that he and some more troops were coming out to Wit Kop in the afternoon, and that we were to proceed on a tour round to the south and the west, and should probably be absent a week.

So next morning, A and H companies, under Major O'Grady and Captain Wisden, paraded at five o'clock and went out to Wit Kop, where we found Captain Lloyd and some of the 8th M.I., and Captain Driscoll and some of his Scouts. It appeared that a party of Driscoll's Scouts had gone out towards Kaffir Kop but had not returned, and it was feared that they had been cut off; during the previous day the few men remaining at Wit Kop had been somewhat heavily fired on by a party of Boers, forty it was estimated, who had crept up under shelter of a donga to within a few hundred yards of our men, and had opened a considerable fire on them. The party on the Kop were not strong enough to turn them out, but had answered the fire and sent in a report to the General as soon as it was dark enough for a messenger to travel.

With our two companies we occupied the Kop, and spent the day watching the surrounding country: Driscoll's Scouts went out and burned a farm, from which the enemy had appeared the previous day, and we sat on the Kop and stared through our field glasses at the open, undulating ground to the south-west, over which we could see some Mounted Infantry moving.

Idly we followed the movements of this little party, evidently a patrol, and we watched five of them, out in front of a few others, riding in extended order across a level space of grass, when suddenly we heard the ping-boom of the Mauser: instantly the patrol wheeled about and galloped back at speed, the firing of the enemy continuing for some moments. After a while we saw some of the enemy riding away and disappearing behind a rise in the ground, to reappear once more and ride off in the distance, a little clump of men, say twenty-five at the outside.

It seems that the Mounted Infantry patrol had noticed some men whom they were approaching, but took them to be the party of Driscoll's Scouts whose return we were all expecting, and so had unsuspectingly ridden towards them; with the unfortunate result that their officer, Captain Willsher, was killed, and one man wounded and taken prisoner.

This incident is only one case among very many, I am afraid, where similar occurrences have resulted in the death and capture of many men, owing to the constant disregard of the saying, "take nothing for granted," to which I have previously alluded; the reputation of the Boers for "slimness," or 'cuteness, has been added to by each of these incidents, which have really often been brought about by crass stupidity on our parts, not always by any clever smartness on the part of our enemies.

It was very sad to sit on the hill-top and observe all this going on in front of us, only about 2 miles away, and to know that we could do nothing; we had insufficient mounted men to chase the Boers, even if they had not already got a long start, and we had no guns with us. Captain Driscoll had had information that his patrol was returning, and had secured two prisoners, from whom information was extracted to the effect that Haasbrook's commando was then about 16 miles away to the south.

About five o'clock we saw, from the cloud of dust approaching from the north, that the remainder of the column was near at hand, and in about an hour they were halted and cooking their tea a mile away from us; the General had come up to the Kop just as the Mounted Infantry were burying poor Captain Willsher, and had received our reports, and then directed me to join the column with our two companies at seven o'clock.

On reaching the camp we found F, G, and the Volunteers, under the command respectively of Captain Gilbert, Lieut. Harden, and Captain Blake, busily engaged at their tea; they were very anxious to hear what was going to happen, but all I knew was that we were to be ready to start at a quarter past seven, at which hour we went off on another night march.

After a couple of hours walk, there was a long halt at the top of a hill, whilst the country in front was reconnoitred by the mounted troops; it was bitterly cold and we could not keep warm, until, at last, the men received permission to roll themselves up in the blankets which they carried on their belts.

Soon nothing was to be seen in the dim light but a long line of black figures stretched out on the road; the Camerons were in front of us and the battery in rear, so we were quite secure. After this long halt we moved on again, eventually encamping, towards half past ten, near a farm about 13 miles from Lindley. Out of this farm a Boer was pulled and made prisoner : he was making ardent love to a blushing Basuto damsel, when he was caught, and handed over to the guard.

At five o'clock the next morning the column marched towards Kaffir Kop, about 6 miles, where we halted until the next afternoon at three, the mounted troops going out to clear the country. This step had become necessary at this stage of the war, and was in accordance with Lord Roberts' orders, in places where disturbances continued. It was distasteful work, but entirely justified by the circumstances.

It was probably never contemplated by anyone that, after occupying the chief towns in the Transvaal and the Orange River Colony, after seizing the railways, dispersing the enemy's forces and driving a large number into Portugese territory, after despatching over 16,000 prisoners to far away islands, after visiting all the towns in each colony, taking the surrender and receiving the allegiance of many thousands of burghers, these same burghers, many of them, would rise again and carry on a guerrilla warfare which could have but one ending.

When Burma was captured and annexed in 1886, after the occupation of Mandalay, a similar state of matters prevailed for several years, armed bands of dacoits roaming the country in all directions ; they were eventually suppressed by the salutary process of quartering garrisons in all parts of the country, and forming numbers of small, mobile, flying columns, largely composed of mounted men, who moved, at a moment's notice, against any Boh, or leader, who appeared in the neighbourhood, and hunted him till he fled or was captured.

By this means, combination was rendered impossible, and the appearance of any force of the enemy was the signal for prompt action being taken against it by every one of the mobile little columns which might be within call, commanded, as these columns often were, by young and dashing officers selected for their energy and zeal. It was for this reason that the latter part of the campaign in Burma in 1885-6 has been called the "Subalterns' War."

Something similar to this procedure was about this time necessary in the Orange River Colony, but the paucity either of mounted troops, or of remounts, delayed the formation of such columns as would be necessary, say for instance, in the case in point on the 4th of October, to recover rapidly the 16 miles which separated us from Haasbrook's commando, and to engage him.

After despatching great droves of cattle and sheep to Lindley, we proceeded in a circular sweep towards the west of that town, and cut the Kroonstad road at Kaalfontein Bridge, which we crossed on the 9th of October, moving beyond it a few miles and camping at Quaggafontein. This place was only a couple of marches from Lindley, to which we expected to return on the 11th of October ; in fact we had to be somewhere by that date, as we had only two days' rations left.

Next morning, to our astonishment, the column headed off to the west instead of to the east or northeast as we expected ; there was only one conclusion to draw—Kroonstad was our destination, and we were not sorry either, as we wanted a new outfit of clothes, boots, and such other articles as tobacco, matches and soap, which are sometimes almost as necessary as a new pair of trousers.

Our half battalion was on baggage and rear guard that day, H company bringing up the rear of all ; a couple of miles from camp the road opened on to a great expanse of rolling veldt, which stretched away in front of us for some miles, to a kopje covered with low trees standing near a drift.

After crossing the drift, there was a farm on the left with several houses, which had been burnt by the Highland Brigade, but in which some women and children were living, temporary roofs of corrugated iron having been erected. Rounding the end of the kopje, which was called Doornkop, we saw, shut away in a recess, another farm house which had been similarly treated : H company had reason afterwards to remember this farm house.

The advanced guard passed over Doornkop, and the remainder of the troops followed along the road and proceeded some distance, halting for the usual ten minutes about a mile and a half beyond Doornkop, where the veldt was level and open like that which we had left behind us.

Whilst the main body was sitting about, resting, Colonel Kennedy, of the Camerons, came up to me and said he thought he heard firing in the direction of the rear guard. We listened, and I distinctly heard our old friend the Mauser; so I rode back to see what was going on. Meeting a breathless man with an incoherent message about Captain Wisden being surrounded (which we found that officer had never sent), I shouted for another company to come back, and rode on until Doornkop and the Valley in which it stood came into view.

The Volunteer company, under Captain Blake, came up in extended order and opened fire on the kopje at a range of 2,000 yards, afterwards advancing somewhat down the slope so as to get within closer range. Captain Gilbert, whose company was marching just in front of Captain Wisden's, had already sent one half-company off to rising ground on the right, and had taken the other to a similar position on the left, so that I had no apprehension as regarded our flanks.

The kopje being rather beyond effective rifle fire, I sent Coleman, my groom, riding back to the column to ask the senior officer to send me a gun from the battery. Evidently not caring to assume the responsibility of so weighty a matter, he sent Coleman on to the General, who was quite two miles away, so that by the time the gun had arrived the opportunity for its use had gone; as the Boers disappeared directly we showed that we meant business.

It might be as well to state here that after this little episode, and to avoid the chance of any similar useless delays on future occasions, the General invariably ordered one gun to accompany the rear guard so as to be handy in case it was wanted.

Advancing down the slope, and still keeping up a fire to keep the enemy under his cover, we came shortly into view of H company. They had, upon being suddenly greeted with a shower of bullets from their rear, discreetly dropped into a donga which, fortunately, lay almost at their feet, and, safe in the security of this cover, had opened a smart fire upon the trees and rocks of the kopje. Not a man of the enemy could be seen, but they could see our men, as a poor fellow of H company, moving from one part of the donga to another, received a bullet in his head and dropped immediately.* The Cape cart which carried the officers' mess property stuck in the drift across the small donga, the ponies jibbed, and no persuasion would induce them to move, so the cart was emptied, the harness cut up, and the ponies turned loose—all this being done under a dropping fire from the enemy.

As soon as the shelling was over, H company withdrew, bringing their dead with them, the

---

* Private C. Shutton, H company.

companies resumed their former positions, and the march was continued. We halted that night at Welgevreden, where the Camerons, being on duty, threw out the usual pickets.

Next morning, the 11th of October, we continued our march, starting at eight o'clock. When about to withdraw, one of the pickets of the Camerons was fired on by some snipers of the enemy. The few mounted men with us who had been advanced guard the previous day had been kept back to carry out the duties of rear guard on this occasion, and on their approach the snipers fled, and we were annoyed no more that day.

Kroonstad, about 11 miles distant, was reached about eleven o'clock, and we camped just beyond No. 3 General Hospital and under Gun Hill. During the day tents arrived for us, and we pitched these, hoping to remain a few days to enjoy them, after having slept in the open for so long—some of us since the 6th of April, but all of us since the 29th of that month, when we left Glen —altogether about five and a half months. Many of the men, however, preferred the fresh open air to the tents, and rigged up their bivouacs as usual.

Late on the night of the 11th of October I received orders to proceed to the railway station at four o'clock the next morning, with a day's rations, but without baggage. The Volunteer company was to remain in camp, as it was expected that they would shortly receive orders to proceed to Bloemfontein, at which place we had heard that all the Volunteers were being concentrated previously to their departure for England.

At the station we were entrained in empty coal trucks, with our water-cart, horses and mules, besides about twenty men of the Royal Engineers, and a quantity of reconstruction material, tools, rails, sleepers and such like, and a break-down gang of natives.

Some reports had come in from down the line which the Staff Officer showed me. The officer commanding at Holfontein reported the line was blown up between the Gangers' Hut No. 60 and Ventersburg Road Station, and that the enemy were too strong for our patrols to encounter them. The officer commanding at Boschrand reported that a number of explosions had been heard on his left, and that the cavalry had been sent out and had fired one volley at the enemy.

One of the hospital trains—full of patients—had been waiting all night to proceed at dawn, but this was now impossible, and the sick men had to spend another day cramped up in the train.

We steamed off as soon as it was light enough—about half-past four—to see our way, and proceeded down the deviation and past the Remount Camp—full of Indian sowars and native syces, or horsekeepers, who waved their hands to us as we went by—until we reached Boschrand Station. The officers were all in the trucks with their companies, and all had been warned to be on the look out for sudden orders, and to be mighty sharp about jumping out of the trucks and at once extending and lying down, should they be ordered to do so. It was quite possible that the train might be attacked when winding along the broken country and numerous kopjes near Boschrand. Luckily this was not necessary, and we steamed along beyond the station to the top of a rise in the ground, where the train pulled up.

Here was the scene of the explosions heard during the night, and a nice lot of damage had been done too. The line was blown up in no less than seventeen places, at the junction of the rails, with heavy charges of dynamite, the cardboard boxes in which this explosive had been carried lying about in several places.

The Boers had chosen the junction of the

rails as the places at which to deposit the charges of dynamite, as two rails would then be rendered useless, their ends being blown up in a curve, in some cases to a right angle, and the steel sleepers also destroyed. The railways in this colony are laid on stamped steel sleepers with the chairs bolted on to them, into which the rails are fixed by steel keys driven in from one side, so that, although it may be an easy matter to lay the line, it is a difficult job to remove a damaged rail, jammed in the chairs by an explosion, in order to replace it by another.

One company of our battalion was sent out on picket to the right and left, up to the summit of the rising ground, from which a clear view could be obtained for some miles, and the remainder were directed to stay in the train, which might have to steam back at any moment. The men of the Engineers were out of the train and at work, coolly and deliberately, each man at his own particular job, before we had done looking about us.

The Engineer officer informed me that the damaged rails would all have to be removed and replaced by new ones, and that all the broken sleepers, a large number, would have to be dug up and others put in their places ; a gang of native labourers were already at work fetching rails and sleepers from the trucks, while the Engineers were clearing away the ballast and exposing the rails to another party, who prized up the rails with crowbars and burst them out of the chairs with sledge hammers.

This was all work which numbers of our reserve men, who had been employed as platelayers on the railways at home, could well undertake, so I asked for volunteers to come and work ; as is always the case with our men, no matter what they are asked to do, volunteers came forward in large numbers ; but only about fifty men were required, who set to work forthwith. In four hours thirty-four damaged rails had been taken up and replaced by new ones, and fifty-four new sleepers had been put in position, and the line was safe enough for our train to pass, after which the native gangs would complete the work. During this time our men had been allowed out of the train by parties in succession to cook their food for breakfast, the company on picket being relieved also for this purpose. We had some telegraph men on board the train, but as they had brought no instrument, the wire could not be tapped, and the railway authorities in Kroonstad could not be informed of the progress of the work until we reached a station.

The damage had apparently been caused by quite a small party of Boers, there being the spoor, or track, of one ox wagon, a couple of Cape carts, and about twenty men on horseback; they had apparently gone off in the direction of the hills lying to the west, towards Bothaville. About eleven o'clock work was concluded, and we proceeded rapidly to the next break, passing on the way the station at Geneva.

The next break was found to be beyond Holfontein; here the damage consisted in four pairs of rails with the sleepers attached having been removed bodily, one pair having been turned over preparatory to being removed, all the bolts and nuts of the fish plates for quite 600 yards broken off, all the telegraph wires dragged away, and the posts, without exception, dragged down and broken and the insulators smashed.

This was the greatest damage that had, as yet, been carried out in this neighbourhood, already famous for the numerous raids on the line. The nuts of the fish plate bolts, four to each rail, had been smashed off with heavy sledge hammers by men who were acquainted with the work, not by ignorant farmers, and to execute this job by night and over an extent of line 600 yards long meant the breaking of no less than 480 bolts. The rails, thus capable of being disconnected, were lifted in pairs with the sleepers, deeply embedded in ballast, still attached, and were turned over on their backs, thus forming a sort of sledge; four pairs had been dragged away by bullocks over a ditch and across the veldt, one pair having been taken more than half a mile away, and the others being about 200 yards from the line. To lift these rails, even with the iron telegraph poles, which had seemingly been used as levers, must have taken at least sixteen powerful men to each pair of rails; apparently the Boers intended to remove more than the five pairs of rails which they had shifted, or else they would not have smashed so many of the fish plate bolts. This was the least damage that was done, and although we could not then replace such a large number, it was of little consequence; there were no expresses likely to thunder along at forty miles an hour, and the track was quite safe for a day or so as it was without bolts.

Having seen the damage done, the next thing was to repair it, but this did not take long; putting a company out on picket on each side of the line, we got another company to work on the rails lying out on the veldt, and, with a long and thick rope that was in the tool van, G company, and afterwards A, soon towed the rails back again (although it was a stiff pull even for 80 men), turned them over and lifted them into their places, where the Engineers soon put them right. Some of the sleepers had to be replaced by others; but as regards the telegraph line and posts, we could do nothing; no less than eight wires, one of them a copper telephone wire, had been removed bodily, and the posts smashed as far as the eye could reach.

It will be easily understood what an interruption this caused, not only to the railway traffic but to the communications with Cape Town : however, telegraph operators were at work everywhere, and a temporary line was rigged up that day ; but it was a long time before all the wires could be renewed.

The Engineers and our men were not long repairing the rails, and in about half an hour we were on the move once more towards Ventersburg Road, in full sight of which was the next, and luckily the last, break ; in this one the line had been blown up in two places, necessitating two new rails being laid, but for fully 200 yards or more the fish plate bolts had been broken off as before; for 120 yards the rails had been disconnected and torn asunder, apparently with the intention of dragging them away over the veldt, and for no less than a mile and a half all the telegraph posts had been torn down (evidently by teams of bullocks) and smashed, and the wires dragged away : every insulator was broken in pieces.

As all this 120 yards of line had to be relaid. the work took us longer than at the last break ; but in about an hour and a half it was done, and away we steamed back again to clear off the line and let the trains pass, which were by now jammed at Kroonstad and Ventersburg Road on both sides of us. At about three o'clock we reached Geneva.

After all, very little real damage had been done, and a very short cessation of traffic caused, as by two o'clock that afternoon trains were running again ; and even in the case of a serious break to the line, such as the destruction of an important bridge, there was always an alternative line, that through Natal, by which supplies could be procured.

CHAPTER XIX.

TO BOTHAVILLE.

Geneva—Kroonstad—New boots and sore feet—Bothaville—A strange souvenir—The town destroyed—Kroonstad again—Home remittances.

At Geneva we received orders to detrain one company there, and to send one to Boschrand, one to Holfontein, and one to Ventersburg Road; there were plenty of trains running both ways by this time, so the companies were quickly got off, H to Boschrand, A to Holfontein, and G to Ventersburg Road, while F company remained at Geneva. In the orders it was stated that our baggage and rations would be sent down, but we did not expect to see them that day, and were not disappointed when they did not arrive until the next morning.

However, the men had all had their rations for that day issued to them, and they also had a blanket each, and we at Geneva, or, rather those who were not on picket, made ourselves snug under some tarpaulins : luckily, it was rather a warm night. I am afraid many men that day had had nothing much to eat after breakfast time ; it is a curious thing that the majority of soldiers never learn to economise their rations or to keep a bit in hand. In this particular case, each man had been issued overnight with a tin of Maconochie's rations, a particularly tasty kind of food, and a relief after much trek ox; but, although we had started at the early hour of half past four in the morning, yet numbers of rations had been eaten and the tins thrown on the line, even inside the station; as we steamed away the few men who had not already finished were busy at their tins.

Geneva was not really a station at all, only a siding, with not a drop of water procurable, except that brought in a tank by the train daily, which tank was not always full. There were a couple of empty tanks at the station, which we filled and kept in reserve, as there was no knowing when the line might again be blown up and communication interrupted, and ourselves forced to drink water out of puddles.

On the 13th of October the Volunteer company passed us in the train going down to Bloemfontein, preparatory to being sent home. They were of course in the highest of spirits, and there was great cheering as the train left the station. They had done well while with the battalion, and had throughout carried out their duties in the field excellently. There were not many men left to go away, only forty-seven, but there were ten more at Lindley, and many others in various hospitals in the country. All day long trains were going down south, and on most of them were Volunteers of many regiments—all in a great state of glee. On Sunday, the 14th of October, we returned to Kroonstad, the train leaving Ventersburg Road about two o'clock in the afternoon, and collecting the companies as it came up the line. We went back to our old camp, and the next day had an opportunity of fitting ourselves out with clothes and boots from the Ordnance stores. No less than 180 pairs of new boots were issued to men of our four companies, and other clothing, socks and shirts to those who wanted them.

It is a curious point in our military administration that on service where boots and helmets, coats and trousers, are issued free, shirts, socks, and drawers, which it is just as necessary to renew, are charged for. This system causes a considerable amount of extra work in the field, as the men have to be charged in their accounts—not to mention that it is not a fair charge to make against a man who is wearing out his clothes in the field and on duty of the severest nature.

It was believed about this time that after a stay of a day or two at Kroonstad, we should move back to Lindley, the convoy of 180 ox-wagons having been loaded and ready for us for some time. Thus there would have been an opportunity of breaking in, by wearing them in camp, the new boots which we had just received, and the marches to Lindley, being fairly short ones, could have been managed without serious disablement.

When, however, the Brigade orders arrived that evening, it was discovered that, far from going to Lindley, we were to proceed in the opposite direction. Camp was to be quitted at half-past five next morning, and the troops were to cross both spruits to the south, and to be at a point on the Bloemfontein Road by seven o'clock, taking with us four days' rations and two days' forage for the animals. It was a terribly long march that day, and the unfortunate men with new boots, thus unexpectedly called upon to march fully 20 miles, suffered considerably, and many were unfit to march for several days, and had to be carried on wagons. Next day was a shorter march of 12 miles to a place called Nels Farm, where we pitched our tents and remained for another day, whilst the cavalry and the mounted troops went out and destroyed the farms in the neighbourhood, belonging to Boers out on commando. There was an unfortunate occurence that day, when one party of Mounted Infantry fired at another party, thinking they were the enemy, and shot a poor fellow through the body, wounding him dangerously.

There have been several cases of this sort of thing during the campaign—due to one or two causes : the similarity in dress of our men and the

Boers, induced first by the absurd fondness in our troops for wearing any headgear except that with which they are provided; and secondly by the habit among the Boers of securing military clothing from the trains they at times have looted. Another reason is the fondness our men have—perhaps due to their over-eagerness and the want of experience of young officers—for opening fire on the enemy, or what is thought to be the enemy, at extreme ranges—any distance from 800 to 3,000 yards—at which it is almost impossible to tell friend from foe.

Field glasses being no part of the equipment even of the higher non-commissioned ranks, how is a party of scouts to tell Mounted Infantry from Boers, except by waiting until they come near enough to distinguish?

Our troops are not sufficiently acquainted with what may be called advanced musketry to understand that a few scattered shots fired at a widely spread target, such as a mounted patrol of five or six men, at the extreme range of 2,000 yards, is worse than useless and a distinct waste of ammunition. The theory of musketry, the curve of the trajectory, and the power of the rifle generally, are points which are far less understood than they might be in our service, and receive as little attention as the important subject of estimating ranges or the no less necessary matter of firing at extreme ranges.

The weather was now becoming distinctly warmer, in fact at Nels Farm, the day we rested there, it was quite warm enough for most of us, and we were glad of the bit of protection afforded from the sun by the bell tents.

On the 19th of October, a warm, close day, we marched about 13 miles to the drift at Tweefontein, two companies being rear guard with a gun and 250 cavalry, who were kept at a good reasonable distance away from the main body, so as to afford us some protection from snipers. Many farms were passed along the road, most of them being burned or blown up; we were now in a local centre of rebellion, this district not having been visited by our troops for some months, and the Boers having swarmed back in crowds in consequence: they used the farms to lodge in, and obtained from them food and information as to our movements.

We camped that night on the near side of the drift, and at early dawn the convoy started moving across and parking on the other side; it was to remain there whilst the remainder of the column went on to Bothaville.

The Buffs Militia, four companies of whom had accompanied us from Kroonstad, were also to remain, together with 40 men of ours and some of the Camerons, as well as one gun from the battery and all the cavalry details; naturally the men still suffering from the new boots were told to remain, and Lieut. Thorne was instructed to take charge of our men.

Bothaville was only 8 miles away, and we soon reached it, and camped on a grassy slope, to the east of the town, running down to the river, which, at this spot, passes through high banks; there were still a few English people in the town, and a Nursing Sister, but most of the residents had either gone or left only their wives and families to represent them.

It was quite a small town, but contained a very fine stone house, quite out of keeping with the remainder, built by the late Government for the use of the Dutch minister. These gentlemen usually seemed fairly comfortable in every town which we had visited, with good houses and gardens and no rent to pay. They were men of much influence; most of them threw in their lot with their parishioners and went with them on commando, for which they can hardly be blamed. The Nursing Sister was very pleased to see us; she had been left behind with a patient by our troops on their last visit, three months before, and had been unable to leave the town since. A good deal of private property (including the valuable telegraph instruments, out of the post office) was found stowed away in the church in the hope that our troops would not touch anything—nor did we.

Two days we halted in this little town, and we enjoyed the rest very much; there was capital bathing in the river, and Captain Gilbert. Lieut. Boevey, and one or two more spent most of their time trying to coax the fish out of the stream, with some success.

As the Boers were still in the neighbourhood, and the mounted troops were out all day destroying the farms of those burghers of whom a good account could not be given, the picket duty was rather hard. Captain Gilbert went out one pitch dark night with a few men to surround some farms close by, which were occupied by pseudo-loyalists, and to try and catch any visitors who might be staying the night; but after some bad walking, falling over ant-heaps and into holes, they returned in the early morning, having visited three farms and drawn blank in each case.

There was a shop in the town with the usual miscellaneous collection of articles, and I was told that such articles as would be of use to the men might be removed; so a party from each company went round to look over the stock, which, however, comprised nothing much worth having. There were a few things, such as writing paper, penny note books, some shovels and other tools, which were useful, and which the men were allowed to take away: but most of the stock consisted of medicines, ironmongery, and some cheap drapery.

I saw one hairy old reserve man going out

with a small bundle under his arm, so I collared him and asked, "What's this?"

He stammered a bit, got confused, and finally said : " Well, Sir, it's—it's—its some calico!"

"Let's have a look at it," said I, and it was slowly unfolded and held up ; it, or rather they, were not calico by any means, but the finest linen, with lace frills.

"What on earth are you going to do with these?" I asked him. He got very red, and still more confused.

"Well, I'd like them, Sir, I want to send them to my girl!" he replied.

So he took them away, to despatch by parcel post, and I hope the young woman was pleased with her present—rather a curious one to receive from the scene of war.

Early next morning, at five o'clock, we were sent to burn and destroy certain houses in the town, which had been apportioned as our share of the work, the remainder being looked after by the Camerons and the men of the Royal Engineers. The church and manse, post office, Landdrost's office and about five or six other houses were not destroyed, but the mill was blown up by the Engineers. In several of the houses which were burned numerous small explosions took place, showing that cartridges were concealed somewhere ; the principal house in the town, filled with English furniture, belonged to the man who owned the shop, and who was then fighting against us with his commando : so it was with no feelings of compunction that we watched the destruction of his home.

All the residents were provided with wagons to take themselves and their property into Kroonstad, and the town was vacated by one o'clock, when we all marched away to our new camp, about three miles distant. There we were joined by the convoy and the men we had left at Tweefontein ; on the way we were sniped at, a few shots being fired at the cavalry rear guard, but no harm was done to anyone.

At six o'clock the next morning, on a lovely day, we marched off towards Beeste Kraal, which we reached before noon ; we had now a very large convoy of wagons with us, in addition to the refugees' wagons and the baggage of ourselves, the Cavalry and the Mounted Infantry, the total making up a very long column.

It was our bad fortune the next day to be rearguard to this huge procession of wagons and carts, which was continually being added to as refugees joined us along the road from the adjacent farms ; the march was a long one, 18 miles, and although we started at seven in the morning, the convoy was so slow that it was past two o'clock when we reached our camp at Driekopjes, or Three Hills. Numbers of farm houses had been burned along the road on both sides ; one farm which we passed belonged to an Englishman, who was with us as a guide, and who had married a Dutchwoman: he had been compelled to leave the country and go to Cape Colony six months before, when the war broke out and all English subjects received notice to quit, and had only now come with the troops, to pack up what he could and bring it and his family along with us.

Driekopjes is within a short distance of the famous Rhenoster Kop, a favourite haunt of De Wet, who was very partial to the three hills which gave the place its name, as they commanded the country for miles round, and formed an excellent advanced position to the larger Rhenoster Kop, rising black and forbidding about three miles to the north. There is a diamond mine close to where we camped, with a couple of shafts and some houses—apparently only a small mine.

On the 26th of October we marched once more into Kroonstad, and a very pleasant tramp it was after our long day's duty as rear guard on the previous day ; it was perfect weather and the road was good, and we were leading battalion of the column, so we stepped along briskly in great form.

After about six hours' march we found ourselves in the outskirts of Kroonstad and camping under Gun Hill, but to the west this time ; many were the speculations as to how long we should remain and where we should next go to, as not one of us believed that we should go back to Lindley just yet ; we had been too often sold before, and had come to look upon Kroonstad as the invariable forerunner of a dash somewhere down the line ; next time we should, perhaps, go north for a change, as a commando was said to be assembling to the north of Rhenoster Kop. Colonel Le Gallais' mounted force had left us at Driekopjes and gone off to the north, and we fully expected to find ourselves next day in coal trucks steaming up the line.

For a wonder we did not move the next day or the next, and the men had a good opportunity of visiting the town. More clothes and boots had been issued to those who required them, and some pay served out also : it was a long time since they had drawn any pay, so every man had about a couple of sovereigns to spend in the shops, which were now all open, crammed full of stock of all kinds, with the owners cutting each others throats in their eagerness to sell to the soldiers ; the price of everything was down to the usual rates and was falling every day, as one could see by the lists of prices outside each shop door. Very many of the men, it was pleasing to hear, went to the Army Post Office at the railway station, and bought largely of the postal orders for sale there, to remit some of their pay to their families.

It was a very great convenience to the men to be able to purchase these Postal Orders and thus send their money home themselves, and it was a great pity that the system was not introduced earlier in the campaign. Another great improvement would be the possibility of buying their postal orders on board the transports, as is done on the ships of the navy. In the beginning of the campaign the men used to bring me their money and ask me to send it home for them, as they could not do so themselves, and at various times I have forwarded to England, through the banks, drafts for over £500; this is a good record and reflects much credit on the men, and shows their consideration for their families.

CHAPTER XX.

VENTERSBURG ROAD.

A midnight start—Column surprised from the flank—Stampede of the animals—Attack of the Boer position—The charge—Boer retreat—The Infantry follow—Final position—A gun comes up—The Cavalry do not appear—The scene of action.

No one was astonished on the 29th of October when we found ourselves at the station entraining again, and bound for our old destination, Ventersburg Road ; this time the mule wagons went with us, and several trains were required to convey us all. The Camerons, half a battalion of the Buffs Militia and half a battalion of the Argyll and Sutherland Militia went off first ; we followed at eight o'clock, and after us came the battery and one of the five inch guns, of which there were two at Kroonstad. The General and his staff came down also by this train, and we camped once more to the west of the station. The Third Cavalry Brigade was there too, and also Captain Pine-Coffin, with his company of the Mounted Infantry from Malta ; but not poor Lieut. Attfield, of the Derbyshire, who, to the great loss of his regiment and the service generally, had been killed in a skirmish with the Boers some time previously : a smarter or cleverer officer of his standing could not have been found.

Reveillé came at the preposterous hour of eleven o'clock at night, when we struck camp and loaded our wagons, marching off at midnight towards Ventersburg town ; it was a darkish night with no moon, but the stars did their best to compensate for the absence of that luminary.

We moved in the following order, preceded by the Third Cavalry Brigade, who had gone out at eight o'clock that evening—first the Camerons, as advanced guard, then the battery and the five inch gun, after that the Buffs Militia, then the other Militia battalion, and lastly ourselves ; each of these units was of course followed by its first line transport—ammunition carts, water carts, and so on, and the rear of all was brought up by the ambulances of the 20th Field Artillery. General Hunter was with us with his staff, but General Bruce Hamilton rode with the Camerons, who were stretched out to some considerable distance in front.

After crossing the drift (which took some time, as there was water in it and we had to get over by the stepping stones), we continued on our way with the usual halts until about four o'clock or so in the morning. It was then just commencing to get light, but it could hardly be called dawn ; and we could distinguish on our left front a dark mass of rock-covered kopje, which lay broadside on to the road, but forming an angle with it, and joining it about a mile further on.

Thus from where we were to the top of the hill must have been at least a thousand yards, but the head of the column could not have been further off than six hundred yards or perhaps less : barring this ridge, which rose steeply out of the plain, the ground around us for a considerable distance was as flat as a table.

The Camerons had gone on some distance, and evidently reached as far as the place where the road dipped into a small valley among some broken hills, and we were still halted, when a Staff officer from General Hunter told me to send a company to occupy the kopje, which it appears was not picketed by the cavalry of the Third Brigade (as it should have been) or even by the Camerons ; owing to a misunderstanding the flank on that side had been left completely alone.

So I nodded to Lieut. Hopkins, who was standing by me and had heard the General's order, and off he went with A company, which was then leading our half battalion; in rear of them, in order of march, came F company, under Captain Gilbert, then G and H, under Major Panton and Captain Wisden, and then a company of details, belonging to the other half battalion, which was commanded by Captain Blake.

We idly watched A company moving off in fours, a dark mass in the dim light, and I was wondering why Lieut. Hopkins did not extend his men, and was on the point of shouting to him to do so, when the thought came into my mind that it would be better to leave the company alone, as the officer knew quite well what he was doing, and would, no doubt, extend as he got closer to the foot of the hill.

They had gone about half way between us and the hill, and Lieut. Hopkins, as he told me afterwards, was just turning round to give the order to extend, when there was the sudden ping-boom of a solitary rifle from the top of the kopje, evidently a signal, as it was followed by a terrible outburst of musketry, somewhat similar to that at Reteif's Nek, but not so heavy.

I was watching A company at the time, and it was very curious to notice how they behaved under this crash of musketry, which spattered the ground all round them with bullets; at the distance it seemed as though the whole company staggered and shook like a field of wheat under a breeze; then instantly the whole were flat on the ground, and they commenced firing without a moment's hesitation. Evidently the orders given were prompt and to the point: the fluttering appearance, like a flock of pigeons just settling down in a field, was caused by the men moving outwards, some to the front, some to the back, to extend; the whole business was over in an instant, but it was very pleasant to see the men so prompt to do what they ought, and so smart in opening fire.

All this passed in the twinkling of an eye, and then we had other matters to attend to, in place of looking on ; F company, now the leading one, had already faced the enemy, and were lying down, waiting for orders ; and the remaining companies were soon doing the same, forming across the veldt at an angle to the road, and, when in position, opening fire over the heads of A company at the Boers on the sky line at about 1,100 yards range ; there was nothing to be seen of the enemy, of course.

There was terrible confusion in front of us. All I could see was a confused mass of horses, bullocks, Cape carts and men moving swiftly and silently, like a great black river, down upon us ; in the middle of all this was a water cart, tearing along with no drivers, and the six mules going all they knew ; there was a mad bullock charging, head down, tail up, amongst the men, and there were loose horses everywhere.

It seems the battery had dismounted during the halt, and the men were lying down when the firing broke out. The Major of the battery was shot dead at once by the first discharge, and several horses were killed and wounded ; instantly, however, one of the gun detachments unlimbered, swung the gun round and got off a shot at the Boers ; but by this time there was a regular stampede going on amongst the animals, which were all rushing back on us to get out of the dreadful fire, and the fearful noise and echoing of rifle shots, which were incessant.

In the battery, several men were run over and seriously injured by bolting wagons, one of the latter travelling several miles before it was brought back ; the team of oxen had swung round with the heavy five inch gun and had smashed the pole, two bullocks had been killed and several injured ; the escort to the battery were apparently men of the Argyll and Sutherland Militia, and they lay down and opened fire.

By this time (and all the foregoing happened in a few seconds), our companies were all extended across the veldt, stretching away from the road, and were parallel to and about a thousand yards from the hill occupied by the enemy, at the skyline of which we were firing.

It was still dark, but momentarily growing lighter and lighter, and our men were blazing away steadily, when Captain Ross, the Divisional Signalling officer, came down with an order from General Hunter for the Royal Sussex to charge the hill.

That was all the Royal Sussex were waiting for: the whistle blew, and the whole line rose to their feet, and rushed wildly across the open ground, a few bullets dropping in front of us; yelling, cheering and cursing, and fixing bayonets as they ran, this wild mob kept on until want of breath necessitated a halt. A moment or two to fill their lungs, and on they dashed again, until checked by a wire fence, A company well in front with the start they had got, and young Wadwicz leading the way; but Cox, of F company, showing us that the reserve man was the best of all. The enemy's fire had ceased as suddenly as it had begun; some of us had our hearts in our mouths as, checked for a moment, we clambered over the barbed wires, dreading momentarily that the Boers were only holding their fire until we were mixed up in the fencing.

Not so, however; the fixing of the bayonets and the sudden onslaught of the long line was too much for their nerves, and they were off; panting and blowing after our long run of a thousand yards, we saw them when we reached the summit, going like smoke in the distance, in two directions; our men did not stop on the summit, but pushed on to gain the next hill.

There was a valley between, about a thousand yards wide, and, beyond, the ridge rose in a smooth slope, extending a long way both to the right and the left; on the left it continued, forking out into two spurs, which ran outwards, that on the left culminating in a lofty, round-topped hill, while that on the right continued round in a half circle. Our party now divided, Major Panton going towards the round hill on the left with two companies, while the remainder pushed on to the smooth ridge straight to our front.

We had opened fire at 800 and 1,000 yards from the top of the hill which we had charged, on the small parties of the Boers, evidently lagging behind the others; one of these men was dismounted, and our bullets hastened his movements considerably, until he disappeared out of sight over the ridge; and we had then pushed on in the hopes of catching him and his friends on the other side. One party of the enemy had gone off towards the round-topped hill on the left, and the horse of one of them, hit at 900 yards, had collapsed in a cloud of dust, so Major Panton and his two companies tore after his rider

While ascending the ridge in front, orders were received not to go any further, so we crept up to the top of the hill and lined the crest; the order was passed along to the companies, now a long way on our left, to do likewise.

Then we had leisure to look about us and fill up our ammunition pouches; it was now about half-past four, and the sun was just thinking of showing himself above the horizon; behind us, coming over the hill, were some companies of the Buffs Militia; in front of us was a huge valley, and beyond, on a small plateau, lay the town of Ventersburg; on our right, a long way off, perhaps a mile and a half, was a small group of mounted men and some infantry, with whom signalling communication was

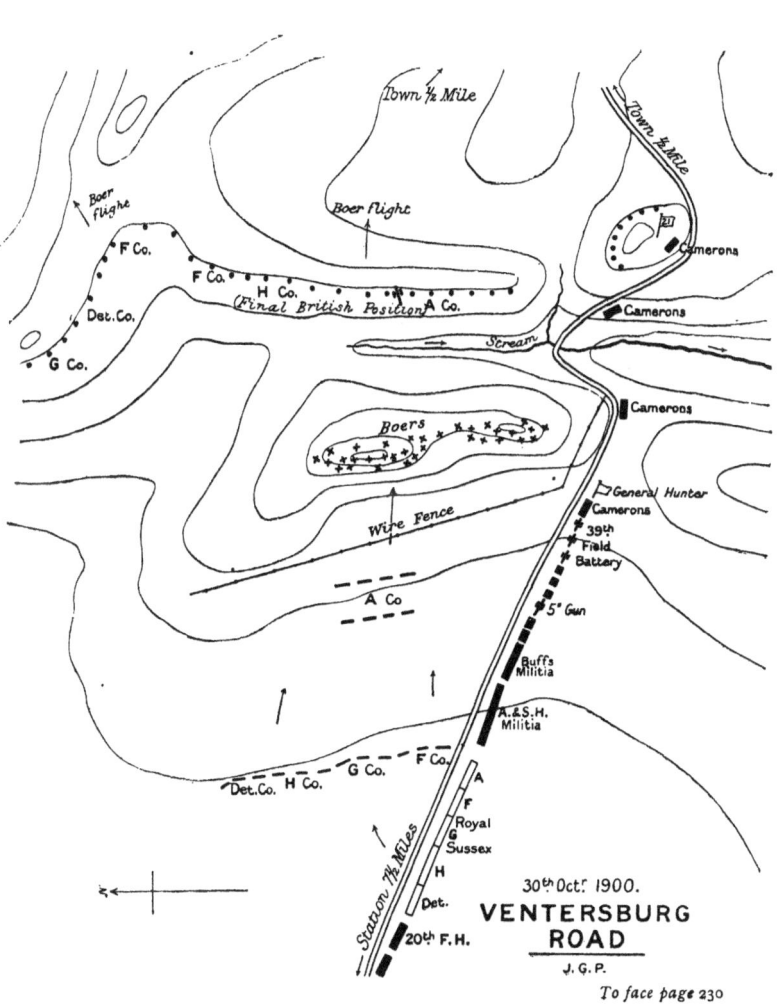

opened, and who proved to be General Bruce Hamilton and his staff and escort, and some of the Camerons. Information was sent to me that the Third Cavalry Brigade was in Ventersburg town, right in rear of the party of the enemy who had fired on us. This news filled us with amazement; what were they doing there, and why had they not tried to cut off the fleeing enemy, some of whom had bolted directly towards them?

In a few minutes up dashed a gun of the 39th Field Battery, under the gallant old sergeant-major; sharp and rapid were his orders, and quickly he asked where to place his shells. I pointed out the range of hills to the left front, right in the eye of the fast rising sun and well away from the town (which I knew it was useless to shell even if the cavalry had not been there), and the shrapnel rapidly began to burst along the circular ridge 3,000 yards in front, searching the reverse slopes. Soon a message, transmitted from the cavalry in the town, arrived, asking the gun to stop firing as the shells had dropped near to them; and so our little fight was all over. Evidently the cavalry were not in the town, as they had said before—although, if they were outside, their conduct in not pursuing the enemy was quite inexplicable.

Our bag was small: three horses, two rifles, and a Boer's hat; but, Lord knows, we ran hard enough and deserved more success. Our casualties were *nil*, to my great wonder and thankfulness: how A company escaped was a marvel, as the ground round them was covered with spirts of dust from dropping bullets until the advance commenced.

After a while, leaving a company on the top of the round hill, we re-formed and moved down towards the General, camping shortly afterwards close by.

It seems the Camerons' advanced guard had crossed the drift and reached the hill, in rear, but a long way to the right, of the enemy's position, and had seen them in the dim light bolting like hares a long way off, and had fired a few volleys at 2,500 yards; but the range was too great and the light too dull to do any good.

Lieut. Nelson, who was acting as Assistant Provost Marshal on the General's staff, had had a narrow escape; he was riding towards the column after the firing began with an order, when he was promptly fired on by some of our troops, and, notwithstanding his shouts and the waving of his helmet, the firing did not cease: so he had to bolt without delivering his message.

Walking over the scene of action the next day, it was interesting to place oneself in the Boer positions, and to notice how admirably they were selected, and what perfect protection from our fire was afforded by the stone walls from behind which they had opened such a galling fire upon the column. Their horses were well placed behind the hill, and, from the traces on the ground, could not have been there more than a few hours at the most; from twenty-five to thirty men must have been employed, and these had posted themselves behind the stone walls (old sheep and cattle kraals), with which the summit of the spur was entirely covered.

Their actual positions were revealed by the presence of their cartridge cases, which showed that four kinds of rifles had been used—Mauser, Lee-Metford, Martini and Stehr—and the Boers themselves were so perfectly concealed and so widely distributed that our column might have remained all day, firing with guns and rifles at the kopje, without disabling more than one or two of the enemy.

Apparently the enemy's picket on the hill could

not see the Camerons passing along (it was dark then, and they were well spread out), or else the Boers intended to devote all their energies to stampeding the battery and the five inch-gun.

Going down into the plain, the positions taken up by the men of A company, when they were suddenly fired upon, were revealed by the little heaps of cartridge cases, showing that the men had thrown themselves down from five to ten paces apart, in line, and with another line of men some little distance in rear, evidently the rear half company. The number of cases in each pile averaged about twenty or twenty-five, several men having fired as many as thirty-two; but a weak point was revealed by the number of unexpended cartridges lying about, as many as thirty-one in one particular spot. This is accounted for partly by the rounds falling out of the pouches when they are opened and the men are lying down; but there is also another reason—the men have a habit, a natural one too, of drawing out a handful of rounds and laying them on the ground to be handy for use; and when a sudden advance is made these rounds are forgotten. As the clip system of loading is pretty sure to be adopted without delay, there is no reason for harping upon the disadvantages of our pouches and our custom of single loading.

There were a number of dead oxen lying about, and two dead horses, one belonging to Major Hanwell, which had been shot at the same time as that unfortunate officer, and the other belonging to an officer of General Hunter's staff; while far away, more than half a mile off, were some dead mules.

Major Hanwell was buried the same afternoon in the little cemetery of the town; he was a smart soldier, and well known in Poona and Bombay.

CHAPTER XXI.

BACK TO LINDLEY.

Ventersburg—Kroonstad—Boer guns captured at Bothaville—Story of the action—To Lindley—Bad drifts and willing workers—Luxuries for the garrison—Their doings during October.

We remained several days in camp, and on the 1st of November a party was sent into Ventersburg to burn and destroy some of the houses ; they were wretched little shanties, most of the better class houses in the town being left untouched. A number of prisoners were taken, and some of the residents were deported and sent off to the railway in our wagons.

It was our turn that day to find the pickets, some of which were a considerable distance away : about dusk it began to rain, and continued to do so, steadily and without intermission, for thirty-six hours, during which time we were practically prisoners, as the roads were too heavy for the wagons to travel.

We were to have moved at seven o'clock in the morning, but as the weather showed no prospect of clearing up, the General decided to remain ; our pickets therefore, after a horribly wet night, were not relieved by the Camerons until about ten o'clock. The men must have had a wretched time on picket, and looked miserable when they came in, wet to the skin : however, an issue of rum, which was sanctioned by the General, was made to them as they arrived, cold and hungry, and soon everyone was cheery and making the best of it. The trouble was the cooking, and wretched were the meals the poor fellows had that day : some of them succeeded in making small fires inside the tents and boiling their canteens on them, but wood was scarce and wet.

By our inability to march on the 2nd we lost our chance of travelling to Kroonstad by rail: three trains were waiting for us at Ventersburg Road, but, owing to our non-arrival, they were ordered away by Lord Kitchener, and the result was we had another thirty miles to tramp.

The rain ceased early on the morning of the 3rd of November, and we were able to strike our tents (still soaked through), load our wagons with our sopping blankets, and move off towards the railway; as soon as we reached the high ground the road was firm enough, but in the neighbourhood of the camp, owing to the constant traffic and the trampling of animals, it was nothing but a sea of mud. We reached the station in good time, and camped, spreading out our blankets to dry directly we got in. Several trains arrived at the station that afternoon with supplies and troops on board: these latter were details and drafts proceeding up country to join their regiments, and among them were about a dozen of our men who had come up from Bloemfontein, and who eventually joined us at Kroonstad; they said there were numbers of men of our battalion still in the Rest Camp at Bloemfontein.

A day or two later I mentioned this to the General, who wired to the General at Bloemfontein, asking him to send up all officers and men of the Royal Sussex; but the latter General replied that he was very sorry he could not, as the men were urgently required for duty in the town; so the regiment had to go short-handed, while a lot of fat fellows were serving in Bloemfontein in the lap of luxury, getting every night in bed, and, many of them, drawing extra pay as well. There were numbers of civilian doctors, chaplains of all kinds, young staff officers, *et hoc genus omne* who each wanted a servant and a groom, or an orderly, and who had only to ask at the Rest Camp to get them.

It was said that General Kelly-Kenny once had a round up of all the idlers and others in Bloemfontein, and the story goes that quite a large number of soldiers were found in shops and hotels and bars, dressed in civilian clothes, and drawing good pay as shopmen and waiters.

On Sunday the 4th of November we marched out of Ventersburg Road once more, at half-past six in the morning; it was a charming day, and our march led us alongside the railway the whole time. All the parties of Militia guarding the line had been relieved by men of the Coldstream Guards who were on their way down country, but had been stopped to relieve the Militia and to furnish one or two new defensive posts near Holfontein.

I was sorry to see that the Guards had adopted the felt hat, which no doubt looks very nice and smart while it is new and retains its jaunty shape; but, after it has been out in the rain once or twice and the owner has slept in it on picket, the thing becomes a hideous shapeless object, a most unsoldierlike head covering, which, to be thoroughly appreciated at its worst, should be seen when worn in conjunction with a kilt and a khaki apron, as in the battalions of the Highland Brigade.

On our way we passed close to the spot where the train had been destroyed at night when we were at Ventersburg Road: the débris was still lying about, although, of course, the trucks had been removed. Most of the contents of the train were Hospital and Ordnance stores, so the ground was littered with the burnt fragments of iron bedsteads and other hospital fittings, with camp kettles, canteens, water bottles, drums which had contained rifle oil and dubbin, and all sorts of other articles. No trace had been left, of course, of the bales of blankets, clothing and boots, or of any of the Supply Stores such as biscuit, beef, etc.

Halting for the night at Geneva, we reached

Kroonstad about half-past eleven on the 5th of November, and camped on our old spot below Gun Hill, where we remained no less than four days.

Volunteers had been called for to serve on the Mounted Infantry, and sixty of our men sent in their names, showing that the spirit of enterprise and adventure had not been knocked out of them by the long marching and the hardships that they had undergone; they went off by train the same evening to Pretoria, where the new bodies of Mounted Infantry were being organised.

All day on the 8th and 9th of November, troops, mostly mounted, had been coming in from the west, and on the latter date, to the great delight of everyone, eight of the enemy's guns were brought in and parked in the market square, together with a large number of prisoners, who were handed over to a guard of the troops in garrison. These were the outcome of a most successful surprise of a Boer commando carried out near Bothaville on the 6th of November.

The guns were a varied lot: there was a 12pr. belonging to U battery and lost by them at Sanna's Post, many months before; there was a 15pr. which had belonged to the 14th Field Battery; two Krupp 9prs. in splendid condition; a Vickers-Maxim, or pom-pom; a one-pounder quick-firing Krupp, a Maxim with a portable tripod stand, and a large quantity of ammunition.

The successful capture of all these guns, prisoners, ammunition and wagons was largely due to our old friend, Major Lean, of the 5th M.I., and after a good deal of questioning (for, like all good soldiers, he was reluctant to talk about his own achievements), the story of the fight was extracted from him.

It seems that Le Gallais' force of Mounted troops, mostly Mounted Infantry, with U Battery, R.H.A., were near Bothaville, when intelligence was received of the presence of a Boer laager in the neighbourhood; so Major Lean with a few men of his own corps, all dismounted, went out one night to reconnoitre. They had to ford the river, the water reaching up to their waists, and then went on for some distance, until Major Lean observed some horses hobbled close to them: thinking this very curious, he went on a little further, and then saw, behind an ant heap, what looked like the head and shoulders of a man: without an instant's hesitation he dashed forward and yelled to the man, "Hands up!"

To his astonishment several other men rose and put up their hands, and he discovered that he had inadvertently held up an entire Boer picket. Handing over the prisoners to his men, he and his party went on cautiously, and on coming to the summit of a rise in the ground saw the whole Boer laager at their feet. The party was discovered, and a heavy fire opened on them at once; but the thirty men of the Mounted Infantry spread out under cover, and devoted themselves to preventing the Boers from inspanning their oxen into the guns and wagons. Word had been sent back to Colonel Le Gallais, who came up rapidly and joined in, U battery opening fire on the Boer guns at a range of 400 yards, but from the other side of a ridge, firing by indirect laying. The Boers answered the fire from their guns, and an artillery duel was in progress for some little time. A message had been sent back to General Knox, who, however, was out of reach, and also to Colonel De Lisle, who was some eight miles away; and the latter with his men came up rapidly, travelling the whole distance without drawing rein. They moved so as to envelope the flanks, but on their approach the enemy fled, leaving a large number of killed and wounded, and a considerable number of prisoners (114 in all), twenty-eight of whom were dressed in the blue uniform of the Staats Artillerie.

Unfortunately our loss had been severe, the gallant and dashing Le Gallais, Lieut.-Colonel Ross of the Durham Light Infantry, and two other officers having been mortally wounded, and seven officers severely wounded, while eight men were killed, and twenty-six wounded; but the success was great, and the rout of the Boers complete. They left the whole of their guns, wagons and Cape carts, and fled on their horses, some not even waiting to saddle up first. The prisoners said that De Wet and Steyn had both been with the laager, but that they had fled directly the firing commenced.

There is no false pride in the Boer commandants, nor any ridiculous notions about sticking to the ship and remaining with their comrades, who follow them so faithfully. Steyn possibly thought that it was time to move the seat of Government to some other place, Hoopstad for instance—probably the only town in the Free State which has not at some time or other been honoured with the designation of the capital of the Free State.

General Knox returned with the troops to Kroonstad soon afterwards, and received many congratulations on his success; at this time there were no less than four Generals in the town—General Knox, General Charles Knox, General Bruce Hamilton and Lieut.-General Kelly-Kenny, who was passing through on his way to Natal, and was just in time to see the captured guns.

It had been at one time rumoured that De Wet was waiting in the neighbourhood with the intention of making a dash at our convoy, while on its way to Lindley; and it was known that many Boers had been seen travelling north, while De Wet himself had been hanging about on the west of the railway. This disaster to his force and the loss of all the guns he had, not to mention his wagons and ammunition, completely upset his little plan, and spoilt our prospects of a fight.

We had been counting upon this, and had even settled that De Wet was to attack us as we passed over Doornkloof; but now there was no chance, unless the enemy round Lindley were to concentrate and give us a show before we reached that town.

The mail arrived just before we left, and we saw in the Gazette that Lieut. Hopkins had been promoted Captain in the Manchester Regiment in recognition of his gallantry at Retief's Nek, when he and two men were recommended for the Victoria Cross. Lieut. Hopkins was now the youngest Captain in the army, as he had hardly completed two years' service.

We left Kroonstad early on the morning of the 10th of November, and moved over to the other side of the drift to the north of the town, about a couple of miles away, where we concentrated.

The convoy, a large one as usual, of about 200 wagons, was waiting for us; the column of troops was not a very large one, consisting only of the Camerons and ourselves: but we had a considerable number of mounted men under Lieut.-Colonel Rimington, besides three guns of the 39th Field Battery, under Captain Brock, and one pom-pom; the Colonial Division was to follow us up as soon as they arrived at Kroonstad.

We camped at night at our old spot, Welgevrede, where H company took the opportunity to erect a fence round and to turf over the grave of Private Shutton, who was killed on the last occasion of our coming this way.

The column moved the next morning at five o'clock, our half battalion with a gun and some Yeomanry being rear guard; there was a long halt just before reaching Doornkloof, while the mounted troops searched the surrounding country: and then the convoy and the baggage were passed over and parked on the open ground on the other side of the kloof. Remembering how our rear guard had been sniped when passing through once before, we took special precautions this time, keeping the pickets out until the convoy had moved again, and giving the latter a good start before our last company left the top of the kopje. Not a Boer was to be seen, so we trekked on in peace, and camped once more at Quaggafontein, leaving that place at five o'clock the next morning. There were three bad drifts to cross on the way, and at one of them we had some hours' hard work. We were advanced guard, and seeing how impassable in its then state the drift was, our companies were set to work in reliefs making a roadway across the mud and slush. There was a broken-down wagon at the drift, the bottom of which we utilised, to the horror of Major Cardew, the Brigade Transport Officer, filling in the space with stones and earth. The Camerons came up soon, and some of them were told off to bring more stones so as to make a solid roadway; yet in places the terribly heavy, narrow-wheeled wagons sank to their axles each time, and there was hard work getting them over, what with the bad driving of the natives and the half wild state of the bullocks.

It was wonderful how the men worked, and how willing they all were to do their utmost to help matters on; there was no shirking or loafing about, but real solid work going on. Of course, we all knew that the sooner the job was got through and the wagons across, the earlier we would get into camp; but, apart from that, the willing cheerfulness to follow the lead of their officers has always been a prominent characteristic of Sussex men.

While we were busy, the Colonial Division overtook us and passed to the front; they were only a small force, composed of the Cape Mounted

Riflemen and their four gun battery, but they were a fine smart lot of men, looking splendid soldiers.

We had a rest of an hour or so while the convoy was being got over, and started again about mid-day. Alongside the road ran the field telegraph wire, which had been dismantled for miles by the Boers, the wire being carried off and the poles broken; with an eye to their camp fires, the men soon began to pick up these poles and carry them along with them, so that we reached camp more like a regiment of dismounted Lancers than tired-out infantry: Birnam Wood coming to Dunsinane was nothing to it!

Before reaching camp at Palmeitfontein we saw troops on the sky-line, and eventually found that they were two companies of our other half battalion, two of the Bedfords, and a gun, the whole under Lieut.-Colonel Donne, who had come out to meet us in case of any opposition among the hills between Quaggafontein and Lindley; there were some Boers about, but a few shots from the pom-pom made them scurry off.

The convoy got under weigh the next morning, at earliest dawn, and trekked the six miles which separated us from the town; and the troops followed a few hours later. Having got permission from the General, I rode on ahead to make arrangements about opening the Brigade Canteen as early as possible; the garrison of Lindley were very badly off for luxuries such as milk, jam and the like, and there had not been a box of matches or a bit of soap in the town for many days. Having secured five wagons at Kroonstad, by the good nature of Captain Atcherly, of the Divisional Staff, and other officers, it had been possible to load these up and bring them along with us for the beleaguered garrison, starving for cigarettes. A house had been secured and fitted up as a shop on our last visit to Lindley, the pioneer sergeant having painted the words, "Canteen, 21st Brigade," in enormous letters over the roof on both sides; they will remain for years as a memorial of our visit. Here the five wagons were off-loaded, the contents stacked inside the shop, and sold in limited quantities all that day and all the next day to the long queue of men at the door, patiently waiting their turn to get inside. About £1,500 worth had been bought in Kroonstad, the traders this time, all smiles and bows, tumbling over each other and quoting lower and lower prices each day, in their eagerness to sell. Of this lot, quite £1,000 worth was sold in three days— of course only to soldiers.

Pay had been issued to our men and to the Camerons, so they all had lots of money to spend: having managed to secure a safe in Bothaville, advantage had been taken of the opportunity to bring out in it £1,000 in gold for the use of the half battalion which had remained in Lindley.

So now the whole battalion was together again, and we had a great deal to talk about, and plenty of news to give: the departure of the Volunteer company, the capture of the eight guns and the death of Le Gallais, and our own adventures during the time we had been away, forming topics of conversation for a long while. We had gone off for a seven days' trek, and had returned at the end of six weeks; we had been constantly on the move, we had been on six occasions under fire, and we had marched 278 miles.

The story of the garrison of Lindley showed that they must have had a somewhat anxious time during our absence—ever on the look out, and entirely ignorant of what was going on in the Orange River Colony, or of what had become of the rest of the battalion and the Brigade.

When General Bruce Hamilton marched out of Lindley, on the 4th of October, he left Lieut.-

Colonel Donne in command of the place, with the following troops in addition to B, C, D and E companies of our battalion:—

    Driscoll's Scouts, 70 men, under Captain Driscoll,
    Three guns, 39th Battery, R.F.A., under Lieut. Maturin,
    Half Battalion Bedford Regiment, under Major Hammond,
    Half Battalion Cameron Highlanders, under Major Malcolm,

and that most comforting and reassuring weapon, the Five-Inch Gun, under Captain Massie, R.G.A. This gun, which has a range for shrapnel of 7,500 yards and for Lyddite shell of 10,500, was ensconced in a gun pit on a hill about 2 miles south of the town, from which it could, and did, dominate the country for miles round, and formed a moral and tangible support to reconnoitring, wood and foraging parties, who always knew that they had behind them this friend in need, at the sound of whose report even Boers would vanish like smoke.

    On the 5th the garrison was reinforced by the arrival of about thirty men of the 7th M.I., under Captain Lloyd of the Lincolnshire Regiment, and about fifteen men of Brabant's Horse, under Lieut. Inglis.

    Captain Garner, of Brabant's Horse, acted as Landrost, and Captain Green, who had lately resigned the Adjutantcy of the battalion, acted as Staff Officer during the period of Colonel Donne's command.

    The garrison settled down to a quiet existence; an Amusement Committee had been formed, and various kinds of games were arranged for: football, hockey, golf and tennis were all engaged in as far as the rather limited supply of appliances at hand would allow.

    The chief elements of excitement were found in the weekly wood parties; to get wood to any extent, it was necessary to go out to Groenvlei, or Green Valley, about 5 miles to the north-east. This farm was a regular oasis in the desert; it was in a pretty little valley, well wooded, through which a running stream, quite unlike the conventional spruit, wandered between old willows. Its situation, however, surrounded as it was by hills, made it a rather dangerous trap, and latterly most elaborate precautions had to be taken to ensure the safety of the wood parties: one or two other sources were tried for the wood supply, but other farms could furnish only two or three days' allowance, whereas Groenvlei was practically inexhaustible.

An occasional foray was made in a south-westerly direction to bring in mealies: these expeditions, and indeed all movements of troops outside the picket lines, brought to light small parties of Boers, who fired a large amount of ammunition to very little purpose—the only casualty being one man of Driscoll's Scouts, who was wounded on a wood party on November the 8th.

On October the 12th, 80 oxen were carried off by the enemy from in front of No. 1 north picket; the Boers fired on the native boys, who promptly bolted, and the enemy drove off the cattle before the picket could move out to the rescue. The scarcity of grass, and the large number of oxen left behind with the convoy, made the grazing of the cattle a very difficult question. However, stringent orders were given that the cattle were not to be allowed more than 800 yards outside the picket lines. Mounted men were also detailed daily to be under the orders of several of the picket commanders, to help the niggers with the cattle if necessary.

Yet in spite of these precautions another successful raid was made on the cattle in front of

No. 1 south picket on October the 28th, and 150 head were carried off; in this case the boys and conductors were held to blame, and were severely dealt with by the Commandant.

From the 10th of October to the 8th of November native runners were sent off weekly to Kroonstad with reports to the Officer commanding there, but only two got through; two were known to have been captured by the enemy, and the remainder returned, generally after having been out a day and a night, declaring that they were unable to get past the Boer patrols. On the other hand, several native runners succeeded in reaching Lindley from Kroonstad; and returned there safely.

On the 5th of November orders were received from Lord Roberts to vacate the town, the troops to proceed to Kroonstad; but these orders were cancelled by others received three hours later, a second lot of runners having come through from Kroonstad in the one night, whereas the bearers of the previous despatch had been upwards of 48 hours on the road. Fortunately the second set of instructions were received before anything had been done in the matter.

On the 5th of November the Supply officer reported that he had sufficient rations to last the garrison at full issues until the 15th; but as no information had been received as to the probable date of the General's return, it was considered advisable to put the troops on three-quarter rations.

On the 10th, runners arrived from Kroonstad with information that General Bruce Hamilton would leave that day with a convoy, expecting to arrive at Lindley on the 13th, and with orders for Colonel Donne to move out on the 11th in the direction of Palmeitfontein, in order to lend the convoy assistance if required. The two forces accordingly met, as has before been said, and marched back to the town without incident.

CHAPTER XXII.

IN GARRISON.

A fruitless expedition—The Brigade goes off—The Volunteers with them—The garrison—Residents—Defences—Communications—A prisoner—A night attack—A complimentary order—No soap—Cordite spills—A trap that failed.

On the 15th of November the General made a dash from Lindley at a Boer laager, which was supposed to be about 7 miles out on the Reitz road, on the other side of a huge kopje easily visible at a considerable distance.

B, C, D, E, and G companies of our battalion were engaged in the operation : we paraded at half past two in the morning, and, with half a battalion of the Camerons, two companies of the Bedfords, two guns, a pom-pom and Rimington's mounted troops, moved cautiously forward and occupied the hill about dawn—only to find the birds flown, and no signs of their nest. It was particularly disappointing to us, as we were the leading troops in the column, and were in hopes of being able to follow the example of Major Lean's little force at Bothaville ; but the enemy had gone the night before, having got wind of our intentions. We remained a few hours on the top of the large kopje, while the cavalry reconnoitred out in front ; there were a few scattered Boers about, but not many. We marched back to the town about mid-day, pretty well tired out; not with the distance, which was only 14 or 15 miles, but with want of sleep—for we had been nearly eleven hours on our feet.

The next morning the General and the Brigade went off, leaving us in sole possession of that important town, and trade centre, Lindley : once, but only for a short time during a somewhat hurried visit paid by Mr. Steyn, the capital of the Free State. Unfortunately for the town, Mr. Steyn's business was of such a peculiar character that he was compelled to transfer the seat of Government to other and less important places than Lindley.

With the Brigade went Captain Hopkins, who, to the loss of the Royal Sussex, was proceeding to join his new regiment. Our two young aspirants for fame on the staff, Lieut. Villiers and Lieut. Nelson, also went off, and with them the remainder of the Volunteer company, to whom the following farewell order was issued by the Colonel.

Extract from Battalion Orders, 16th of Nov., 1900.

" In bidding farewell to Lieut. D'Olier and the Volunteer company of the Royal Sussex Regiment, Lieut.-Colonel Donne wishes to express the feelings of all ranks in the First Battalion at losing such good comrades in many a long march and hard fought action. They will go home to Sussex carrying with them the proudest insignia of this campaign—the memories of Welkom Farm, Zand River, Doornkop, Capture of Johannesburg, Capture of Pretoria, and the hard fought battle of Diamond Hill on the 11th and 12th of June; the subsequent march south to Heidelburg and Bethlehem, the operations in the Caledon Valley, the brilliant action at Retief's Nek, and the surrender of the Boer forces at Golden Gate—these are records they can well consider as second to none of the Volunteer companies in South Africa.

" But these marches and victories have not been achieved without grievous losses to mourn. Their best of leaders and bravest of men—Sir Walter Barttelot—fell gallantly leading them to the attack on Retief's Nek. His sterling worth as a soldier will live long in the records of the regiment. He gloried in fighting for his country, and his death at the head of his Volunteer company will serve not only as a pathetic incident in the campaign, but as an illustrious example for all time to the Volunteers of Sussex ; it will knit more firmly together in the bond of *esprit de corps* all the battalions of the Royal Sussex as one great county regiment.

" Whilst the path of the Volunteer company is towards home, that of the First Battalion is outward bound, far out into the British Empire for many a long year; but we shall never forget the comradeship which has been cemented on the fields of South Africa in 1900. All Sussex will welcome her citizen soldiers who have shared our hardships, and added fresh glory to our old flags, which will shortly find their resting place in the County Cathedral. We wish them a speedy and safe return home after work so well accomplished. We wish them the hearty reception that we know awaits them in the old country, and long life to enjoy the honour of having served in this memorable campaign."

The garrison left in Lindley on the departure of the Brigade comprised our battalion, two companies of the Bedfords under Captain Rowe, two guns of the 39th Field Battery under Lieut. Harrison, the Five-Inch gun, two companies of the 15th Battalion of Yeomanry under Lieut. Shepherd-Crosse, and a few of Brabant's Horse under Lieut. Friedlander. Lieut. Lloyd, the Supply Officer, had gone with the Brigade, but had left his Sergeant-Major behind with an enormous mountain of stores of all sorts, as we were rationed up to the 15th of the next month, January. Lieut. Goodman had been left also to look after the transport : the hospital and medical arrangements were supervised by Major Ritchie, of the R.A.M.C., who had been some time in Lindley, and who had under him Civil Surgeons Barr and Twigg, Captain Knapp, the medical officer of the Cape Mounted Riflemen, and Lieut. Duncan of the R.A.M.C. There were a good many men in hospital belonging to various corps, and the large church in the centre of the market square, which from the first had been used as a hospital, was nearly full; there had been one or two deaths from enteric.

There were a few civilians in the town: it seems the Boers allowed each business house in the towns to leave either the owner or the manager in charge, all the other assistants having either to go on commando or to pay a heavy fine. Of course those of them who were British subjects cleared out altogether; but the unfortunate owner of the shop, if he was in possession of burgher rights, gained by long residence in the country, was in rather a fix, and saw every prospect of losing his money either way. One of the merchants in Heilbron provided a case in point: he was an Englishman with burgher rights, and, when war was looming in the distance, he went to Cape Colony, leaving his manager in charge of the store. The Boers under their rule exempted the manager from service, but sent the owner a notice to turn out and join his commando; no notice being taken of this by the man, a fine of £500 was inflicted, which the unfortunate trader had to pay, and did pay, because if he had not done so the Boers would have distrained on the goods in his shop, and would have probably taken several times the amount of the fine. There was a branch of the National Bank in Lindley, and the manager and a clerk had remained throughout all the troubles, and the various occupations and evacuations by our troops and the Boers: the Boers always respected the Bank, and gave no annoyance whatever.

Several families of doubtful loyalty had been removed by General Bruce Hamilton, and taken away with the Brigade; their property in Lindley was respected, however, in view of their return. One or two of those who were left made themselves useful to us and added to their own income by making up the men's rations of flour into loaves. It will hardly be believed that the greater part of our bread ration was flour only, while at Kroonstad thousands of boxes of biscuits were being used to form houses for the supply subordinates to live in.

The town and the vicinity were in a filthy state after so many mounted troops, cattle and horses had been quartered there; but after a while it was gradually cleared up, and the carcases of the dead bullocks and mules left behind by the Brigade dragged away or buried. The river was a disgusting sight, with dead bullocks strewn about from one end to the other, half in the water: still some men did not mind, but bathed frequently in the deeper pools.

From its situation, in a hollow, surrounded by extensive hills, the town needed a good many pickets to adequately protect it; there were three permanent posts to the north and four to the south, each consisting of an entire company, and some furnishing subsidiary posts in the neighbourhood, on roads or prominent spurs. Each post was well defended, and in some a reserve of rations and water sufficient for three days' consumption was stored; there was, it need hardly be said, extra ammunition kept by each, and all were defended by earthworks or stone sangars on prominent points, the tents being pitched in each case so as to be out of the line of fire, should the enemy take it into his head to snipe at long range at the pickets.

The remaining three companies of the infantry were quartered on the three sides of the town to act as a reserve, and also as a second line of defence, should the Boers penetrate the picket line and rush into the town. The pickets were relieved every ten days or so, and their positions changed, as the sentry work at some was harder than at others. The men were allowed into the town to go to the Canteen or the Soldiers' Club during the afternoon; it was quite 40 minutes' walk to some of the pickets, so that most of the men usually remained at home.

The two guns of the battery were quartered on the outskirts of the town, but the five inch gun was kept in its gun pit on No. 2 picket to the south, where it dominated a very large tract of country. On one occasion it was taken at night to the opposite picket, about 4 miles away, whence it very much astonished some Boers who were wandering about in front at a distance of no less than 6 miles.

The Yeomanry and a few men of Brabant's Scouts were utilised to furnish a picket by day on the top of Tafelburg, a high square-crowned kopje, about 3 miles to the north-west, from which an extensive view could be obtained; and a couple of mounted men were kept by day at some of the pickets, in case of necessity, to carry messages or go after suspicious passers-by. All the pickets were in signalling communication with each other and with headquarters in the town; sometimes helio messages were received from Bethlehem, about 35 miles to the south-east, whose garrison was apparently similarly situated to ourselves; and occasionally, at long intervals, a runner arrived from Kroonstad with microscopic messages—usually containing news, unimportant to us at all events, such as the state of the Czar's health, but very little information as to how things were going on with regard to our move to India, about which we were most concerned.

Occasionally a few of the mounted men would go out at night, and surround a farm or two in hopes of catching a few Boers who might be indulging in the unwonted luxury of a night's rest in a bed; but only once did they meet with any success, and then they caught a solitary Boer who gave us a deal of trouble to look after. Lieut. Harden and Lieut. Montgomerie had the honour of catching this sportsman, who seemed to have been a fighting Boer from the yarns he told with regard to the fights in which he had taken part; but most of his stories had to be taken *cum grano salis*.

On the 3rd of December, however, the Boers treated us to an alarm about half-past nine at night: they crawled up a donga which ended in a short outcrop of rocks within four hundred yards of one of the detached posts then occupied by B company. The rocks afforded splendid natural cover in capital positions for firing from, and the Boers, about a dozen of them, opened a smart fire at the eight men occupying the small defensive work, who, nothing loath, replied with vigour, blazing away at the flashes of the enemy's rifles. One Boer must have been hit, as some blood was found on the grass the next day. The enemy fired about 500 rounds, judging from the cartridge cases lying in little heaps behind the rocks, and our men got rid of about the same number. One or two of the Boers had the impertinence (it was nothing less!) to try and stalk the picket by dodging up towards them from post to post of a line of fencing which ran in their direction; but, coming to a gap where one or two posts were missing, their hearts failed them, and they went no further. None of our men were hit, but the stone loopholes and the parapet of the post were splashed with bullet marks in five or six places.

Firing commenced also against Captain Aldridge's picket, about a mile further off, where bullets came plunging through the tents, to the astonishment of the men there. These, however, quickly dropped into their places in the various sangars, and replied briskly to the enemy's fire, which, as could be seen by the flashes, was coming from a ridge over 2,000 yards away. After half-an-hour or so the firing dropped on both sides.

The remainder of us had, of course, turned out at once and got into our various positions. About half-past ten, everything being quiet, we turned into bed again. In a few minutes there was a furious clatter of about a dozen shots fired rapidly from the north-east, and later, two more outbursts of firing from the north; and as none of our pickets on that side had fired, we concluded the Boers were ending the evening's amusement by firing at each other, an original idea, and one that we hoped they would regularly carry out—if possible, without causing us to turn out also in the dark. We never heard the cause of this firing, and the only possible solution was that two parties of Boers must have met in the dark. There was, however, a very good reason for the sudden firing on the pickets to the east and north-east, as we found in the morning, when Swannepool, a loyal farmer living to the north-west of the town and some miles away, arrived in a furious passion, swearing vengeance against all and every Boer; and, when he had cooled down somewhat, announced that some Boers had held him up in the night, and had driven off all his stock, his cows, his bullocks and horses, and had taken away his Cape cart. *Hinc illae lachrymae*, he said, and we sympathised with him.

The few men of B company on the detached post were in a nasty corner for some time, and fully deserved the complimentary remarks which the Colonel made the next day, and which were published in battalion orders. They were as follows :—

Extract from Battalion Orders, 6th of December, 1900—

"The Commanding Officer wishes to express

to Lance-Sergeant Ockelford and the eight men who defended the outpost of No. 1 picket, South, on the night of the 3rd of December, his approbation of their soldierly conduct in defending a small breastwork against a superior force of the enemy.

"An incident of this sort shows what a few men can do who are determined to hold their own, and the Commanding Officer has made a report of their creditable conduct to the General Officer commanding at Bloemfontein."

Our humdrum existence continued now for some little time, our days commencing by standing to arms at dawn (which was pretty early, usually between three and four o'clock), and concluding by our going to bed about eight o'clock in the evening. Almost every day there were cricket matches, and there were *al fresco* concerts three times a week. Beyond this mild form of entertainment, it cannot be said that we lived in an exciting whirl of constant pleasures.

Soap was at a premium; there was not a scrap to be had anywhere. All that the Brigade Canteen had brought had been commandeered by the Supply people for the use of the hospital, and, beyond a meagre issue of one ounce a man, the troops had had none for nearly two months. Matches were also conspicuous by their absence. The soldier is always a large consumer of this article, and spends a good deal of his time daily in striking matches and lighting his pipe; he was not, however, to be defeated by the absence of matches: some ingenious man had discovered that the thin sticks of cordite out of the cartridges made an excellent spill for lighting cigarettes or pipes at the fire, and, until the practice was peremptorily stopped, it became quite a fashionable pursuit.

Some of the Boers must have developed quite an affection for Captain Aldridge's picket, because, on the 8th of December, they fired a few shots about half-past nine in the morning at the men of the picket employed in repairing their sangars. To this fire E company disdained even to reply, and the disgusted Boers, finding their overtures received with apathy, rode off, six of them being observed passing through a gap in the hills quite 2,500 yards away.

On the night of the 9th, some of the mounted troops went out to lay a trap for a Boer picket which was in the habit of coming to a kraal, about three miles to the north and in full view of our pickets on that side; and a field gun was sent out early next morning to No. 2 picket to cover their retirement, if required.

The little plan failed, owing to the too eager and inexperienced Yeomen showing themselves just as the birds were entering the trap. There was a certain amount of shooting, however, as towards breakfast time our men withdrew; but it was all long range firing, which seldom harms anyone.

In front of the picket where the gun was posted was a splendid expanse of open country, with an occasional small kopje; and the whole panorama was backed by a range of hills, which limited the view to about five miles. Over this country were a few groups of Boers dotted, moving about aimlessly. One small party riding towards a donga, whence possibly they might have attempted to annoy our Yeomanry, were fired at by our gun at 4,500 yards: the shell sang through the still air and burst with a "ping" some hundreds of yards short. With one accord the four or five Boers mounted and spurred vigorously away, nor did they draw rein so long as they remained in sight.

(*End of Colonel du Moulin's manuscript.*)

CHAPTER XXIII.

THE RAISING OF THE MOUNTED COLUMN.

Evacuation of Lindley—Regiment split up—Major du Moulin's detachment—Men mounted at Bethulie—On convoy—The chase of De Wet—Strydenburg—Colesberg—Edenburg—A vast convoy—Bloemfontein—Smithfield—Action at Commissie Bridge—the Fighting Column—Raw Yeomen—Deep Dene Drift—Jammersberg Bridge—Springfontein.

The wearisome stay of the Regiment in Lindley came to an end in January, 1901. On the 13th of that month the filling in of the entrenchments was begun, and orders to evacuate the town were finally received on the afternoon of the 20th. The piquets were sent out as usual, but by 9 p.m. the town was cleared, and the force (consisting of the Royal Sussex, two companies of the Bedfords, and Col. Munro's column) started for Kroonstad. There was great confusion at the drift outside the town, several lines of wagons converging on it in the dark; and by dawn only 3 miles had been made. The secret, however, had been very well kept, and the Boers had no inkling of the departure of the troops until well on into the morning of the 21st. They then harassed the rear, but made no other use of their considerable numbers, and the force reached Kroonstad practically without incident.

Here the regiment was split up, and B, E, and H companies were sent up the railway to Heilbron. From Heilbron they trekked to Frankfort and back with Col. Williams' Column, assisting in the evacuation of that place; and they then railed with Head Quarters down to Norval's Pont, where the railway from Cape Town crosses the Orange River, and enters the Orange River Colony. They relieved the Essex Regiment there, taking over the piquets on the hills north of the river; subsequently detachments were sent to Donkerpoort, and to Providence Siding, further up the line.

On June 3rd these Companies were relieved by Militia, and sent to join various columns, all men who would ride ultimately reaching the Sussex column. Head Quarters remained at Norval's Pont till July, when they were moved, first to Springfontein, and then (December 6th) to Bethulie, on the Port Elizabeth line. Col. Donne had previously gone to Kroonstad as Commandant of that place.

To return to January, 1901—A, C, D, F, and G companies entrained at Kroonstad on the 25th of that month, under Major du Moulin, for Ventersburg Road; and from there they moved out as escort to an ox convoy on the evening of the 27th. The weather was appalling—very heavy rain lit by vivid flashes of lightning, that showed men and oxen in a sea of mud. Progress soon became impossible, and the column halted, waiting where it stood for dawn. The crossing of Zand River on the 29th gave great trouble, the huge convoy taking fifteen hours to complete it. Smaldeel was reached on the 30th, and there the convoy was left, the five companies entraining for Bethulie, where a great concentration was taking place in view of De Wet's intended raid into Cape Colony. On reaching Bethulie, the kit was reduced to one blanket and one waterproof sheet per man, great-coats and tents being returned to store.

A bad railway accident involving several trains took place here on the 1st of February. The Sussex men turned out, and cleared the line after the greatest exertions. Trucks had to be broken up, and great pieces of them dragged out of the railway cutting by main force.

Want of mounted men was being most keenly felt at this time, and General Lyttleton (who was at Bethulie) suggested that the Regiment might provide the mounted escort required for a convoy. The idea was enthusiastically taken up; many more men volunteered than could be mounted. By the 7th of February an M.I. Company of 120 men had been organised under Lieut. Harden and 2nd Lieut. Leachman; and in addition to these, a number of men of C, D and F companies were mounted, and left under their own officers.

The scenes that ensued during the two or three days, which were all that could be allowed for training, had their humorous side. Many of the men had never had anything to do with a horse before, and hardly knew one end of it from the other. However, they stuck to their mounts nobly —as long as they could. On one of the first treks, an officer, coming under the eye of the authorities, and wishing to show off the accomplishments of his men, gave the command "Trot!" The result was a surprise to all parties. With a thundering of hoofs, a mob of galloping horsemen swept past the officer, scattered the authorities, and disappeared in clouds of dust. They knew how to start their horses—but had not yet learned the art of stopping them.

Great difficulty was experienced in getting saddlery. This had to be obtained locally, and the stuff in the town turned out to be mere rubbish. Some more serviceable equipment was got from the Mounted Infantry, but, when the detachment moved out on February 9th in charge of a convoy, many of the men were using blankets as saddles, and looped putties as stirrups.

The horses supplied were also very indifferent. A large proportion had been cast by the columns for sore backs and wrung withers, from which they had hardly recovered. However, all obstacles were surmounted, and the convoy, consisting of some 300 ox wagons, crossed the main line at Prior's siding on the 10th of February, and reached Philippolis on the 11th, after marching that day 24 miles.

The total strength of the detachment under Major du Moulin at this time was 12 officers and 558 rank and file. This included two companies of the Royal Irish Rifles, which were attached.

Striking down into the Colony, two days were taken up in crossing the Orange River at Sand Drift, where many columns had collected, the river being in flood. The water on the Drift was five feet deep in places, so that the wagons were awash. The bottom was sandy, and the track had constantly to be changed. A steep bank of heavy sand on the south side added to the difficulties. The constant rain at this time was very trying to the troops; the roads were knee-deep in slush, the camps became marshes, and, as there were no tents, wet blankets were the order of the day.

By the 17th the line was again reached at De Aar. Here more men were mounted, Lieut. Ashworth having brought up a further instalment of saddlery, and on the next day a start was made with a full convoy for Britstown, to the west of the railway line.

At this time De Wet had crossed the Orange River with his raiders, had reached Britstown, and had been headed off to the west in the Strydenburg direction. A large number of columns had been thrown into the Colony to deal with him, and the convoy under Major du Moulin was to serve the Northern section of these. It reached Britstown on the 20th, after some fighting; for it was actually ahead of the columns, and the Boers only evacuated the town as the convoy came up.

An average trek of 20 miles a day brought the convoy to Strydenburg (by way of Prieska) on the 23rd of February, hot on the trail of the Boers, whose recent camps were found at farms along the road. Maxwell's column was already in the town, and Munro's arrived with the convoy. Bethune's column was in rear. De Wet, who could not re-cross the Orange River on account of the floods, lost on this day a 15 pr., a pom-pom and 100 men, captured by Plumer.—The return journey of the convoy to Paau Pan, on the railway, was completed on the 26th.

The long marches to and from Strydenburg were wearisome and hot. Day after day the convoy plodded on, while the Karoo country stretched all round, brown, dusty, waterless, and quite flat. There was little sign of life—a few sheep, perhaps, a few ostriches, and a very occasional farm. The scrubby bush was most trying to the horses' legs. A "pan" here and there promised relief to the thirsty men and beasts, but the water as often as not turned out to be salt.

De Wet managed to cross the River on the 28th of February, and the column's next piece of convoy work consisted in taking 100 ox wagons and 19 mule wagons from Orange River Station to Colesberg, a distance of 100 miles. This was done in the remarkably quick time of six days, making an average of 17 miles a day in spite of bad weather. As 2½ miles an hour is fast for an ox wagon, this entailed eight hours a day actually on the move. The convoy reached Colesberg on the 8th of March, after a trek that formed a delightful contrast to the preceding one. The road led through a green and smiling country, lying among its hills by the Orange River. It was the season of fruit, and there was a great abundance of all kinds. Colesberg itself was a pleasant and friendly town, behind which rose the towering sides of Coles Kop. It seemed impossible that a gun should have been taken to its summit, but the feat had been accomplished, and the gun was there. A signal station on the top maintained helio communication within a radius of 30 or 40 miles, and exchanged occasional messages at 70 miles or more.

On the 10th of March the force under Major du Moulin started by rail for Edenburg. The men were not yet very skilled at entraining horses, and one company omitted to look to the bolts of the door on the far side of its truck. A few miles from Colesberg, a telegram overtook the train to say that horses were dropping out. The side of the truck had swung open, the train was going slow, and, looking back, three or four horses could be seen careering about the veldt. The door was quickly secured, and the train went on.

Soon after passing Norval's Pont, the train again came to a standstill. A swarm of locusts was on the rails, and the wheels of the engine could get no grip. The men had to turn out, and throw sand in front of the engine till the swarm was passed.

The country south of Dewetsdorp and east of Edenburg is intersected by a series of long ridges from two to five hundred feet in height, between which lie valleys and plains of irregular shape, often many miles across. At this time these valleys were full of stock of all kinds, the inhabitants were on their farms, and the local commandos, under Commandant Brand and others, had lived undisturbed upon the fat of the land. The size of the country, and the power of splitting up possessed by the commandos, made it extremely difficult to get at the latter. An effort was therefore made to cut off their supplies, and General Lyttleton's columns were turned into the district to clear it. Major du Moulin started from Edenburg with a convoy of 152 wagons for these columns on the 13th of March, reached Dewetsdorp on the 16th after some sniping, and on the 21st handed in at Bloemfontein 2,000 horses, 5,000 cattle, and 80,000 sheep collected during the week. A number of refugees were also brought in. The Boers had been engaged at Geluk on the 19th, two of them being killed and three wounded. Some South African Light Horse had been attached, to assist the escort of the convoy.

This trek into Bloemfontein from Dewetsdorp was a truly remarkable one. The convoy had grown so enormously in taking over the captures of the various columns, that it was no less than 10 miles long. Sometimes the rearguard did not leave one camping ground until two hours after the advanced guard had reached the next. The rearguard had a very difficult job. The great masses of sheep were very slow, and often a kopje had to be held until it was difficult to get away in the face of the Boer snipers, who constantly harassed the rear. This sniping continued right up to the outposts of Bloemfontein.

Here a great change was noticed in the look of the troops in the town. Instead of the torn and dirty uniforms of Lord Roberts' advance, neat new Khaki was to be seen all round, while at the Club starched collars and red tabs seemed the rule.

At Bloemfontein Capt. Montrésor joined the column, and there the Royal Irish Rifles left it. The weather continued extremely bad, the heavy rain causing the greatest discomfort to the troops.

Entraining for Springfontein, the force started thence with another convoy for the east of the line on the 27th of March. There were then under Major du Moulin 12 officers and 375 men of the Royal Sussex, of whom 250 were mounted; and a section each of the 39th and 85th batteries R.F.A.

The convoy was constantly sniped; but a trap laid by the Boers near Leeuwfontein failed, the widely extended flank guards getting in their rear without being conscious of the fact. The want of a pom-pom was very much felt, as the guns could not leave the convoy.

Smithfield was reached on the 30th, and some cycles found there formed the nucleus of a cyclist section, subsequently elaborated under Lieut. Crawley-Boevey. From Smithfield a four days' trek brought the convoy to Bethulie, after destroying by the way a Boer supply depôt, with ovens for the baking of bread, at Gryskop. Near the same place D company (under Capt. Montrésor) found itself in a warm corner at a farm to which it had been sent foraging, and lost four horses killed and three wounded. The guns, however, galloped up, and the Boers retired under a heavy fire.

Smithfield was reached on the return journey on the 7th of April, and Edenburg on the 10th. At the latter place, prisoners, refugees and stock were handed in.*

While trekking, the Mounted Infantry furnished the advanced and rear screens, and the flank guards, the latter keeping well out. The order of march of the remainder was as follows:—

>   Advanced Guard:—
>   > Section R.F.A.
>   > 1 Coy. Infantry in wagons (when available).
>
>   Main Body:—
>   > 1 Coy. Infantry in Cape Carts.
>   > Baggage Column, R.A. leading.
>   > Supply wagons (mule).
>   > Ox wagons.
>   > Refugee wagons and ambulances.
>
>   Rear Guard:—
>   > Section R.F.A.
>   > 1 Coy. Infantry in wagons (when available).

The company of Infantry at the head of the main body was used as a species of mounted (or rather carted) infantry; on the convoy being threatened, the Cape carts were turned in the required

---

* 20 Prisoners, 9 Male Refugees, 41 Women, 124 Children, 6,179 Sheep, 337 Cattle, 136 Horses.

direction, and galloped across the veldt, disgorging their occupants at points of vantage. All the mounted men were thus freed for more important duties further afield. Each Cape cart contained one or two boxes of ammunition, and thus acted as ammunition reserve for any other troops who came up.

In April, General Lyttleton gave up command of the Southern District of the Orange River Colony, and on doing so published the following order:—

The Officer Commanding
1st Royal Sussex Regt.

Lieut. General Lyttleton desires me, before he leaves this command, to convey to you his appreciation of the very efficient manner in which the men of your Battalion, under Major du Moulin, have carried out the arduous duties of escort to convoys, on which they have been frequently employed.

They have been admirably trained and handled by that Officer, who has singular qualifications for that sort of work, and O.C.'s of columns in the field have reported in high terms on them.

General Lyttleton hopes that his good opinion may be conveyed to all ranks, in Battalion Orders, or in whatever way the Commanding Officer thinks best.

A. J. M. MacAndrew, Capt.
Edenburg, for C.S.O.
April 12, 1901   Genl. Lyttleton's Force.

A convoy of 120 wagons was again taken out to Dewetsdorp on the 11th of April, 250 I.Y. and 50 South African Light Horse (all freshly raised) being added to the escort. Dewetsdorp was cleared of inhabitants, and also all the farms along the route; and a vast body of refugees was brought in on the return to Edenburg, many having been handed over by the columns.* There was a good deal of sniping during the trek, in which one man † was severely wounded. A bicyclist of the advanced guard had been captured, with his machine, on the first day out. The man was of course set free : the bicycle was recovered months afterwards in a farm some distance away.

The force then set out for Smithfield with a convoy, reaching that place on the 24th of April, after having had a brush with a party of Boers near Rietput the day before. The town was cleared, and all the ovens and cooking utensils found in the houses were destroyed. On the morning of the 26th, when the convoy moved on, the Boers attempted to hold Commissie Bridge over the Caledon River. A sharp engagement followed, during which 2nd Lieut. Thorne collected men from among the wagons, dashed across the bridge, and seized a kopje on the further side, thereby gaining a mention in column orders. The Boers were driven off, but followed the convoy almost to Rouxville, which was reached on the 27th of April; and from this date to the 20th of May the force under Major du Moulin was occupied in escorting a convoy between Aliwal and Rouxville, bringing out stores from the latter place, and returning with refugees and stock taken over from the columns working the district.

On the 20th of May orders were received from General Bruce Hamilton that the column was to clear the country north of Smithfield as a fighting column. The task of watching the trek ox plod slowly and gloomily through the dust was over, to the great delight of all ranks, and, with a roving commission, the column set out in a northerly direction. In addition to men of the Royal Sussex

---

* 100 prisoners, 30 male refugees, 300 women, 980 children, 400 black refugees, 30,000 sheep, 6,000 cattle, 300 horses.
† Pte. Pruce, E Company.

(5 companies M.I. and an Infantry escort), Major du Moulin had under him at this time a company of the Connaught Rangers M.I. and a section of the 43rd Battery, R.F.A.

On the 22nd a retreating Boer convoy was sighted—probably belonging to Brand's Commando, then at Rietput. On the 24th the baggage of the column was well sniped by some sixty Boers at Kopjeskraal, on the way to Vaalbank. What followed was characteristic of Major du Moulin's methods. The cooks and other duty men, together with the wagon escort in Cape carts, were immediately set to charge round the flank of the hill at a gallop, Cape carts and all. This was too much for the nerves of the Boers, who streamed away. The guns came into action, without, however, any luck, the retreating Boers having separated in all directions.

The work of clearing farms continued, two companies of M.I. being sent out daily on each flank for the purpose. In many cases the farms were found empty, with every sign that the occupants had just hurriedly left. Sometimes a room had been bricked up, in which a supply of grain or the family treasures were stored.

On the 3rd of June the line was again reached at Jagersfontein Road, in cold and snow. A trek northwards along the line brought the column to Edenburg, where a new batch of mounted men from the Regiment joined. The 30th and 31st Imperial Yeomanry were also attached, and the much-desired pom-pom (under Capt. A. A. Montgomery, R.A.) was obtained. Two guns of the 39th Field Battery were with the column.

This batch of Yeomanry consisted of men utterly raw and untrained. They knew nothing about the work, so that it was necessary to assign each Yeoman to a Sussex man for instruction. As the pay of the latter was only one shilling a day, while the Yeoman was receiving five shillings, the position was rather absurd. On the first day out a spare wagon was filled with stuff that the Yeomen had left in camp—saddles, blankets, ammunition, etc. While on trek they were constantly losing horses and rifles. A system of heavy fines, propor-portionate to their pay, was instituted for these offences. In one case it was strongly suspected that a horse had been shot and left, saddle and all, by its rider when out on flank guard—presumably because he had no turn for mounted work, and disliked his animal.

No doubt some of these men developed into useful soldiers. Under the circumstances, however, the process was an annoying and even dangerous one for their instructors.

On the 6th of June the column set out to the West of the line. Capt. Gilbert raided the farm of Lokshoek on the night of the 6th, and Capt. Montrésor that of Kranzhoek on the 7th, capturing 13 and 11 prisoners respectively. At Lokshoek was a laager of women and children, with Cape carts and wagons. During the following days this process was repeated elsewhere, with the result that on the return of the column to Edenburg on the 15th, 53 prisoners were handed in, besides many refugees and a large amount of stock.*

In Army Orders of the 4th of June, Major du Moulin was granted the local rank of Lieut.-Colonel. He was subsequently awarded a brevet Lieut.-Colonelcy.

			Refugees.		
* Prisoners of War	..	53	White men ...	..	3
Rifles	..	4	,, women	..	131
Ammunition	..	500 rounds	,, children	..	467
Dynamite..	..	10 lbs.	Black men ...	..	2
Horses	..	558	,, women	..	7
Ox wagons	..	36	,, children	..	70
Cape carts	..	30			
Cattle	..	.. 2052			
Sheep	..	..15000			

At Edenburg, Lieuts. Crawley-Boevey and Bond, and 2nd Lieut. Paget joined the column— the latter with 50 mounted men, who had been raised at Norval's Pont, and employed round Edenburg.

On the 18th, the column set out to the East of the line, and worked once more in the now familiar country south of Dewetsdorp. Parties were constantly sent out to surround farms at night on the chance of finding Boers. The enemy had, however, realised by this time the danger of sleeping under a roof.

The 25th of June provided a long day's work. The column was fired at in the morning at Koetzee's Post, some 300 Boers being among the hills west of that place. The troops turned into the hill, successfully forcing the difficult nek to Klip Huis. Fourteen Cape carts and two wagons containing women and children were captured, but the commando was in flight, and the mounted troops chased them as far as Helvetia, 12 miles off, getting back to camp at Klip Huis after eleven hours in the saddle without food. A signal lamp stuck up in camp helped the tired companies to find their way in.

On the 28th of June some Boers successfully trapped a small flanking party at Mooifontein. The column had gone by Hex River, a pass some miles to the south; the baggage and escort were to cross the ridge by a road running close to Mooifontein farm. While the baggage was crossing the nek, a message was received by the Yeomanry Officer commanding the left flanking party that a Boer woman at the farm wished to be brought in to a refugee camp, and had asked for a wagon to take her and her boxes, which were ready packed. The Officer accordingly rode up to the farm, after passing the message on, and waited there with seven men of the Yeomanry and G company till a wagon should be sent back. It seems that the men paid more attention to catching chickens than to keeping a look-out. At any rate, as soon as the baggage was out of sight over the nek, some Boers, who were in hiding behind the farm, opened fire at the party point blank, killing three in the first volley and wounding two.* The bugler only escaped, and missing his way, arrived at the camp of the column late at night. A party sent back of course found the farm unoccupied.

On the 29th of June a special company was organised under Capt. Montrésor to perform scouting duties, raids, and surprise visits to farms by day and night. The men were to receive a daily ration of rum, with an extra issue to those engaged in night work; while they were to be exempt from piquets and guards. One hundred men were easily obtained, and the " Raiders " came into existence.

On the 5th of July Lieut. Woodruffe was left with 14 men in ambush at Weltevreden, the camp of the night before, to wait for Boers, who were expected to visit the camp when the column had left, in the hope of picking up food or ammunition. Three Boers came along, one to the farm where the men were hidden. He would not surrender when challenged, but turned and galloped away, and so was shot.

Thirty Boers now opened fire upon the farm, and four of the horses of Woodruffe's party broke loose, delaying his retirement. His difficulties were further increased by one of the Yeomen with him, who became panic-stricken, and refused to mount. The Boers surrounded the small kopje upon which Woodruffe took up a position (not, however, before a boy had been sent back with a note to the column), and, working among the rocks, gradually closed in upon him. He was slightly

---

* Pte. Boniface, of G Company, was killed there. On the same day Pte. Shorney, of H Company, was mortally wounded at Hex River.

wounded in the head, and one of his men (Weston) was hit. Things were looking rather black, when Lieut. Howes, I.Y., with 25 men of the rear guard, came back to his support, and the Boers retired with two killed.

On the 5th of July Dewetsdorp was raided in conjunction with Col. Rochfort, but the Boers were not there. They sent a letter by a released prisoner, saying they were sorry not to be at home.

Moving down to the Caledon River, the column arrived at Deep Dene on the 7th of July. There was no drift over the river at this point, and Col. du Moulin determined to make one. The banks, which were very steep, were dynamited, and horses and oxen were put to trample down and harden the loose deep sand of the river bed.

Great care had to be taken to avoid the quicksands. Five small donkeys got involved in these, and sank lower and lower, in spite of all attempts to haul them out by ropes. They made the most pitiable noise in their terror, and ultimately had to be despatched, when little but their heads remained visible.

After enormous efforts, all the mule wagons were got across by 8 p.m., but the drift was found impassable for ox wagons; these, accordingly, moved on the following day up to Jammersberg Bridge, being shelled by another column on the way, and joined the mule wagons again at Wepener.

On the 10th of July, Col. Rochfort and Col. du Moulin, reconnoitring over Jammersberg Bridge with the Raiders (under Capt. Montrésor) and the pom-pom (under Capt. Montgomery), found seventy Boers holding the kopjes on the further side. Attacking at once, the hills were stormed on foot, and the Boers were turned out of their position and pursued for some miles. One prisoner was taken, and four saddled horses. Serjt. Nightingale was killed during the action, when very pluckily leading his section over the bridge.

The column was shortly ordered into Edenburg, and thence down the line to Springfontein, in order to operate on the west of the line. Orders had by this time been given that every man of the Regiment who was willing should be mounted, and join Col. du Moulin ; and accordingly Major Church with the mounted men of H company, and Capt. Beale with those of the second Volunteer company, were waiting for the column at Springfontein. Major Church and the Volunteers had been trekking with Williams' and Byng's columns respectively.

CHAPTER XXIV.

TWO DISTRICTS.

A derelict town—The district—Entertainments—British "commandos"—Hertzog's Adjutant—Back to Springfontein—Vlakfontein—The scene of a disaster—Caledon River—Edenburg—Stranded traction engines—Ventershoek—"Commandos" again.

Col. du Moulin moved out of Springfontein on the 21st of July to take over the district which had been assigned to him, and which lay west of the line, and north of the Orange River, round about the town of Philippolis. He had under him about 600 men of the Sussex, nearly all mounted, and a section of the 7th Battery (Capt. Geoghegan and Lieut. Chamier), besides the pom-pom.

Philippolis, which for the next two months was used as the headquarters and rendezvous of the column, lies at the head of a valley some 15 miles west of the railway. The usual stone Church looks down the usual main street of one-storied tin-roofed buildings. Two other parallel streets and a few cross roads make up the town. It is surrounded by bare veldt; a eucalyptus or two and a couple of rows of cypress down the main street are the only trees to be seen for miles round.

At this time there were still a few inhabitants remaining, although most of the houses were quite empty. At first, here as elsewhere, the town had been left undisturbed under authorities appointed by the British; but, when the local commandos again took up arms, authorities and townspeople had alike to be brought in to the line; and now the last of them was to be removed, Lord Kitchener's order being not to leave a living thing. For if inhabitants were left, food must be left too; and what was food for the inhabitants was food also for the local commandos—or the fragments of them that lurked in the hills round. Besides this, information, more valuable even than food, would be spread as to the movements of columns. The supreme object at this juncture was to make life impossible for the Boers under arms.

It was a strange sight, this derelict town. Doors were open, and it was possible to turn out of the silent street into a house, where the very music lay as it had been left upon the piano in the sitting room : to sit down at the piano and try a few bars, momentarily expecting the owner to appear and protest against such intrusion. Yet the only representative of the owner would be perhaps the watch dog lying in the yard where it had been necessary to shoot him, when the house was searched (very likely with success) for ammunition. The town was placed out of bounds for the troops of the column.

The Boers of the neighbourhood were not in very high feather. Except for bodies of men passing through from the surrounding districts, they consisted only of small parties of a dozen or less, living precariously upon the much-cleared country. They had established a certain number of depôts to which they could come for grain, but beyond these there was very little food to be found ; and nearly all the farms were empty.

Colonel du Moulin's task, therefore, consisted of netting as many stray Boers as possible, and destroying all stock, grain, cooking utensils, and anything else that would help to support life, besides being prepared to meet any commando that should attempt to cross the district.

For these purposes he divided the column into three sub-columns or "commandos" of about 150 men each, under Major Church, Capt. Gilbert, and Capt. Montrésor. Two of these were always in the field, while one was usually resting in Philippolis. In order to enliven the time of the resting "commando," he detailed a few men with a bent in that direction as permanent entertainers, and these used to give nightly performances in the Town Hall, with the help of one of the many pianos in which the town abounded. Songs, dramatic sketches, and clog-dances used to form items of the programme.

During the first week (which was cold and snowy) a number of farms were cleared. Twenty-five sacks of wheat were found by the Colonel, bricked up at the farm Poortje. The dam there was destroyed, as was done in other cases. On August the 4th the ox convoy bringing supplies from Springfontein joined the three "commandos" at Brandkraal. Lieut. Bidder and 2nd Lieut. Cole from the 3rd Battalion of the Regiment arrived with it.

For the next month the "commandos" worked up and down the district with comparatively little incident, picking up a few prisoners here and there, and sending in refugees. Captain (now Brevet-Major) Gilbert searched the kloofs along the Orange River: there were several families living there, who supplied food to the fighting Boers, and these were transported to the line. In one place the Major was just leaving a valley that he had searched in vain, when the strange behaviour of a horse directed his attention to a large bush. Investigation followed, and from the recesses of the bush emerged an entire family of three generations.

By surprise visits at night to likely places, Major Gilbert also captured a number of armed Boers—on the 11th of August in particular two raids resulted in the taking of thirteen prisoners.

On the 16th Major Church's "commando" chased a party of twenty Boers, who had come to unearth a store of boots they had buried near Tafelkop. A signalling piquet on Tafelkop disturbed them as Major Church was coming up, and the Boers got away through Otterspoort, after being turned out of the farm there by the pom-pom.

On the 17th of August, information was received that 200 Boers under Kritzinger were at Buonapartfontein, on the east of the line, working north with horses very done up. Orders were sent round at once to the three "commandos" to hurl themselves across the line, and they accordingly met at Driekuil Siding early on the 18th. Kritzinger had, however, already moved north, pursued by Gorringe's column—the information being twenty-four hours late.

On the 25th of August Major Gilbert's "commando" captured Cronje, Adjutant and Chief of Scouts to Hertzog, the local Commandant. The actual capture was effected by Liliveld, a Colonial Scout attached to the column, who did some brilliant work.

That same evening, Major Gilbert, who had been talking to Cronje, told him to follow him across the camp, wishing for some reason to shift his quarters. The Major carried his hand in his pocket. The Boer, who looked very white and anxious, suddenly said "Well, when are you going to do it." He thought he was being taken out to be shot, and that the Major had his hand on his revolver. It appeared that the Commandants had persuaded their men that the Proclamations as to surrender, published at this time, were only decoys, and that any man surrendering would be shot. Cronje said that many would come in if they knew they would be well treated. "We shall have a score to settle with the Commandants when the War is over," he added.

He was one of the men chased by Major Church a few days before. "They had had nothing to eat for twenty-four hours," he said, "and had bolted another 25 miles." He was offered good pay to act as guide to the column, but to his credit he refused.

On the 30th of August, Captain Montrésor and Lieut. Morphett, with thirteen men, surrounded the Jansfontein Hills in the dusk, and crept up just before dawn, by starlight. They captured four Boers with rifles on the top without a shot being fired. Captain Montrésor's "commando" returned to Philippolis on the 5th of September with twelve prisoners.

On the 31st of August, two Boers with rifles came in to surrender to Major Church at Osfontein. They had been living for a fortnight in a cave near, that contained the household treasures of Ospoort farm—clothes, dried fruit, a violin, pillows and a coffee machine. There was also a little ammunition, the remains, perhaps, of a larger supply.

Later in the day Boers were reported on a neighbouring hill, which was accordingly surrounded, Major Church taking one party, Captain Montgomery and Lieut. Harden another. Eight men were captured and seventeen rifles. They had no idea a British force was near, the camp being very well hidden. They had orders from Herzog not to stay long in the district, as there was no food. One of them was a Secret Agent of the British.

Two days afterwards, Major Church came upon and destroyed another Boer supply depôt consisting of two large tin-lined boxes hidden among bushes, and containing eight sacks of wheat and stores of all kind. Round about were rough beds of heather and branches, and fire holes for cooking.

On the 17th of September orders were received for the whole column to march in to Springfontein, and entrain for the North. Rain had been falling heavily for a week, and the roads were almost impassable. The oxen were weak with overwork, lung disease and inoculation; dead oxen lay every few yards of the way. Relief wagons were sent to meet the convoy, the end of which struggled painfully in to Springfontein at nine o'clock on the night of the 19th. This convoy, which had been working backwards and forwards between Philippolis and the line with supplies for the column, was left at Springfontein when the column moved North. Lieut. De La Pryme, A.S.C., who had admirably managed the supply arrangements, accompanied the column.

On the 19th September news arrived of the disaster at Vlakfontein, not far from Thabanchu, in which two guns of U battery, and their escort of newly-raised Mounted Infantry, were taken. General Bruce Hamilton's troops were accordingly despatched into the district round the scene of action. The Sussex column entrained during the 20th, and the work of hauling and shoving recalcitrant mules and horses into trucks went on all that night by the light of flares. There was a sharp frost at dawn; the helmets of men who had slept upon the ground were white, and the ditch by the railway was covered with ice. The sixth and last train reached Bloemfontein on the evening of the 21st; the column marched for Vlakfontein itself, after being inspected by General Tucker, and on the 23rd camped close to the scene of the fight.

The Boers and their prisoners had of course gone, but there were many traces of what had occurred.

In a kloof in a long low kopje lay two dead gunhorses. The ground all round was trampled down, probably by the horses of the escort, which had perhaps been put there under cover when the action began. The guns had come into action on the slope of the ridge against a kopje to the north, as the marks made by the spades shewed. Boers had apparently crept up from the direction of Slangfontein farm (which lay to the south), and had taken the position in rear.

On the top of the ridge were a number of bayonets, some artillery harness, haversacks, canteens, bandages stained with blood and other traces of the fight. Little heaps of cartridge cases behind stones here and there shewed where men had made a stand. The graves of four soldiers were found—so shallow that it was necessary to dig them afresh. The gun tracks led away from the ridge towards Slangfontein farm.

It was found afterwards that the officer in charge of the guns had indeed made a fine stand. The escort, consisting of untried Mounted Infantry, had not supported him. Attacked in front and rear, he fought the guns till the last moment, and then died beside them. His gunners, and a few of the escort who held out, were shot down almost to a man. The officer was Lieut. Otter Barry, R.A., whose brother is now (December, 1906) Adjutant of the 2nd Battn. of the Royal Sussex Regiment.

At this farm, a newly-made grave in the family burial ground aroused the suspicions of Major Gilbert. It was opened in spite of the protests of the inhabitants, and was found to contain nearly fifty rifles. Some more rifles and gun harness were in the dam. The people of the farm were removed, as well as a wounded Boer who was there. Most of the farms in the district were occupied at the time.

The tracks of the guns were followed for the next two days, without however catching up the enemy. The Boers put their prisoners over the Basuto border and dispersed; the column halted at Jammersberg Bridge on the Caledon River. Its strength at this time was 800 Europeans, 220 natives (drivers, etc.), 830 horses and 540 mules:

The District was swept by various columns (those of Lowrie Cole, Hamilton, Plumer and Williams) during the following week, without any great result. Col. du Moulin's column arrived at

Edenburg on the 6th of October, and left the next day for the new district which had been assigned to it, in the familiar ground south of Dewetsdorp and east of Reddersburg. Before settling down to work, an expedition was made to the North to protect a convoy of coal on its way from Bloemfontein to some traction engines, which were stranded on the veldt for lack of fuel. The escort to the convoy consisted of the mounted men of the Third Battalion of the Royal Sussex Regiment under Capt. the Hon. J. S. R. Tufton.

Ackerman's commando was met on the evening of the 9th, but did not wait. A terrific rain storm that night covered his retreat.

One of the guns lost at Vlakfontein had already been recovered, and the second, with harness, was found on the 12th at Weltevreden. Reddersburg was reached next day, and building materials were collected in the town, with a view to establishing a fortified camp and depôt at a convenient centre.

During the expedition north, much stock had been collected, and the inhabitants of farms brought in. At one of the farms, a mad woman who objected to clothing was kept in the stable, and presented a difficult problem to the officer sent to clear it. The people of the house refused to assist in any way; some Kaffir women, however, dressed the poor wretch, who proved, indeed, on the return journey, the only cheerful member of the party.

Colonel du Moulin decided to make his headquarters at Ventershoek, a farm 11 miles S.E. of Reddersburg, surrounded on three sides by high ridges. On each of these a permanent piquet was established, for which a stone fort was constructed. Roads were made to these forts, and the two guns were sent up.

Two ranges of hills met at Ventershoek, one from the north-east and the other from the north;

and the Camp lay between them at their point of junction. The piquets thus commanded the flat country to the south and west, the ridges dropping abruptly down into wide plains.

The column was again divided into "commandos," Major Gilbert and Captain Montrésor being assigned 200 men each, and a pom-pom and maxim respectively. On the 17th of October these "commandos" moved out—Major Gilbert to Hardewater, Captain Montrésor to Mooifontein. At Hardewater, a lofty hill (the end of the N.E. range) gave a magnificent view over the surrounding country; and here Major Gilbert remained. The Boers were said to be massing in the East of the Colony, and moving towards the line; and a sharp look-out was kept from the top of Hardewater Hill, on which the helio had some busy days. No one was seen, however, except men of other columns, who answered the enquiring flash.

Before leaving Hardewater, it was discovered that every drop of water used in camp came first over the body of a sheep that had fallen into a cutting some months before. No one appeared to be any the worse!

In a farm near, a notice, of which the following is a translation, had been left for the column:—

11th October, 1901.
" Droogfontein.

" May it herewith be notified to every British Officer and to all men that the true Africanders, who are still under arms, are determined to sacrifice themselves for the freedom of their Country, and with God's help they will defend themselves till the last man is killed or captured.

" N.C.P. in the name of true Africanders."

CHAPTER XXV.

DE PUT.

New Boer tactics—The column goes to relieve Lean—A brush with the enemy—Camp at Rietput—Brand appears at dawn—Start of the column—De Put Ridges—Held by Ackerman—Engagement—The position finally turned—Brand effects nothing—Casualties—The Boer version.

As has been said, the Boers to the south and east of Bloemfontein had at this time adopted new tactics. Hitherto they had roved the hills in small bands, and even in twos and threes, and the British forces had accordingly been split up into a number of small columns, in order the more easily to sweep the country. It occurred to Commandant Brand of Edenburg that, if he collected the scattered local commandos, he would be sufficiently strong to deal with the average British column; he therefore combined the Boers under Koetzee, Joubert, Ackerman and others, and found himself with a force of 600 men and more at his disposal. The first fruits of this policy was the capture of the two guns at Vlakfontein: since then, Brand had surrounded and captured a patrol of fifty yeomen at Snyman's Post: and on the 24th of October he attacked Col. Lean at Klein Zevenfontein, about 20 miles S.E. of Ventershoek. On the evening of the 24th Col. Rochfort ordered all available columns to go to Col. Lean's relief—the latter being considerably outnumbered.

Col. du Moulin started at once from Ventershoek with Captain Montrésor's 200 men and the maxim, sending a runner to Major Gilbert with orders to join him on the march. The two forces met soon after midnight at Koetzee's Post, halting there till dawn. With the first light they marched towards Klein Zevenfontein. In all they numbered about 400 fighting men.

The plains to the south of Ventershoek are divided by a lofty ridge (the Ospoort Ridge) covered with large rocks and bushes, that runs generally north and south. Of this Ridge the southern four miles form a horse shoe, from the Dam Plaats Pass to De Put farm. Between these two points there is no means of crossing the Ridge, except by the very rough and stony track at Ospoort, where a narrow Kloof runs through the hill. Through this it is just possible to lead a horse.

At De Put a series of low foot hills meets the main Ridge. A road from the south approaches the Ridge, and then divides, one branch crossing these foot hills by De Put farm, the other running north-east, parallel to the Ridge.

At sunrise on the 25th of October, the Sussex column was moving south parallel to the Ospoort Ridge and about 5 miles to the east of it. Captain Montrésor, in charge of the advanced guard, saw at a farm on the right front (Twyfelfontein) a group of horsemen in Khaki, with blue cavalry cloaks and white haversacks. They appeared to be men of the South African Constabulary who were expected in the neighbourhood, and Montrésor rode over with four men and a signaller to speak to them. Two of his men and the signaller (Sergt. Skeat) were on ahead, and passed over a rise; they were immediately disarmed by Boers waiting on the other side. As Montrésor rode up the rise, three men came into view less than thirty yards off, and shouted " Hands up." Montrésor and the two with him turned and galloped for it. A bullet through Montrésor's helmet and a flesh wound in one of the horses was all the damage done.

Firing now broke out, and two companies were sent to line the high ground on the right, while the pom-pom came into action against the farm.

The Boers, however, had no intention of joining issue with the column that day. Their main body, several hundred strong, retreated along the foot of the Ospoort Ridge towards De Put; and the column proceeded in the direction of Klein Zevenfontein. The three captured men returned without their equipment: in Sergt. Skeat's case the Boers took, besides his heliograph, a pair of presentation field glasses, which he subsequently recovered in the successful raid of Christmas Eve in another part of the country.

Col. du Moulin camped that night at Rietput, having ascertained that Klein Zevenfontein was untenanted. The graves of four men (two Boers and two British) were found there.

Early on the morning of the 26th of October Commandant Brand with about 300 men (including those under Joubert) and a machine gun worked round the Sussex camp, expecting the column to continue its march in the same direction as on the day before. If he had any intention of attacking the camp, a very heavy rain storm put it out of the question. The piquets opened fire on some of his men, and Major Gilbert with his company was sent to investigate matters. He first met Brand's advanced guard, driving them back: one Boer was wounded, but rescued by a comrade, and some horses were captured. Then some 200 Boers came in sight. Major Gilbert occupied a ridge behind the camp until the column had moved off, when he retired, to successive positions. Brand did not attack, but moved after the column on its right rear, Major Gilbert moving parallel to him.

There was no object now in going to Klein Zevenfontein, and Col. du Moulin had decided to retrace his steps towards Ospoort, where the Boers had been met the day before. Ten miles across the plain the blue Ridge lay quiet in the sun, and for the Southern end of this the advanced guard (H. Company) was ordered to make. A screen of ten double files was spread out over a front of about two miles. Nearer and nearer they drew to the Ridge, which showed no signs of life. Then, as they reached the very foot of it, a heavy burst of firing broke out on the right. The time was about 11 o'clock.

A few horsemen had been seen through the Ospoort Kloof on the far side of the Ridge, and Col. du Moulin had sent Lieut. Gouldsmith with C company to reconnoitre the pass. He arrived there at the same time as the right flankers of the advanced guard, who had been collected together for the same purpose. White, the Intelligence Agent, had galloped on in front of all with a few boys, and rode first into the Kloof. Not a shot had then been fired from the Ridge.

A large number of Boers under Ackerman were, however, waiting among the stones on the hillside, and, as soon as White got far enough in to the gully to see them, they were forced to open fire. When they did so, Gouldsmith with some men of his company and of the advanced guard had just come through a wire fence, and were within 100 yards of the ridge. White was mortally wounded (he died the next day). Farrant of H company was shot through the heart, and one or two horses were hit; but the range was too short for the Boers, and the others got back over the wire and took cover without further casualties. The pom-pom and maxim were brought into action; in a short time the fire from the Ridge died down, and the column moved on, working round towards De Put with a view to crossing the foot hills there. The road runs over the latter close under the western extension of the main Ridge.

Meanwhile all had been quiet on the left. The left flankers and centre of the advanced guard, who were holding some low rises facing the western extremity of the Ridge, had not been fired upon, when Colonel du Moulin joined them. A solitary post stuck up prominently on the sky-line: and this was constantly being reported as a Boer.

"The next man who tells me of that," said the Colonel, "will have to go up and have a closer look at it." No Boers were in fact to be seen among the rocks and bushes of the lofty crest.

The Colonel now sent on the advanced guard, and Captain Montrésor with the "Raiders," to seize the foot hills at different points, first searching them with the pom-pom. During the process, the baggage was closing up on the left of the troops at what appeared to be a safe distance from the Ridge.

The advanced guard went off first, and galloped for a point some little distance from the main Ridge. A stone wall ran along the crest of the low hills, but the Boers had not had time to get round and hold it: and, somewhat to their surprise, this party reached the wall without opposition. Leaving a piquet there, they descended on the other side.

As Montrésor, who was sent along the road, neared the foot hills, a very heavy fire broke out from the crest of the Ridge above him. The road runs by the side of a dam, and the water of this was lashed as if by a hail storm. The baggage, which was really within 1,200 yards of the Ridge, at once stampeded, the black drivers bolted, and for a few minutes all was confusion. The Boers did not make good practice, however, and the wagons were collected again at a safe distance, after some mules had been killed and a few of the escort and drivers wounded.

The pom-pom now came into action in the open against the crest line of the Ridge at about 800 yards, and continued firing there for three quarters of an hour—a feat which much impressed the Boers. "Three times," they said afterwards, "we drove the gunners away from the gun, and three times they came back." The companies who had not been otherwise employed scattered and lay down in the open by the pom-pom, and along the rising ground: and soon a heavy rifle fire was developed, the horses having been sent back under cover. The Colonel had already arranged for the supply of ammunition from the reserve in the wagons to the men in the firing line, and this arrived before they began to run short. He himself remained near the pom-pom.

The pom-pom shield was hit in ten places, and Captain Montgomery was wounded in the knee. He had the gun (which was steaming like a kettle) moved back under cover of a hillock, and fired thence for another half hour. He found that the greatest effect was produced by firing one or two shots at a time—then pausing—then firing one or two more. This kept the Boers behind their rocks.

Captain Montrésor, with Lieut. Woodruffe and 2nd Lieuts. Paget and Thorne, had safely reached the low hill above the dam: but he was here too close under the end of the main Ridge (now held by the Boers) to effect much. It was impossible to stir without attracting a shower of bullets. One or two of his men were wounded there, Sergt. Finucane being shot through the shoulder.

The men of the advanced guard who had crossed the low hills turned and rode towards the Boer position over the open; but they were met and stopped by a heavy fire. There were only five or six of them, and they waited in a donga for reinforcements. Meantime an attempt by the Boers at Ospoort to work up the bed of a spruit in rear of the column had been checked. Major Gilbert, with Brand on his right, had closed up. Brand, finding no troops left between himself and the Ospoort Ridge (the whole column having by now been moved to its left), turned northwards to Twyfelfontein. Major Gilbert left his men as rearguard, and went to find Col. du Moulin. It had been the Colonel's idea to turn the rear of the Boers, but this had not yet been done; and he sent Major Gilbert forward to try and accomplish it.

The Major rode over the low hills in front, where the advanced guard had already gone, and picked up some of G company by the way. With these and the party in the donga he went on, making for the rear of the Boer position, and keeping out of range of the Ridge.

The ground in rear of the Ridge rises and falls in long swelling mounds. As soon as the Boers realised that the British were making for one of these, Field Cornet du Toit with 25 men left the Ridge and raced for it. The Field Cornet and his men could not be seen by the advancing soldiers; the latter, however, were galloping for all they were worth, not knowing whether the mound were held or not. The two or three whose horses were freshest drew ahead, and neared the top: at last they got high enough to see over the crest. There, within 300 yards, was a bearded Boer, galloping towards them; beyond him another two, and behind them others again.

The British jumped off their horses and lay down behind ant-heaps. The nearest Boer raised his hand in signal to the others that the rise was held; they stopped, fired from their saddles, turned their horses' heads and galloped off, while their friends behind blazed away to cover their retreat. The Field Cornet had lost.

By this burst of firing one of the horses of those upon the rise was killed, but no other damage was done. The rest of Major Gilbert's party were coming up through it, and soon the rise was lined. The retreating Boers were, however, quickly out of range.

Ackerman and his men were now taken in rear. Not liking this, they abandoned the whole position,

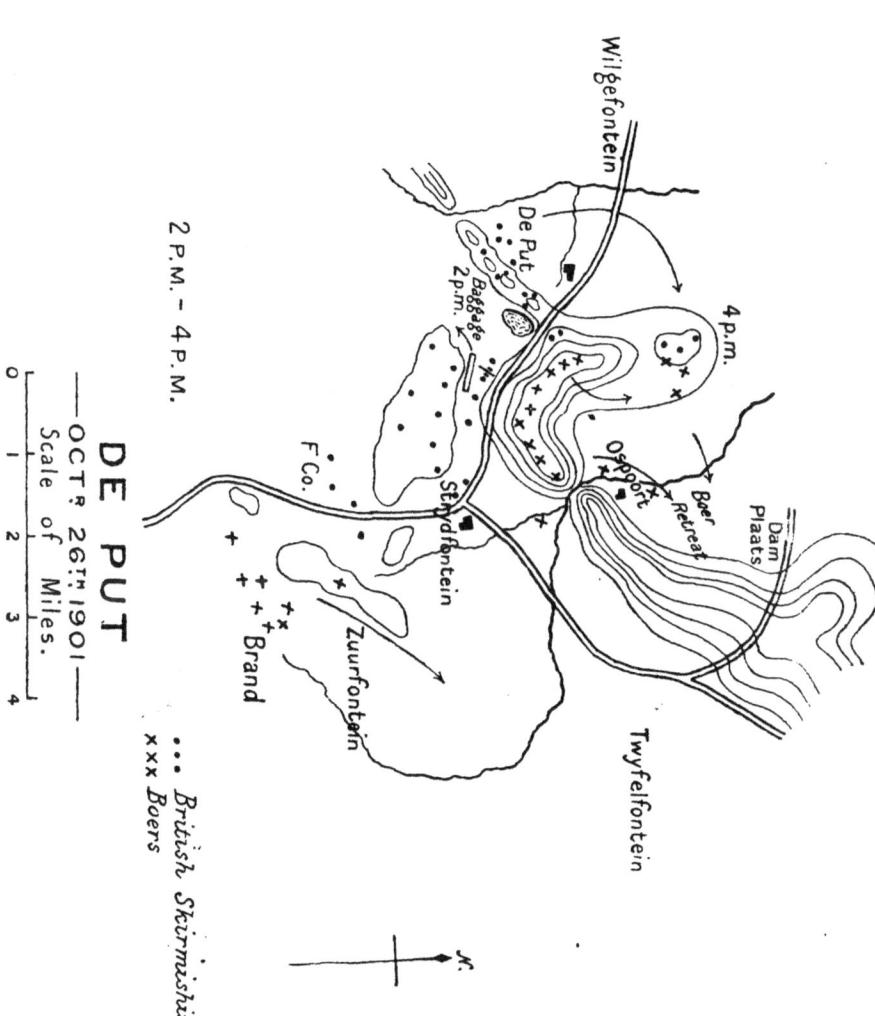

and those on the rise watched them streaming away through the Dam Plaats Pass. Ackerman had with him between two and three hundred Boers.

It was now 4.30 p.m. The baggage had been successfully passed over the low hills, and the column moved forward to Wilgefontein, camping there for the night. Major Gilbert and the men with him returned over the west end of the Boer position. On the crest lay a man, hit in the head by a pom-pom shell; a notice was pinned to his coat: " This is —— of ——; please let his father know that he is killed."

To return to Commandant Brand: he had so far played a singularly ineffective part in the day's proceedings. With a considerable force of Boers under him, he had been out-manœuvred and kept at a distance in rear by Major Gilbert and his company, although the resources of the column were fully employed against the Ridge in front, and, till that Ridge was forced, a dashing charge of two or three hundred Boers from the rear would have been at least a serious matter.

It appears that Brand had not left Ackerman any orders to hold the Ridge, as he did not expect the column to go that way. When firing broke out in that direction, he did not know how many Boers were involved, or which side was on the Ridge. He, therefore, sent round two men to find out what was happening, and to tell Ackerman (if it was he) to hold the Ridge as long as he could, and he (Brand) would attack the British in rear.

Ackerman got this message, and held on (which he had not intended to do), momentarily expecting Brand to turn up: Brand waited for an answer from Ackerman, which Ackerman omitted to send. So Brand lay, checked and ineffective, until the Ridge was forced and the chance had gone.

The retreating Ackerman became involved

with a small column of S.A.C. under Captain Malcolm. His Khaki clad Boers again deceived a squadron, who rode up to them thinking they were Malcolm's main body. The Boers opened fire at forty yards; luckily, however, the gun on the south piquet at Ventershoek opened fire at the same time upon the real main body of the British, driving them down upon the scene of action. The forces became considerably mixed, but were eventually disentangled without many casualties.

After the fighting at De Put was over, two men with white flags left the Ridge and came to surrender with their rifles. They said that they were tired of fighting (one of them had a bullet through his hat) : that they were Transvaalers, and had only promised to fight for two years, which were up : and that the camp was to be attacked that night. The column accordingly lay ready and waiting ; but the Boers thought better of it.

The report of the action spread by the Boers was that they, with 150 men and a machine gun, had surprised and routed a column of 400, with pom-pom and maxim The British losses they put at 150—in actual fact they were two killed and nine wounded (including four natives).* It was said that the Boers had three killed and six wounded ; but the man who lay upon the hillside provided the only certain piece of information.

The pom-pom fired 900 rounds; while over 30,000 rounds of small arm ammunition were expended.†

Civil-Surgeon Leach did very well during the action, riding with a large red cross flag through heavy fire to assist the wounded.

---

* *Killed :* Intelligence Agent White ; Pte. J. Farrant, H Co.
Wounded : Sgt. Finucane, H Co. ; Cpl. E. Manning, Vol. ; Pte. F. Webb, C Co. ; Pte. C. Dymock, F Co. ; Pte. M. Hunt, G Co.

† The bulk of this ammunition was fired at the jagged crest-line of the Ridge, and kept the Boers down under cover, checking their fire. The Boers themselves remained invisible.

CHAPTER XXVI.

TO VLAKFONTEIN.

The King's Road—On the track of a commando—A stern chase—Wearing out the Boers—Kritzinger appears—The column goes to meet him—Kaffir's Kop—A mélée—A gallant death—Kritzinger gets through—Moving westwards- Night march on Jagersfontein—Boers surprised at dawn- -Captures at Vlakfontein—Christmas Day—Fauresmith—Vlakfontein again.

After the fight at De Put, the column again divided into two " commandos," of which Major Gilbert's returned with Head Quarters to Ventershoek. Very heavy rain on the 29th and 30th of October flooded the camp there.

Col. du Moulin had from the first determined to shorten the route from this camp to Edenburg. The convoy, in bringing supplies from the line, had to go round by Mooifontein, 6 miles north of Ventershoek, in order to cross the ridge running in that direction. Close to the camp, this ridge was cut by a small stream (Hex River) running through a stony gorge. The gorge was of considerable length, and was strewn throughout with great boulders of ironstone. Through this gorge the Colonel decided to make a road, and the cyclists had been for some time employed in preparing it. All the men in the camp were now turned on to the work. Chains were fastened to the larger rocks, and they were hauled to one side or rolled into the stream. Boulders were blasted and embankments made, and by the 31st of October the convoy on its way to Edenburg was able to pass along "King's Road." Frequent use was subsequently made of this road when moving troops out to the west and south, and Boers of the neighbourhood who were brought in by it, were considerably astonished. The people of the district probably still find it a great convenience.

The country round Ventershoek was constantly patrolled by parties of ten or twelve men under an officer, who went out at night so as to reach positions from which they could see the country round, by dawn. One of these patrols under Lt. Bond located a Boer commando at Lakensvlei, to the south-west, on November 7th; and on November 8th, a general move of columns was begun with the object of surrounding it. Col. du Moulin moved out with the whole of his force at 2 a.m. on the 9th, getting into touch with the other columns that afternoon. A Boer hospital was found among the hills, and the three ambulances with it were ordered to rejoin their commando.

On the 10th two Boers were captured by Liliveld at Lakensvlei, and others were seen in the distance; and on the 11th, Ackerman's commando was found in the middle of the circle of columns. Col. du Moulin had made an early march from Lakensvlei to Parys (a farm some miles south of Ventershoek) that morning; and while the column was breakfasting, a helio message came from Ventershoek to say that a party of Boers were being driven by Col. Hamilton towards Parys. The column was off in ten minutes, and chased Ackerman for the remainder of the day, capturing his Cape cart, eighty horses and twenty-five rifles. A halt was made that night at Mooifontein, after a day's trek of 30 miles for the baggage and 40 for the mounted troops, the Boers being still ahead. Col. Hamilton had taken seven prisoners.

One hundred men under Lieut. Bond were sent out at midnight to a hill (the Bulsberg) where the Boers were last seen. Silently they rode through the darkness, and, nearing the hill, took one end of it at a gallop; but the Boers had gone. This party was, during the morning, itself attacked by another small column that had come on the same mission. Fortunately the attack was stayed before any harm was done. The Boers escaped out of the ring of columns—so harried, however, that twelve went straight to Bloemfontein to surrender, five of whom were too weak from want of food and sleep to reach the town, and had to be fetched in in Cape carts.

On the night of the 23rd November, Lieut. Crawley-Boevey was sent with 100 men (cyclists and mounted men) to search the hills at Parys for stray Boers. At dawn he saw a couple of Boers watering their horses at a dam near; he despatched a dozen men to cut them off, but these soon returned, having found a commando of sixty on the other side of the hill. The Boers at once moved off towards Ospoort, where Captain Montrésor lay hidden; took fright at the smoke of some fires there and moved north; were headed off by column after column, and lost twenty-six prisoners before the day was over, four of them falling to Crawley-Boevey. At dawn on the 26th Captain Montrésor was sent to Lakensvlei, where the Boers were reported to have gone; but Col. Pilcher was before him, and had captured twelve more. Thus the commando, which was Joubert's, was practically wiped out.

At this time Kritzinger with 300 men and a number of led horses was making his way down to the Colony; and on the 27th of November Col. du Moulin got orders to move out and try to intercept him, 150 South African Constabulary under Major Vaughan and fifty Edenburg M. I. under Lieut. Kentish (Royal Irish Fusiliers) being added to the column. By the evening of the 28th he reached Roodepoort, 25 miles east of Ventershoek as the crow flies and considerably more by road. The baggage, with which were one of the guns (under Lt. Warren, R.F.A.) and the pom-pom (under Capt. Harrington, R.G.A.) went by a different route from that taken by the main body. On emerging from De Rand pass, fire was opened by both gun and pom-pom upon Captain Montrésor's "commando," which was crossing the front—fortunately without inflicting any damage. By the evening six Boers had been captured, with four rifles.

Kritzinger was known to be close to Roodepoort, and likely to break west; Col. du Moulin therefore decided to occupy a line north and south, and after dark sent Captain Montrésor with two companies two miles to the north, and the S. A. C. the same distance to the south.

The men, who were carrying Maconochie rations, were served out that evening with a ration of raw meat. It was late however, and many did not trouble to cook the meat, eating the tinned stew instead; as a result they went short the next day.

The column started again at four the next morning. The Colonel moved out with the main body at a fast trot in a N.W. direction towards a long high ridge called Kaffir's Kop. The S. A. C. were on his right; Captain Montrésor was on the left, but the ground there was so broken that he could not be seen. Owing to a misunderstanding, the advanced guard took a wrong direction, and a second one had to be sent out somewhat hurriedly. Shortly afterwards Boers were reported on the left. The Colonel and his staff, the main body (in close order), the gun, pom-pom and escort all turned on to a rise to the left of the road, and saw a large body of Boers going west at the foot of Kaffir's Kop, a couple of miles away. Almost at the same moment, a smart fire was opened from a small kopje 1,000 yards in rear, which, owing to the pace and the change of advanced guards, had not been searched. Colonel, staff, men and guns all turned sharp to the right again and galloped under cover of the rise, the crest of which was at once lined, while the guns opened fire. The Boers in rear did not wait, however, and streamed away from the other side of the kopje—to which gun, pom-pom, and troops followed them. Their course lay directly over a ridge on which were half of Captain Montrésor's men, and a general mêlée ensued, the two sides getting so involved that in one case a drummer and a Boer took shots at each other at ten yards distance, and then threw down their rifles and closed. Lieut. Woodruffe fired his revolver up at a Boer as he jumped his horse over the depression in which Woodruffe was lying.

Unfortunately the pom-pom had again opened on Captain Montrésor's men by mistake—it being almost impossible to tell which of the scattered parties were Boers and which not. Beset by friend and foe, they had a bad quarter of an hour, losing two men killed by the Boers (Sergt. Waters and Private Elphick) and one mortally wounded (Corporal Robinson).* Elphick (whose horse had been shot) died splendidly: he was found behind an ant-heap, his bayonet fixed, all the cartridges in his bandolier used—killed by a shot from a Boer who had worked round behind him. The Boers also lost two killed and one wounded.

Another column was pressing the rear of the main body of the Boers, who hurried west some miles to the north of Col. du Moulin, and then turned south in a wide circle. The Colonel turned and followed them. On their way the Boers picked up and looted one of the company kit wagons that had broken down, taking the mules and a native guide away with them. The latter they shot.

The column followed the Boers till three in the afternoon without a halt, and stopped then at Ganspoort, unable to go further. The first meal of the day was at 4 p.m. Kritzinger's men, however, had got through; the columns ahead were not in position to block them; and on the following day they crossed the line to the west, shifting their laager half a mile further from the railway

---

* Pte. L. Greenfield, E Co., was also wounded.

when they found that the gun on the armoured train could reach them.

The local Boers were at this time finding the eastern district too hot to hold them. They were harried by the columns and short of food; for although a certain amount of grain was still left, hidden in broken down sheds and under bushes, meat was getting scarce, and the few wild sheep on the hills were growing wilder.* A general movement of the Boers therefore set in to the west; and towards the end of December the columns followed.

Col. du Moulin's column moved into Edenburg on the 19th of December, and down the line to Jagersfontein Road on the 22nd. Capt. Griffin had joined it on the 12th.†

On the evening of December 23rd, the column moved out of Jagersfontein Road and made for Jagersfontein Town, 25 miles to the west. The camp was not struck till dark, and the baggage was left to follow in the morning.

It was known that the Commandants had been summoned by De Wet to a conference in the North, and it was intended to attack the local commandos (believed to be at Jagersfontein) during their absence.

Col. du Moulin started at 7 p.m., having with him about 300 mounted men of the Sussex and the pom-pom; and the column trekked along in bright moonlight till midnight, and then halted and off-saddled for a couple of hours under the black mass of Boomplaats Hill. Starting again at 2 a.m., they went forward till the setting of the moon, which occurred shortly before dawn. A halt was then made to wait for the light.

---

* The report of Commandant Brand upon the District, at the Vereeniging Meeting of Commandants in May, 1902, was that everything had been carried off; there was, he said, not a sheep left.

† Capt. Griffin had been sent from Malta to South Africa at the beginning of the war on special service. He had been invalided home with fever, and now returned to the Regiment.

The advanced guard (H. Company) were now on the edge of a broad plain that stretched across to Jagersfontein and the hills behind it, 6 miles away. Lt. Crawley-Boevey and his cyclists were to the left front of the advanced guard. As the light grew stronger, two farms could be seen half way across the plain, about a mile apart; and a number of horses were made out grazing round them. The Colonel ordered the advanced guard, and F Company under Major Gilbert, to gallop these farms. The two companies spread out into a line nearly two miles long, and set off at a canter. Other companies supported them in rear.

The sun was just rising, shewing up a row of eucalyptus trees that stood out between the farms like the teeth of a comb, and casting long shadows in front of the galloping men. As H Company got nearer to the farm house on the left (Vlakfontein) figures could be seen making for the horses. Nearer still, and across a spruit, and they were in among the dazed Boers, those who had not been able to jump on a horse and get away throwing up their hands and surrendering.

On the right Major Gilbert came upon a donga in which Field Cornet du Toit and a number of Boers were sleeping. These rolled out of their blankets, and started firing, wounding two men.* The advancing Company was checked by a wire fence, and there was an awkward moment till the wire was cut; then the donga was taken, and the Field Cornet and his men surrendered. A desultory fire was kept up for a short time from a kopje on the extreme right, but soon ceased.

All the Boers had now either got away towards Jagersfontein, or been taken prisoners. Two companies were sent on towards the Jagersfontein hills; but there was no chance of stopping the retreating

---

* These were Cpl. A. Palmer and Pte. R. Smith, of F. Co.

Boers, and the companies soon returned to Vlakfontein. Heaps of rifles, saddles, bandoliers and other equipment were brought in and piled against the verandah of the farmhouse, the Colonel and the other officers assembled on the verandah, the horses were picketed in lines in front of the house, the men started to brew their coffee over little fires, and a general air of cheerful satisfaction pervaded the place; for it had been a very successful raid. Besides twenty-eight prisoners, the column had taken 52 rifles, 78 bandoliers, 2,500 rounds of ammunition, 105 horses, 96 saddles, 130 blankets, 25 cloaks and 8 bags of wheat.

One shadow however fell upon the day. One of the Boers taken was in a complete suit of Khaki, regimental badges, slouch hat and all. Too many British had been killed, deceived by a British uniform upon a Boer, for it to be possible to be lenient: and he was accordingly tried by Court Martial, and shot in the evening.

Companies were sent out in the afternoon to search adjoining hills and kloofs; no Boers however had remained within reach. In the afternoon the explosion of Mauser cartridges which were being destroyed by burning sounded to those who had not been warned like a counter-attack, and caused a momentary sensation.

It was thought very probable that the Boers would rally and try to take their revenge, and with the first light of Christmas morning the column stood to arms, and waited. Nothing occurred, however, until soon after sunrise, when guns were heard from the south. Col. du Moulin started off as soon as possible in that direction, and trekked through the long midsummer morning. Very hot and dusty, the column arrived about mid-day at Fauresmith, without, however, having come across anything more aggressive than a swarm of locusts, many miles in length.

The guns had been those of Col. Hamilton, who, with Major Driscoll, was co-operating with Col. du Moulin. Col. Hamilton had surprised a commando at dawn that morning, taken fifteen of them and chased the remainder, but in turn got his own baggage cut off at Kok's Kraal by a party of 150 who slipped behind him. A number of his wagons were looted and burned.

Fauresmith was a deserted town (three streets of tin-roofed houses and a market place) lying at the foot of a high, boldly-shaped hill : the column camped outside, and soon parties were making their way in to explore.

At the entrance to the town was a spring running freely. The water was clear, not muddy; cold, not tepid ; it did not smell ; there was plenty of it. The explorers filled themselves, and passed on.

There was not much to be said for the street. The doors of the houses were open ; here and there in front of a house was a bed, or a mattress, half destroyed : for all bedding that could not be used for the Refugee camps had to be burnt. But the gardens at the back were Paradise. What if much of the fruit had not ripened, for want of water ? There was still enough and to spare for everyone : apricots, figs, mulberries, small peaches. Men shook the trees or lay along the branches, and blessed their luck. The padré attached to the column (the Rev. — Hood) had given out that he would hold a service in the Dutch church, as there was sure to be an organ there. There was : but it had been damaged—so had that in the Anglican church. Then he decided to hold his service in the street ; a piano was found, and placed on the verandah of a house ; chairs and sofas were borrowed and arranged in the road, and the bell in the market-place was rung. A small congregation collected, the men, of course, all fully armed, and the service was carried out. "Oh, come, all ye faithful," was lustily rendered; and the walls of the empty houses echoed it back.

One more excitement, and Christmas day was over. Late at night, a shot from one of the piquets and a cry of "Stand to!" turned everybody out. It was only Driscoll, however, riding in with his Scouts. The string of tired men and horses made its way through the camp, and silence fell again, this time unbroken.

On Boxing Day Col. du Moulin moved to Jagersfontein, an absolutely deserted town with a diamond mine like a vast quarry, the bottom of which was full of emerald green water. The Boers in passing through had been living in the schoolroom of the convent there, and they had chalked on the black board their names and various messages. The hills round were searched without result, and the column moved back to Vlakfontein.

This place was made the Headquarters and depôt for the columns of the district, and Col. Rochfort came out there on the 2nd of January, 1902. On the 3rd, Col. du Moulin moved out with 350 mounted men, the cyclists and pom-pom, at 8 p.m. It was the beginning of a combined move of all Col. Rochfort's columns against the Boers, who had again collected together in the west.

The generous Christmas gifts from the County of Sussex, consisting of pipes and other useful articles, besides luxuries in the way of food, had been served out to the men while at Vlakfontein.

CHAPTER XXVII.

ABRAHAM'S KRAAL.

Ramah's Spring—Belmont—In touch with the Boers—Jagersfontein—Nieuwoudt turns North—On his track—Camp at Abraham's Kraal—Description of ground—Boers rush the piquet—The defence of the camp—The Colonel's charge—The Boers retire—Next morning.

The Sussex column, which was working in conjunction with Col. Western and Major Driscoll, reached Luckhoff on the 11th of January without having come across the Boers. It then crossed into Cape Colony, going by Ramah's Spring to Witteput. The sight of a farm, cultivated, and occupied by friendly people, was a strange one. The owner of Ramah's Spring in particular was most hospitable.

On the 15th the column camped at Belmont. A terrific thunderstorm in the evening struck some trees in the camp, but did no damage. A patrol of fifty men under Major Gilbert got into touch next day with 300 Boers moving south : these Boers turned east, and the column accordingly followed them back into the Orange River Colony, and reached Luckhoff on the 18th, after a long trek.

On the following day the Boers were only 10 miles off; but the horses of the column were too done to move until the evening. At Liebenbergspan a number of mules and horses, taken with Hamilton's transport, were recovered. It was necessary now to draw fresh supplies ; Col. du Moulin accordingly went to Jagersfontein on the 22nd and drew supplies from Vlakfontein. Over 10,000 rounds of mixed ammunition were destroyed, which had been found in the town, sunk in a flooded mine.

The Boers (three commandos under Nieuwoudt) had turned north, and the column started after them on the 23rd. The Riet River was crossed at Jagersfontein Drift on the 24th, and Witdam was reached on the 26th. On the following day Col. du Moulin got again into touch with the Boers. The column had started at 5 a.m., and, while it was halted for breakfast, four men were seen by Capt. Beale, the Intelligence Officer, leaving a farm some miles off. Capt. Griffin was sent out with his company to reconnoitre, and came upon the spoor of a large party. Mounting a high kopje, he saw the four join a large laager of some 400 Boers, with spare horses, cattle and three Cape carts, which was on the move. The column followed, passed through the Boers' camp at De Dam, and by the evening arrived at a drift over the Riet River. This drift lay under the farm of Abraham's Kraal, and here the column bivouacked. The Boers, expecting them to take a different route, had crossed the River a few miles lower down, and were waiting on the further bank.

At Abraham's Kraal, the farm houses are at the open end of a semi-circle some 200 yards in diameter, formed by a low ridge that rises here and there into small kopjes covered with large stones. Beyond the buildings and facing the semi-circle is a garden with a stone wall. Standing with one's back to the garden and buildings, on the right is a large stone kraal, divided into several compartments. In front is the highest part of the ridge, beyond which the ground drops very quickly to the Riet River. On the left, the ridge ends in a conical rocky mound, with a small kraal at its foot. On the outside of this mound a donga leads up from the river, and curls in towards the farm.

The horse lines were placed across the semi-circle, parallel to the garden wall. On the river side of them, the officers' valises were laid out. The Colonel and his staff slept in the farm house, which was at the end of the ridge near the largest Kraal. The pom-pom was at the foot of the conical mound, on the road that here entered the semi-circle. The transport was along the garden wall, to the right rear of the horse lines.

Three piquets were put out, one of them on the highest part of the ridge, looking towards the river and drift. It will be convenient to called this the camp piquet. The river could not be actually seen from this piquet, owing to the rapid drop of the ground. The two other piquets were placed upon small kopjes, one to the right of the camp piquet outside the semi-circle, and one in rear of the garden. The men in camp, done up with many days of continuous trekking, turned in.

At about 1 a.m. a Sergeant got up to put the nose-bag on his horse, as a patrol was to go across the river at 3. As he was walking back to his place, he heard a shot fired on the piquet, and shouted " Stand to !" Almost immediately a tremendous fire was opened upon the centre of the camp. The men woke to hear shouts and yells of "Come on you Bob-a-days"—"Vorwatz Burghers"—and to see through the misty moonlight (for the night was cloudy) swarms of dark figures topping the crest of the piquet within 200 yards of them, and rushing down the slope, firing from their hips. Nieuwoudt, after being chased so far by the column, was striking back at last.

The Boers had been forced into action. Col. Western with his column was closing in upon them from the west, Major Driscoll was coming up from the south. If they were to avoid facing a combinaton of columns, it was necessary to attack one of them at once. Col. du Moulin was close on their heels, and his force was numerically inferior.[*]

Nieuwoudt therefore planned this night attack, entrusting the execution of it to Commandant Theunissen.

---

[*] Nieuwoudt had three commandos with him, making a total of about 400 men. Col. du Moulin had about 300, with a pom-pom.

The attacking Boers had crossed a drift, worked up the river bed (out of sight) till they were below the camp piquet, crept up the steep hillside, and then rushed the sentry and piquet, killing two men and having two men killed—one of them the owner of the farm. They then started firing down into the camp, while some rushed across the saddle to their left and occupied a large kraal, and others began to work along the ridge to their right. One or two ran straight down the slope.

Major Gilbert, sleeping in the officers' line, woke up to see a dark giant come bounding down the hill, shouting "Hands up." The Major dashed across to the small kraal at the foot of the conical mound, and, finding Lieut. Thorne there, sent him to the garden wall to get men who had taken cover there up on to the mound. Colour-Sergt. Weston was already going up, shouting "Come on, chaps, come on!"; he was killed on the top, by a bullet in the head, before he could fire. Major Gilbert and Thorne, with Lieuts. Crawley-Boevey, Bond, and Paget, continued working men up onto this ridge, getting a steady fire to bear in the direction of the Boers, and driving back those who were attempting to work along the ridge.

Captain Harrington, who, with his pom-pom, was at the foot of the mound, hid the gun under a tarpaulin, and then disposed his men to check any attempt to creep up the donga from the River. Thorne took a party to search this donga, but the Boers made no flank attack.

The men behind the garden wall had also by this time developed a steady fire, aiming at the flashes on the ridge. Neither side realised how very small the area of operations was, and the firing was mostly high; still a hail of bullets swept the horse lines. In a small sheet of corrugated iron found there afterwards, were seventeen bullet holes; ninety horses were killed.

The Colonel, sleeping in the farmhouse, woke at the first onset. Shouting "My God, they're in the camp," he dashed up the ridge behind the farm.

Lieut. Ashworth, signalling officer to the column, and 2nd Lieut. Leachman, staff officer, ran up there too, the Colonel calling out to Ashworth "Look after this end."

Men were worked up to the ridge from the garden wall, Captain Beale bringing across several parties, and here too a steady fire was gradually developed. The noise of the firing and the shouting and yelling was infernal.

The Colonel had collected a little knot of men, and with them had cleared, with the bayonet, the compartments of the large Kraal, one after the other. The Boers still clung to the further side of it. The Colonel now determined on a charge along the lower edge of the kraal; shouting "All who have boots follow me" (a shout that could only be heard by the men close to him), he dashed along the lower wall of the kraal. The moment he cleared the corner he fell, shot through the heart and leg; two of the men following him were mortally wounded.

This charge appears to have shaken the Boers' nerves. They were making no progress; they held one side of the camp, and had certainly done a great deal of damage to the horses; but the British were firmly established on the other, and, far from being on the run, were taking the offensive. At any rate, shortly after the Colonel's charge, a whistle sounded loudly several times from the piquet which the Boers had first rushed: it was then about 2 a.m.

A curious hush fell on the camp; yells and firing ceased as if by common consent, and for a moment their was absolute silence. Then a shout rose from the British side—"They're off"—and heavy firing again broke out. The whistle was Theunissen's signal for the Boers to retire. This they did as suddenly and as quickly as they had come. Back from the Kraal wall—back over the piquet—back down the hill and over the drift they went: and in a few minutes the only Boers in camp were the two they had left dead behind them.

It was not at once realized that the Boers had altogether gone. The survivors of the camp piquet shouted to the men below to stop firing. Major Gilbert learned of Col. du Moulin's death, and assumed command. Fresh piquets were sent out, and all prepared to meet another attack. None, however, was made. The groans of the wounded horses had been painful to hear during the night, and as soon as it got light these were slaughtered with revolvers. When this task was finished, more than 120 dead horses and mules lay about the camp. They were piled literally in heaps.

It was now possible to make up the list of casualties. Besides the Colonel, two Sergeants (Col. Sergt. Weston and Sergt. Green) and four men were dead, and nine men wounded, of whom one died very shortly.*

At half past seven, all the available men paraded, Captain Montrésor read the burial service, and the Last Post was sounded over the

---

* The casualties were as follows:—

KILLED—
    Lt.-Col. du Moulin.
    C.-Sgt. A. Weston. G Co.
    Sgt. C. Green. B Co.
    Pte. W. Covington. D Co.
    ,, T. Hill. D Co.
    ,, R. Pimm. E Co.
    ,, G. Tomlin. F Co.

DIED OF WOUNDS—
    Pte. A. Brackpool. A Co.
    ,, J. Clarke. C Co.
    Pte. B Gaston. E Co.
    ,, T. Light. E Co.

WOUNDED—
    Sgt. E. Simmins. Vol.
    Pte. G. Langley. D Co.
    Dr. S. Sproston. D Co.
    Pte. T. Bostock. F Co.
    ,, J. Coles. F Co.
    ,, A. Cox. F Co.

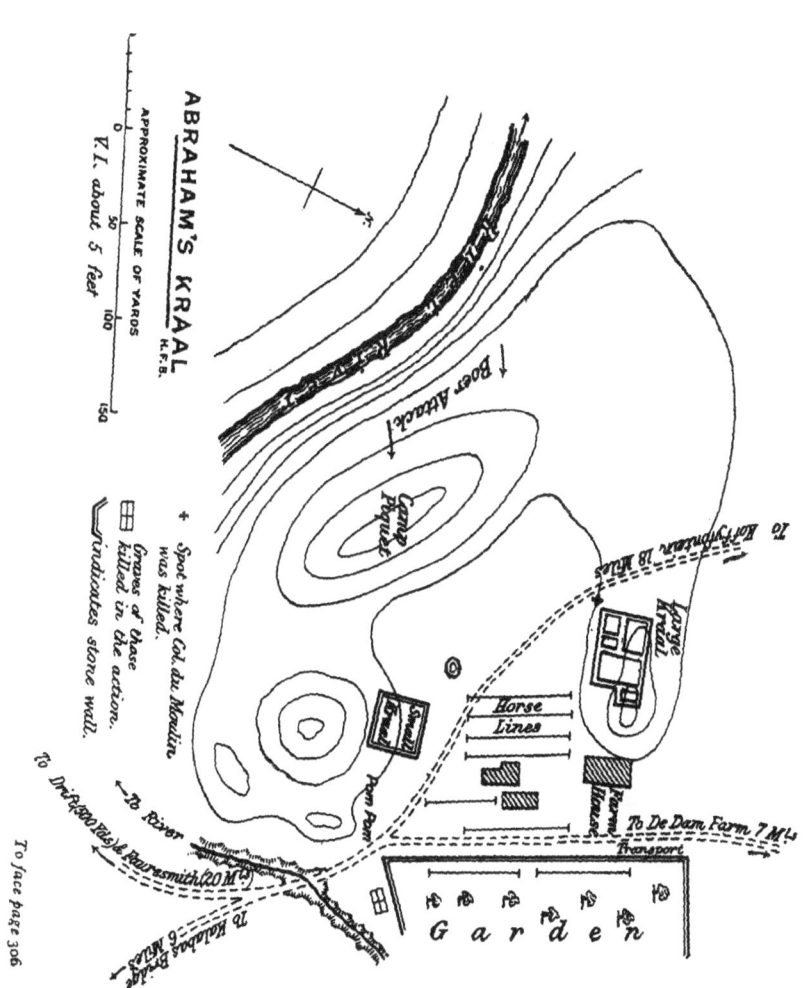

grave of the man to whose initiative and energy the column owed its existence, and who had died most gallantly in its defence. It sounded, too, over the men who had followed him to his death, and over two of the enemy who had paid the forfeit.*

---

* It is interesting to notice that after this Nieuwoudt's opinion of night attacks was that they were not worth while, and he declared himself against them in the future. This was learned from prisoners, and also from some correspondence between him and Cdt. Erasmus, which was subsequently found. The latter was urging a night attack upon Nieuwoudt, saying that although they had been unable to capture the camp at Abraham's Kraal, still they had killed many horses.

CHAPTER XXVIII.

NORTHWARDS—AND THE END.

Vlakfontein—A circular tour—Northwards—Boshof—Baas Berg—A pom-pom exhibition—A night march—The Boers overtaken—Action at Scheer Pan—Charging the Ridge—Hoopstadt—Commando Drift—A Delarey drive—Klerksdorp—The Drift again—The column broken up—Last stage—Peace—India.

Major Gilbert and the column left Abraham's Kraal at 8.30 on the morning of the fight. Before that, a white flag had come in with a request for an ambulance to bring in a wounded Boer. It appeared that several of the enemy had been hit.

Half of the men being dismounted, the column made slow progress; the Boers, however, had no intention of attacking by daylight, and Jagersfontein Drift was reached after a trek of 30 miles.

Several of the Kaffir drivers had bolted at the first alarm that morning, two of them with nothing on at all. They had made a bee-line through barbed wire, cactus hedges, and mud holes; and, during the march, sorry figures came limping back to the column, and rejoined the wagons. One Kaffir got right through to Vlakfontein, doing the 45 miles in ten hours, and said the column had been wiped out. The garrison there had an anxious time till runners arrived from Major Gilbert on the following morning.

The column reached Vlakfontein on the 29th, three of the wounded British and the wounded Boer having died on the way.

A convoy from Edenburg arrived on the 1st of February, bringing a few remounts with it; and on the 4th Major Gilbert moved out with a force consisting of 150 mounted men of the Sussex and the 90th I.Y., with the pom-pom. A tour was made in the direction of Philippolis, but the

Boers were not met with. At Alwyn's Kop some Kaffir scouts from the Orange River reported the column as a Boer commando; this piece of intelligence was sent on to Vlakfontein, and Major Gilbert was stopped on the return journey and sent, together with Major Driscoll and his Scouts, to chase himself.

As might have been expected, nothing resulted, and the column returned to Vlakfontein on the 17th of February. A terrific hailstorm had done a great deal of damage here a few days before, stampeding the horses. Some dashed into the house, while others got away altogether, and were never seen again.

On the afternoon of the 21st Major Gilbert started again (the Yeomen had been transferred to Col. Western), with supplies for Col. Rochfort, who was on his way north. Calabas Bridge over the Riet River was reached shortly before midnight, after a trek of 27 miles. Joining Col. Rochfort the next day, the column took part in a general move to the north. They marched 26 miles that night, and crossed the Modder River near Paardeberg in the early morning.

Boshof was reached on the 26th of February. It stood in the middle of vast plains, covered with deep grass that reached up to the horses' shoulders. An occasional kopje sticking up darkly here and there only served to mark the great distances.

The local commandos, under Commandants Badenhorst, Jacobs and Erasmus, had been having things very much their own way in this district; Boshof itself was garrisoned by the Scottish Rifles Militia, but they had practically no mounted troops. The country had never been effectively cleared; it contained plenty of stock and crops, and many of the farms were occupied.

Before reaching Boshof, Major Driscoll and

his scouts had found and rushed Jacob's laager, capturing six men, five wagons, and nine Cape carts. Driscoll's men were many of them Boers (it was said that more Dutch than English was to be heard in passing through his lines), and one of the first to rush the laager was greeted by his grandmother with a magnificent flow of abuse.

The Boers were believed to be to the north of Boshof, and Col. Rochfort's columns accordingly surrounded and attacked at dawn on the 1st of March a large hill, the Baas Berg, said to be their stronghold. The Boers had, however, moved away, and, though they could be seen, it was hopeless to chase them.

On the night of the 1st a party of fifty Driscoll's scouts, who had been sent to surround a farm, got entangled with 350 Boers; and half the Sussex, with the rest of Driscoll's and the pom-pom, were sent out to relieve them. The Boers retired, and the force returned, bringing with it 150 sheep. As they reached camp, three men with five horses appeared about a mile away, making for a farm. At first they were taken for British scouts, but, when it was realised that they were dressed in black, this seemed unlikely. A pom-pom shell was put over them, and they immediately scattered, and made in the direction of the Boers. They had mistaken the troops for a commando.

They had two miles of open ground to cover, and the pom-pom made beautiful practice. Shells burst just behind them, just in front, just beyond and even (as it seemed) right under them, but they got away and behind a ridge, uninjured. The effect of a pom-pom is more moral than material.

During the next few days several laagers were captured by the other columns, and 6,000 sheep and 300 horses taken, besides some cattle. On the evening of the 5th Col. Rochfort organized a night march of all columns to the north in the hope of catching up the Boers, who had retired in that direction. The Sussex column and Driscoll's Scouts were now working together, and Col. Rochfort accompanied them.

The horses were not saddled nor the wagons inspanned till after dusk. Great fires were left burning in the camp when the combined column moved out. During the night a Boer Hospital was met. The sick Boers had got wind of the column's approach, and had not waited for it. After a trek of 20 miles a halt was made at Scheerpan. The wagons were out-spanned, hidden in the garden of the farm, and the men were allowed to snatch two hours' sleep.

The farm at Scheerpan looks across an open plain to a long ridge about 2 miles off. This ridge (known as Busch Kop) is crossed at the right end of it (as you look from the farm) by a road from the north-east. To the left of the road the ridge is covered with very thick bush for some distance. A sugar-loaf hill and a small kopje stand in front of the ridge at about the centre. At the extreme left end a spur runs out from the ridge into the plain.

Behind Scheerpan farmhouse is a rocky hill, and on this Col. Rochfort, Major Gilbert, and Major Driscoll waited for sunrise.

All seemed quiet. As the light grew stronger, nothing could be seen moving on the ridge opposite. Then twenty men came round the corner of the ridge and down the road, and more behind them.

Were they Boers or British? It was difficult to tell. Touch had been got with Col. Western's column on the right; it seemed more likely that they were a patrol of his.—They saw the wagons in the garden and turned back.

Even that was not conclusive; a patrol might well have done the same. Major Driscoll went down and took out a few men to reconnoitre. From the top of the kopje he could be seen going out; then a dozen men left the ridge and went across to the sugar-loaf hill, opening fire from there. The Scouts dismounted and returned their fire from the open. At the same time thirty or forty men appeared round the extreme left end of the ridge, working round to cut Driscoll off; and it was clear that he could not see them. It was an anxious moment for those watching on the kopje.

There was no doubt now as to who was holding the ridge. Two squadrons of Driscoll's were sent to clear the sugar-loaf hill. Driscoll's attention was at length drawn to the men beyond him, and he retired on the camp. The Boers followed him up, and, occupying a hillock, opened fire on the camp at less than a mile. Capt. Griffin with his company was sent to charge the hillock, and the pom-pom opened upon it. The Boers were cleared off. Major Gilbert went out and took charge of this flank.

Meanwhile the two squadrons had occupied the sugar-loaf hill and the small kopje, which were about 1,000 yards from the main ridge. It was thought that there were no Boers upon the left end of the latter, as the heavy fire which had been opened came from its right end only. Col. Rochfort and Major Driscoll had come up, and it was decided to charge the ridge with a company of the Sussex and the two squadrons.

A few men were left on the sugar-loaf hill to fire at the crest opposite; the squadrons and the Sussex men were drawn up in lines under cover.

"Trot till you get into the open and then gallop," shouted Driscoll, and off went the lines. The first line charged towards the centre of the ridge, the second line (consisting largely of Sussex) followed 500 yards behind, and rather to the left.

As soon as the men got into the open, a heavy

fire broke out from the spur of the main ridge, at the foot of which the left hand men were riding. At the same time the rest of the Boers (there were about 200 of them among the bushes) turned their fire upon the charging lines. The ridge is about 1½ miles long.

Bullets fell very fast, and kicked up the dust among the horses' feet; but the men were moving at a good pace, and very little damage was done. One man of Driscoll's was killed and two were wounded.

The first line reached the ridge at about the centre; the second line turned to the left and charged up the spur, which was occupied by about fifty Boers. These did not wait for the attack, and, as the leading men reached the top, they saw the last Boer disappearing into the thick bush 500 yards down the other side. The British followed, but were soon recalled, as pursuit would have been useless.

The first line made their position good on the centre of the ridge; the pom-pom was brought into action against the right half of it, and the Boers evacuated the whole position, leaving one prisoner behind them. They could be seen streaming away in batches northwards and westwards, and they were followed with long range rifle fire, which, however, only made them move a little quicker.

During the next few days the other columns came into line, but the Boers were not heard of again.

The movement was continued northwards, and Major Gilbert with the Sussex column, Driscoll's, and 100 I. Y., marched on Hoopstadt by a circuitous route to the west. Two nights were spent in trekking, the column lying up in farms in the daytime.

At the end of the second night, Bornemansfontein was reached, a well-wooded farm with stone-walled paddocks, in which the men were disposed. Soon after dawn, some mounted men were seen bearing down upon the camp at a gallop. As they came nearer cries of "Hands up!" were heard, and it became evident that they were executing a gallant though quite hopeless charge. The stone walls were lined, and a few shots fired, killing one of the advancing horses. By this time it had been realised that the men were South African Constabulary. The troops were well hidden, and they had mistaken the encampment for a small Boer family laager.

Major Davis of Driscoll's very pluckily rode between the lines, blowing his whistle. Firing ceased, and explanations followed.

The farm was inhabited, and the wife of the owner said that her husband was on commando, but that she had not seen him or the commando for two months. Her little boy, however, was more communicative, and said he had been there two nights before with five horses.

Hoopstadt was reached on the 11th of March. It was a small town, the inhabitants of which had been removed. The church was used as a hospital, and most of the houses were occupied by troops, for the place was one of the S. A. C. Headquarters. The only water supply was from the Vet River, which ran a rich thick brown. It was said that, if a spoon was placed upright in the middle of a cup of tea, it would stand there.

In the past five weeks some of the horses of the column had done 500 miles, practically trekking every day.

The great combined movements in the northeast of the Orange River Colony had at this time finally broken the power of De Wet, and he crossed the railway line south of the Vaal on March 5th, with President Steyn and about 200 men.

Delarey was in considerable strength in the

Western Transvaal, and it was thought that he and De Wet might attempt to effect a combination. A line was therefore held running along the Vaal and Valsch Rivers, and the column, composed of the Sussex and Driscoll's Scouts under Major Gilbert, moved on the 12th of March from Hoopstadt for Commando Drift. After a mid-day halt at Wegdraai, an attempt was made to march on in the evening; rain, however, fell in torrents, and the night was pitch-dark. Having gone a few miles with the greatest difficulty, half the transport (following in rear of the mounted troops) led off on to a wrong road, and progress became impossible. Thoroughly wet and uncomfortable, the column halted for the night, and before morning the lost wagons returned. Commando Drift was reached on the 14th, and here the news was made known of Delarey's successes: first, the capture of Col. Von Donop's convoy, and then the taking of Lord Methuen and a number of men. The column proceeded to Strydfontein, a drift 3 miles above Commando Drift (which was occupied by S. A. C.), and held it during the following week. It had been expected that Delarey with his successful commandos might attempt to break south and join De Wet. The latter, however, slipped across the Vaal with President Steyn by a little known bridle drift on the night of the 15th, and joined Delarey.

Meantime the troops that had been operating in the east were being brought across the line, and by the 23rd of March there were collected at Commando Drift under Colonel Rochfort the columns of Lord Basing and of Cols. Bulfin, Sitwell, and Western, besides a force of South African Constabulary. Major Gilbert and Major Driscoll having moved down to Commando Drift, Col. Rochfort crossed into the Transvaal during the evening of the 23rd with 3,000 men. No wheeled vehicle or gun was taken, every man carrying two days' rations for himself and his horse. Before starting, Lord Kitchener's message had been read out to the troops, in which he said that the operations would tax their endurance, but that he relied upon their using every effort, working with the greatest dash and spirit, and utterly defeating any enemy they might meet.

The scheme provided that Col. Rochfort should come up at night from the south, and get touch with the large bodies of troops that would be sent westward from Klerksdorp, and that the whole should turn eastwards in the morning, forming a gigantic net which would be drawn in upon the Schoonspruit blockhouse line, specially reinforced.

The moon was full, and Col. Rochfort's men marched through the night, making Wolmaranstad by 3.30 a.m. There the black masses of troops closed up and dismounted, till the whole slope by the townlet was covered with horses and men. Then the columns separated out to take up their positions in the line.

Major Gilbert and Major Driscoll again worked together. At dawn, Driscoll's, who were leading, captured twelve Boers asleep round their wagons; they were an outpost of Delarey's, and they had no idea that any British could be in the vicinity. They said that a commando of Delarey's was ten miles ahead. This commando, however, managed to slip through between two columns. Through the day the net was drawn tighter, and by the evening of the 23rd Major Gilbert and his men had ridden over 60 miles in twenty-one hours. At six o'clock they bivouacked in the rain in some scrub at Matjespruit. There had been a heavy hailstorm during the afternoon.

On the next afternoon Klerksdorp was reached. Some hundreds of Boers had been caught altogether, besides three 15-pounders, two pom-poms, and a quantity of ammunition. Perhaps the greatest effect produced, however, was upon the nerves of the Boers. They got into a state of "nervous tension," as they never knew when or where the British would turn up next. A district miles away from the nearest troops in the evening was swarming with columns in the morning. The absolute abandonment of transport by the British had been the key to the situation.

On the evening of the following day Col. Rochfort's columns started to return to Commando Drift. They marched 30 miles during the night, and got to the Drift the next evening, having covered 150 miles in four days. The lights of the camps that stretched along the river for a mile or more shone through the trees like the lights of a town.

On the way in, two Africander guides of the Intelligence Department had ridden on ahead of the columns, and, coming up to a farm, were taken by the woman there for Boers. She gave them seven rounds of ammunition (all she had, she said) and told them they must not stay, as there were thousands and thousands of Khakis on the river—more than she had ever seen—with Lord Roberts and Lord Kitchener. Asked how she knew Lord Roberts was there, she produced a photograph of him out of a packet of cheap cigarettes, and said she recognised him as he rode through.

On the 29th of March the Sussex column was finally broken up. It had been ten months in existence not counting the months of convoy work; it had covered thousands of miles. It had had its days of success, and it had come through its black hour of tribulation. For some months it had been dwindling in numbers, more and more men becoming dismounted and being left at the various bases. The column had done its work.

The remaining mounted men were turned into an M. I. Company under Captain Montrésor, and attached to Col. Western's column, of which Major Gilbert was made second in command. The dismounted men were sent to Hoopstadt, at which place the officers, men and stores left behind at Vlakfontein had arrived.

From this time until the declaration of peace on June 1st, the dismounted men worked between Hoopstadt, Bloemhof and the line, sometimes as escort to convoys, sometimes as stops for drives. The mounted company joined in the latter, of which the most important took place on the 9th of June and following days. Col. Rochfort's columns moved to Schweizer Renecke, where they surprised some Boers, capturing sixty. They then formed, in conjunction with Gen. Ian Hamilton's columns from the north, a line in single rank 50 miles long. For the next three days this line moved west, the men sleeping in their positions at nightfall. The sight, when an extended view could be got, was a strange one. As far as the eye could reach the line of mounted men stretched away, here dipping into a valley, there topping a rise. There were some 21,000 troops driving.

The Kimberley railway was reached on the 11th of May. Nearly 400 Boers were captured, and a great deal of stock. Severe sniping was experienced on the way back to Bloemhof—several mules and horses, and one or two men being hit.

News of the declaration of peace was received on June 1st amidst general rejoicings, and the scattered regiment was gradually collected at Bloemfontein, to which place Headquarters moved up from Bethulie. From Bloemfontein the time-expired men, the volunteers, and the reservists (regular and militia), were sent home, leaving only a skeleton Battalion, due for India, where fresh drafts would await it.

CHAPTER XXIX.

THE THIRD BATTALION.

The Third Battalion of the Royal Sussex Regiment was embodied, under the command of Col. the Earl of March, A.D.C., from December 11th, 1899, to September 11th, 1902—probably the record embodiment for a Militia Battalion during the war. The Battalion assembled at Preston Barracks, Brighton, and, shortly before Christmas, 1899, volunteered as a whole for service in South Africa. This offer was not, however, utilized until early in 1901.

On the 30th March, 1900, the Battalion was moved to the Shaft Barracks, Dover. Both Line Battalions being abroad, line details were attached to it, ultimately amounting to three Companies.

The Battalion marched to Shorncliffe on the 30th April, and remained there under canvas until the 18th October, forming part of a Militia Brigade. On that date they moved into Napier Barracks. The latter part of the time under canvas had been extremely wet and cold.

On the 2nd February, 1901, the Battalion took part in the lining of the streets for the funeral of Queen Victoria. They paraded with the Colours at 2.15 a.m., and entrained for London, where they were stationed near Apsley House.

Early in February, orders were received for the Battalion to hold itself in readiness to proceed on active service; and after many delays it embarked on the "City of Cambridge," at the Albert Dock, on the 29th of March. The numbers proceeding to South Africa were twenty-four officers and 480 men. Already 123 men of the Battalion had been sent out to join the 1st Battalion as Militia Reservists. One officer (Capt. Blake) had also been attached to that Battalion for duty a year before.

Capetown was reached on the 23rd April, and the Battalion was at once entrained for Bloemfontein, arriving there five days later. On the way, a call was made at the Headquarters of the 1st Battalion at Norval's Pont, and a football match played with them.

At Bloemfontein, the 3rd Battalion camped at Spitzkop, 4 miles west of the town, and took over the "B" section of the outposts, which was placed under the command of Col. the Earl of March. On the suggestion of Col. Long, R.A., commanding the troops at Bloemfontein, a number of men of the Battalion were trained as Mounted Infantry for local defence purposes, first under Captain Papillon, and then (on his falling sick in June) under Capt. the Hon. J. S. R. Tufton. By August, the 3rd Battalion M. I. numbered eight officers and 225 N. C. O.'s and men.

There must have been, at this time, over a thousand men, in all, of the Royal Sussex Regiment, doing mounted work in South Africa.

The mounted duties round Bloemfontein consisted of patrolling beyond the outposts, and of escorting convoys to columns in the field. The men for the most part knew nothing about horses to start with; they were, however, very keen, and, under careful instruction, quickly learned the rudiments of horsemastership, and finally constituted a really useful body of M. I.

Capt. Tufton took over the post at Fischer's Farm with fifty men, in July; and in September another seventy-five of the M. I. were sent, under Lieut. Wilson (4th Suffolk Regt., attached) and 2nd Lieut. Nicholson, to occupy Warringham's, beyond Thabanchu.

Although no opportunity is allowed for a militiaman to learn signalling, yet the 3rd Battalion had taken this up on the voyage out; some signalling equipment was obtained at Bloemfontein, and classes were started, with the result that when, in July, the regular signallers at Spitzkop had to be withdrawn, the 3rd Battalion signallers were able to take over the station.

Capt. Hankey and Lieut. Parkin, with 100 men, had been sent to the Supply Depôt in Bloemfontein, in place of coming to Spitzkop. Shortly afterwards Capt. Hankey went as A.D.C. to Col. Long.

On November 23rd the M. I. was broken up. Col. Long wrote the following letter upon the subject:

> The O. C. troops regrets to have to publish an order to-day for the withdrawal of the ponies of the Sussex M. I. The Remount Department have to furnish 600 horses for columns on the move in the next week, and they are at present so short of fit horses that they are obliged to call upon the Sussex to hand in the ponies they have so well looked after and converted into serviceable animals. The greatest credit is due to you and all concerned for the way you have cared for these ponies. The G. O. C. regrets having to take this step, but feels sure you will understand that this step has only been taken owing to extreme pressure and the urgent requirements of the service.

In December the Battalion was moved down to Volksrust, on the Natal border. The first detachment left under Lieut.-Col. Godman on the 7th, escorting a batch of Boer prisoners as far as Ladysmith.

On the 12th of December the following order was published at Bloemfontein:

> The Third Royal Sussex Regt. having been ordered away from this station, the O. C. troops wishes to take this opportunity of expressing his appreciation of their uniform excellent conduct, and of the cheerful and thorough manner of carrying out the duties in garrison by all ranks of the Battalion during the eight months they have been at Bloemfontein.

Major Clarke, with seven officers and 181 N. C. O.'s and men, moved down the line to Ingogo, in Natal, and took over a district and a line of posts along the railway between that place and Mount Prospect; other detachments were at Laing's Nek, Iketeni Nek (Majuba), and along the line north of Volksrust. Col. the Earl of March took over command of the troops at Volksrust, Capt. and Adjt. P. E. P. Crawfurd taking up the duties of S. S. O.

At Christmas time the county of Sussex sent out to the Battalion a generous gift in the shape of good fare and useful presents.

On January 5th, 1902, Capt. Aldridge came as Adjutant to the Battalion. During the following months several attemps were made by Boers to cross the railway at night; they were, however, frustrated by the heavy firing of the block-houses.

On the anniversary of the embarkation of the Battalion, three officers and forty-nine men had been invalided home, fourteen men had died, two officers and fifty-two N. C. O.'s and men were in hospital, and twenty-three officers and 452 N.C.O.'s and men were doing duty. A draft had been received from the depôt in February.

In May, the Peace negotiations were on foot, and Boer delegates arrived at Volksrust on their way to Vereeniging. In accordance with orders, they were treated with lavish hospitality.

Peace was declared on June 1st, and on the next day the Battalion received orders to move to St. Helena for duty in guarding prisoners. The various detachments collected at Ingogo, and moved down on the 9th to Durban, where the "Wakool" was waiting for them; the weather was however too rough to embark until the 14th, the intervening days being spent at Umbilo Prison Camp. Major Clarke now commanded the Battalion, Col. the Earl of March having returned for the Coronation.

St. Helena was reached on the 24th June. As the "Wakool" steamed into the Jamestown anchorage, the signallers on H.M.S. Dwarf gave the news of the King's illness, and of the consequent postponement of the coronation, which should have taken place next day.

After five days quarantine the Battalion disembarked, and marched to Broadbottom Camp, at the N.E. end of the Island, relieving the Buffs Militia. Gen. Cronje watched the men go by from the house where he lived apart; he was not very popular among the other prisoners—mostly Paardebergers.

There were about 2,000 Boers at Broadbottom, including Gen. Ben Viljoen. They were at this time just trying to make up their minds to take the oath of allegiance. They were too loyal to their old Government to do so without orders—which, however, they ultimately received. Those who took the oath beforehand did not have a pleasant time.

The weather was extremely bad, and the camp a sea of mud. On July 19th, a gloom was cast over the Battalion by the death of Colour Sergt. Penfold, who was killed in trying to climb down a steep cliff.

On August 9th, Coronation Day was celebrated. A *feu de joie* was fired, and the Battalion was inspected by Col. Wright, commandant of the camp. In the evening an enormous bonfire was lit upon the hillside. In the crowd round it, Boers and British mingled freely, the latter tanned from exposure, the former pale from a year or more mostly spent in their tents. After loyalty had been satisfied, Col. Wright called for three cheers for " our friends and fellow subjects, our late gallant enemies," which were heartily given. The Battalion embarked for England on board the " Dominion " on August 11th, and arrived at Chichester a month later, having travelled by way of Cape Town. At Chichester they were welcomed by the Mayor and Corporation, and marched to barracks through decorated streets.

The medals earned by the men were presented to them by Mrs. Kilgour (Col. Kilgour then commanded the Regimental District), and the embodiment, which had lasted two years and nine months, was at an end.

APPENDIX A.

THE 13TH M. I.

By Capt. G. P. Hunt, Royal Berkshire Regiment.

In November, 1900, four new Battalions of M. I. were assembled at Pretoria : and of these the 13th M. I. was one. It was made up of detachments from various regiments, and No. 1 Co. consisted of seventy N. C. O.'s and men of the Royal Sussex, brought up by Lieut. J. S. Cameron from Lindley, and fifty-five of the Royal Berkshire Regiment under Lieut. G. P. Hunt. The Battalion was commanded by Capt. (afterwards Brevet Maj.) Pratt, of the Durham Light Infantry. Early in 1901 Lt. Cameron took over command of No. 1 Co.

December and January were mostly spent in training the men. Many of these knew nothing about mounted work, and had first to learn to stick on their horses (raw, untrained Argentines for the most part) somehow. However, in a creditably short time a body of useful mounted men, if not of expert horsemen, was turned out.

The 13th M. I. were first under fire at Hekpoort on 19th December, with General Alderson's column. Gen. Clements was then conducting a combined movement westwards up the Magaliesberg Valley. The Boers were eventually driven out of their Hekpoort position. The Company came under a smart rifle fire, and their led horses were pom-pomed : but they sustained no casualties and saw no Boers.

From January to April, 1901, Gen. Alderson's column was engaged on the operations under Gen. French in the eastern and south-eastern Transvaal. This column consisted of the 13th and 14th M. I., the Canadian Scouts, the Yorkshire Light Infantry, " J " Battery, R. H. A., and a pom-pom ; it trekked along the Swaziland border to Ermelo, encountering very few Boers by the way. The column waited for supplies at Ermelo for ten days ; but continuous rain and flooded rivers prevented the convoys coming out from Newcastle, and mutton and mealies were all that men and horses had to live on. The horses suffered severely from the lack of food, and from standing about in the wet camp. Full rations were not obtained till 26th March, more than a month later.

During April the column trekked through the difficult country between Vryheid and Zululand, arriving at Newcastle on the 20th of that month.

By this time more than half the 13th M. I. were dismounted, and the men were in rags. Gen. French's operations had cost the Boers 1,000 casualties, and the districts involved had been cleared, cattle being driven in, and sheep used for rations or destroyed. The Boer families were brought in to Refugee camps.

The 13th and 14th M. I. were remounted, and joined Gen. Bullock's column at Volksrust. The horses supplied to the Company were mostly large raw Hungarians, quite unsuited to the work.

Gen. Bullock's column, which was a large one, first trekked about the Standerton and Wakkerstroom districts, and then worked in the northern Free State, finishing up at Heidelberg in the end of July. There was no serious fighting, although every day Boer skirmishers were encountered. These would lie in wait for the scouts of the column, on the chance of shooting them at short range, and then making off. Dogs proved very useful to scouting parties : going on ahead, they would, by their actions, give warning of concealed Boers.

The men kept wonderfully fit and in very good spirits ; they were just the type that Kipling describes in his poem " M. I." The horses, however, suffered severely from the cold, which was very severe, particularly at night.

At Heidelberg, Brig. Gen. Spens took over the column, which worked from July to September in the N. E. Free State. This was a very eventful time for the 13th M. I. ; night marches were the rule rather than the exception. Numbers of Boers were captured, wagons, cattle and horses were brought in, and farms were destroyed. The column worked sometimes by itself, and sometimes in conjunction with others ; occasionally single battallions went in different directions. The Boers had difficulty in avoiding the troops, and were deprived of their wagons, spare horses, shelters and means of subsistence, with a view to forcing them to surrender.

One occasion in particular may be mentioned. On the night of the 6th of August the column divided into two, acting in conjunction with Rimington. After a night march, a laager was surprised at dawn, many prisoners being taken.

The Company captured a number of Boers and wagons after a long gallop : they only just avoided an engagement with Gough's M. I., which was coming up from another direction.

On the 15th August Lieut. J. M. Hulton joined the 13th M. I. at Kroonstad from the 5th Bn. Royal Fusiliers, and was posted to No. 1 Co., and given command of one of the Sussex sections. He had his horse killed on the 18th, when on flank-guard, by some Boers who crept up a donga just as the scouts were moving on. He fell under his horse, but one of the section galloped back, helped him to get clear, and took the saddle on to his own horse while Hulton ran by his side.

On the 3rd September the column rode down a Boer convoy and 300 Boers. Cameron was in command of the advanced guard. Nearly all the wagons were captured, some falling into the hands of Rimington's and Wilson's columns. Many Boers were taken, and a number killed and wounded. Many of the horses of the column had subsequently to be destroyed : for the men rode over 50 miles that day, and the horses were utterly done up.

Towards the end of September Botha threatened to invade Natal, and Gen. Spens' column, with others, entrained for that colony. Gough's M. I. had suffered a serious reverse near Vryheid, the Boers being in superior numbers. Botha had then attacked Major Chapman and his small force at Fort Itala on the Zulu border, but had been repulsed after two days' most severe fighting. He afterwards stated that it was here that his power was finally broken.

The 13th, 14th, and Gough's M. I. moved out of Dundee on September 22nd, crossed Rorke's Drift, passed Isandhlwana, and hurried on to help Chapman, leaving the convoy to follow. The columns of Spens, Pulteney, and Allenby, under Major Gen. Bruce Hamilton, formed up along the Zululand border, and worked northwards through the mountainous Vryheid district ; Gen. Clements coming in from Dundee.

APPENDIX A.

The main body of the Boers appeared to have gone, but a number of those wounded at Itala were found in farms, and a number of fresh graves showed that Botha's forces had suffered considerably in attempting to capture Chapman with his small force and two guns.

Wagons and carts were found in the most incredible places on the slopes of mountains, and were destroyed. A good number of cattle also were captured from the few Boers looking after them. In the meantime, the convoy had such difficulty in getting up the roads that for three days it could not reach the battalion, which had to do without rations; and both men and horses felt rather done up and very empty after climbing up and down the rugged hills in the rain. Several horses were unable to get on and had to be shot, but fortunately only two of the Company's.

Gen. Spens' column reached Vryheid on the 22nd October, and, returning to Newcastle, got fresh supplies for a trek in the Orange River Colony. Standerton was reached in November, after operations along the Drakensberg.

At the end of November began the series of captures by Gen. Bruce Hamilton, made possible by the wonderful intelligence obtained by Col. Wools-Sampson. Half of Spens' column and half of Col. Rawlinson's, with the corps of surrendered Boers, made a night march of some 25 miles from Ermelo on the 4th December.

Led by Wools-Sampson's native boys, they came on a laager at dawn the next morning. Unfortunately there was not time to surround it, and another small laager beyond was warned by the firing, many of the Boers jumping on to their ponies and galloping off. However, the columns pursued and captured a good many, and all the wagons, etc., were captured. The totals were ninety-one prisoners of the Bethel and Standerton commandos, including the Landrost of Bethel, twenty wagons, thirty Cape carts, 2,000 head of cattle, and 5,000 sheep, many rifles, ammunition, etc. During the pursuit the Sussex section captured fifteen Boers, and one man killed a native with the butt of his rifle, who had just fired at and missed him.

The column now camped at the head of the Standerton-Ermelo block-house line, which was progressing at the rate of about two block-houses and one mile of barbed wire fence a day. December was spent in clearing the surrounding country. A number of Boers were brought in, and a great deal of stock.

On the 19th December, the 14th M. I. were surprised by Britz's commando at Tweefontein, while searching farms; they lost two officers and thirteen men killed, and several officers and men wounded.

The Boers were dressed in khaki, having red cloth tabs with B.S. (Britz's Scouts), and numbered some 300 or 400. It was noticed that after the fight they destroyed their own rifles, taking away those they captured, as they preferred ours. The remainder of the column, which moved to join the 14th M. I. in the morning, did not hear of the attack by the Boers in time to assist, but drove off the commando, inflicting on the Boers some few more casualties. The column moved towards Amersfort, where Christmas was spent, and then made two successive night marches (27th, 28th December), towards Tweefontein and Standerton, in which twenty-seven Boers, six armed natives and 600 cattle were captured, and forty-four Boers were obliged to surrender on the block-house lines. Some of the

APPENDIX A.

arms and equipment of the 14th M. I. were recovered from the prisoners.

For about six weeks the column had its headquarters at Ermelo, which became an important station at the junction of three lines of block-houses. Bruce Hamilton now had five or six columns under him, which he sent out in any direction according to the Intelligence obtained by Wools-Sampson's boys.

The night marches that ensued resulted in the capture of a great many Boers, including that of Grobelaar's laager and 100 men. The scattered pursuits that followed the discovery of a laager became very like hunting without hounds—with the added excitement that occasionally the enemy would stop to fire. Only the fittest horses were taken out, and the Boers were ridden down or driven onto lines of block-houses. The men had to act by themselves in following up single or small parties of Boers, as a column often got spread over many miles of country.

From 23rd February to 8th April the column was detached, still under Brigadier General Spens, and acted in the low veldt and the Vryheid district, also going through Utrecht and Wakkerstroom. The principal idea of this trek appears to have been to complete the clearing of those districts of cattle, and for this purpose some 200 Zulus were called for, under a chief of north-western Zululand, to assist in bringing in the cattle. The majority of the natives in those districts with whom the Boers had left their cattle were of Zulu origin, but it was difficult for the troops to sort the Boer from the Zulu cattle. This, however, the "impi" did with ease. Going out into the kraals at night, they would persuade the natives to bring in the Boer cattle themselves, as they were allowed to kill as many as they could eat ; and the "impi" grew and grew until it was more than ten times its original size. By day it would trek along at a jog trot beside the convoy, the men singing their war songs ; for they were not allowed to carry rifles, but only carried assegais for self-defence at night. When the column returned to the high veldt, the Zulus, though loath to do so, had to return to their own country.

The final stage of the war was now reached. It was short. The Boers that were left in the field were practically all enclosed in areas surrounded by lines of block-houses and barbed wire fences, which they themselves called "Kraals." Single men were known to have got through from one area to another, but it was practically impossible for many to do so without storming a block-house. It therefore only remained for us to sweep one area after another, and this was done by an extended line of mounted troops with its ends marching along block-houses. The block-house lines on either flank and in front of the sweeping line were strengthened by infantry trenches between the block-houses, which made them impassable by day or night ; and when either of these happened to be a railway line, armoured trains patrolled the line to assist. The mounted troops remained in their column organisation, and each column was bound to keep in touch with the next by day and night, in order that every hiding place should be searched and the Boers prevented from breaking through as far as possible. By day a continuous chain of scouts advanced supported by small bodies, at intervals in rear ; and mule wagons followed in rear of the centre of each column with supplies, blankets, and entrenching tools. At night a continuous line of trenches about 50 to 200 yards apart was formed, and as far as possible a continuous obstacle of barbed wire was put up in front of the trenches.

1ST DRIVE.—The 13th M. I. were always on the right of Spens' line, the 14th M. I. in the centre, and Gough's M. I. on the left. The Company being No. 1 of the 13th was on the extreme right, and consequently on them fell the onus of keeping touch with the next column through all the drives.

On 10th April the columns under Bruce-Hamilton lined up from Ermelo, through Carolina, to the Middelburg-Belfast line, and in three days' swept the area to the Standerton-Heidelberg line.

On the last night of this drive some Boers made a determined effort to get through the line, attacking Gough's M. I.; but not more than forty were supposed to have succeeded, the remainder being beaten back. The column picked up altogether ninety-five Boers out of a total of 134 captured, and a good many Boers were killed in attacking the line.

On 12th April some of the advanced scouts were ambushed by a party of Boers, Pte. Leadbetter, of the Royal Sussex Regt., being killed and two temporarily captured.

2ND DRIVE.—From the 18th—20th April the columns swept the area from the Vaal-Springs line to the Bronkhorst Spruit—Middelburg line.

There were six columns extended, the Scots Greys joining in from Springs; but the results were very small, the Boers having got through a gap between two other columns on the left.

3RD DRIVE.—On 26th—27th the line went back over the same ground, going over forty miles on the second day.

4TH DRIVE.—From the 3rd—5th May the columns swept the country from Standerton—Heidelberg—Vereeniging southwards to Frankfort—Heilbron and the main railway line, and then on in one day to the Kroonstad-Lindley line; Elliot's columns holding the Liebensberg Vlei on the left. The Boers made a great effort to break through the next column, and some 200 succeeded; but the result of the whole drive was 294 prisoners and eleven killed, which was very satisfactory after the long and arduous drive. The distance traversed on the 6th alone was over forty miles, as the crow flies, which meant a good deal more for everyone, if the unevenness of the land and the continual straining of a line some sixty miles long be taken into account. But this told more on the poor horses, which had to be sacrificed to accomplish the necessary steps for finishing the war. Officers and men not only rode these long distances, wearied by the monotony of trekking hour after hour at the walk, on tired horses, but were hardly able to sleep at night during the drives on account of the possibility of having a trench rushed at any moment, and also on account of the continual firing all along the line, everyone being ordered to fire on the slightest suspicion of Boers being in front. By this time many of the horses were considered incapable of keeping up with the line in a long day's drive, and were sent in to the railway, leaving the Company only about half its original strength. Everyone looked forward to the rest which Lord Kitchener promised us we should soon have, but we had one more drive to accomplish—the return drive to Heilbron and Frankfort, and this proved to be one of the most eventful days for No. 1 Company.

LAST DRIVE.—The drive took place on 9th May, 1902; the 13th M. I. started from Lindley, and finished at a point about twelve miles out of Heilbron towards Frankfort. Starting at dawn, No. 1 Company joined hands with McKenzie's column at 7.30, and the line halted for an hour at 10.30. The units being so weak, about four scouts per Company were sent about half-a-mile in front, and the remainder of the men extended to keep touch. The guide on the left of McKenzie's column, at the time of the halt, said he had already come a mile over his line of advance, and refused to come further; meanwhile Garratt's column on the left had gone off to their left, leaving several miles to be covered by Spens' column. The columns on the left were evidently under the impression that the majority of the Boers were opposite them, and some firing was heard in that direction on moving on again. But the Boers had chosen their piece of ground well, and it turned out to be just in the line of advance of the Company, a very few of the Boers having attracted attention by firing on the left. The scouts had just reached the top of a rise, when they saw a number of Boers cantering towards them only about 150 yards to their front. The Company was then extended to about fifty yards between men. The scouts fired, and the Boers fired with their rifles laid across their saddles; but there was no time to warn the line, in fact a low rise divided the Company, so that only some twenty men could see the Boers coming on, in a long disordered crowd, with natives leading spare animals. About ten men, immediately in front of the Boers, galloped together, forming a small group round a sergeant, and fired at the column of Boers which was coming straight towards them. The remainder of the Company came galloping in from the left one by one, and formed another group which opened fire, but not until the Boers had already passed through the line. They had steered off from the first group and cantered on, and nothing remained to be done but to pick up what they had left, as the long driving line was going further and further away. Several horses and mules were found loose; some were wounded and had to be destroyed. One man was captured with a dislocated shoulder, having fallen off his horse, and another was found in the grass, shot through the temple. About twelve rifles were picked up and destroyed, and other signs were found indicating that men and horses had been wounded.

As the Company went on to join the line, two more Boers were captured in a farm and taken on, the line arriving at its destination in driblets an hour after dark. The number of Boers which passed through was estimated at from 150--200, said to be under Mentz; they were evidently the same party that had broken through McKenzie's column on the 6th. It seemed a pity that they have got off so easily within a mile of the stronger line of McKenzie's column, but doubtless these last two experiences, with the prospect of more, influenced them in the peace meetings they were now allowed to hold without molestation.

The Column was ordered to make its way to Heidelberg, where it stayed inactive until it was broken up. On 6th August, 1902, the horses were taken to the remount depôt near Johannesburg. And on the 8th the two detachments started to rejoin their regiments.

APPENDIX B.

THE 21ST M. I.

By LT. E. C. BEETON, Royal Sussex Regiment.

1901.—The two Companies of the 21st M. I., made up largely of men of the Royal Sussex Regiment, were trained at Shorncliffe during March and April, 1901. No. 2 Co., commanded by Major Anderson (late 60th Rifles), was composed entirely of men of the Regiment, and was 130 strong, though, with the exception of Lieut. Drinan, it was officered from other regiments. No. 3. Co., commanded by Major Hearn, late 21st Lancers and K. D. G.'s, was 136 strong, and was made up of a section of Royal Sussex under Lieut. Beeton, a section of Dublin Fusiliers, a section of Buffs and a mixed section of the West Kent and Loyal North Lancs. Regts.

No. 2 Co. left England at the end of April, and was followed three weeks later by No. 3 Co.; the latter Company disembarked at Durban on the 14th June, proceeding to Elandsfontein for remounts, and thence by train to Klerksdorp. Meanwhile No. 2 Co. had joined the 21st M. I. on Colonel Williams' column in the Western Transvaal, where it took part in various minor engagements against Potgeiter's and Vermas' commandos, and did good work in the Orange River Colony, and on the Magaliesberg mountains, assisting in the capture of several Boer convoys during July, August, and September, 1901. During the latter part of September Col. Williams' column succeeded in taking nearly 100 prisoners and over sixty wagons of the enemy. About October 20th No. 2 Co. was sent into the base at Klerksdorp for garrison duty, and was relieved by No. 3 Co., which had been on almost continuous convoy-escort duty between Potchefstroom and Ventersdorp, with headquarters at Potchefstroom. Though no serious fighting had occurred, the convoys were frequently threatened and fired at by small parties of Boers. No. 2 Co. had also been working with General Wilson's column, assisting in the capture of Cdt. Holls. In six weeks Gen. Wilson took 140 prisoners, and cleared a large stretch of fertile country.

In October, the 21st M. I. was operating on Col. Hickie's column in the Western Transvaal. From Nov. 10th to Nov. 20th this column, then only 800 strong, was held up by the combined commandos of Generals Delarey, Kemp, and Liebenberg, about 2,000 strong, at Brakspruit, 14 miles west of Klerksdorp. The column was very strongly entrenched, and the entire perimeter of the camp encircled with barbed wire. The enemy did not attack, and the column was subsequently relieved by Lord Methuen's (1st Division) column coming up from the south, and Col. Kekewich's from the east. A squadron of the 11th Yeomanry, belonging to Col. Hickie's column, were surprised and captured by Delarey on Nov. 12th, when on reconnaissance. The 21st M. I. were sent out in relief, and met the squadron of Yeomanry returning on foot, stripped of all rifles and clothing.

On Dec. 8th Major Hearn was relieved of command of No. 3 Co., and appointed commandant of Col. Kekewich's Base Depôt. Lieut. Beeton took over command of this Company

APPENDIX B.

From Dec. 8th, 1901 to Jan. 23rd, 1902, Col. Hickie's column was trekking through the Western Transvaal and down to the Vaal River without much result; very few Boers were found owing to the very heavy rains. Many small expeditions for mounted troops, with four days' rations on the saddle, were undertaken.

1902.—On Feb. 3rd an attack was made at dawn on Commandant Alberts' commando by the 21st M. I., Scottish Horse, and 11th Co. I. Y., in which General Alberts and fifty Boers were captured, together with a number of wagons. The British casualties were one officer killed and two men, and about twenty wounded. The Boer casualties were four killed and about twenty or thirty wounded.

At the end of February the 21st M. I. were transferred to Lord Methuen's column, subsequently commanded by Col. von Donop.

On Feb. 25th Col. von Donop's empty convoy of 160 mule wagons (2,000 mules) was attacked and captured at daybreak 8 miles from Klerksdorp by General Delarey and 1,500 Boers. The convoy was trekking from Wolmeranstadt to Klerksdorp for supplies, under an escort of 360 men, composed of Yeomanry and two or three companies Northumberland Fusiliers, with two field guns and a pom-pom and a maxim—all of which were taken by the Boers. Major Anderson, commanding the escort, sent in to Klerksdorp for reinforcements, and Major Hearn, with Lieut. Beeton, and about thirty men of the 21st M. I. (who had been sent in to Klerksdorp for remounts) moved out of the town towards Wolmeranstadt about 7.30 a.m., and were subsequently joined by two troops of Scottish Horse, some men of No. 2 Co. 21st M. I., with Lieut. Drinan, and other details, making up a total of perhaps 250 men. This force, commanded by Col. Grenfell, 1st Life Guards, galloped 6 miles towards the scene of the disaster, subsequently reaching high ground from which the captured convoy could be seen, turned about and moving off in an opposite direction. The woods on the right of the road were occupied by large numbers of Boers, who could be clearly seen, as well as a great number trekking away over the hills. Col. Grenfell's men dismounted and opened fire at 1,000 yards. Part of the force charged down the hill in an attempt to recapture half-a-dozen wagons, which had been blocked and overturned in the Spruit; whereupon the Boers in large numbers formed up and galloped, firing from their saddles, down the hill opposite, towards the British, compelling them to retire, with a loss of several horses killed and two men of the Scottish Horse wounded. The Boers did not continue the pursuit, being satisfied with the capture of the entire convoy, and the guns, with the exception of the maxim, which was galloped into Klerksdorp on a pack horse. The casualties among the convoy escort were over over 200. Two officers of the Northumberland Fusiliers were killed, and three severely wounded.

On March 14th Lord Kitchener concentrated a large force in the vicinity of Klerksdorp with the object of destroying Delarey's commandos. Col. Grenfell, 1st Life Guards, took command of all mounted troops belonging to the three columns (Col. von Donop's, Col. Kekewich's, and Col. Grenfell's), together 1,500 strong. The first of the combined drives began on March 16th and occupied five days, the enemy being driven from S.-W. to N.-E., in the direction of Klerksdorp. Owing to a gap left by General W. Kitchener's column, most of the Boers escaped over the hills, near Brakspruit,

9 miles from Klerksdorp. The 21st M. I. came in touch with a party of Boers quite unexpectedly at nightfall, and after galloping a few miles in pursuit drove them in the direction of General Kitchener's column, where sixteen subsequently were taken prisoners.

From March 16th to April 1st, small three days' operations took place from Vaalbank (50 miles W. of Klerksdorp), the men carrying rations on their saddles. Many men had to be sent on to Klerksdorp for remounts, owing to considerable losses in horses from exhaustion and horse-sickness.

On the evening of April 4th the mounted troops moved from Middlebult at 7 p.m., rationed for three days, in very heavy rain. The night was pitch dark. At daybreak they attacked and captured a Boer convoy and large herds of cattle and sheep, after a long gallop.

On April 9th the mounted troops of the combined columns started from Middlebult to join General Ian Hamilton's big drive and enveloping movement against General Delarey's commandos. After two days' march they arrived at Rooival, passing the scene of Col. Cookson's engagement, which had occurred five days previously, when Delarey surrounded the column, killing all Cookson's horses. Col. von Donop's troops finally took up their position in the driving line on the extreme right, and entrenched for the night. On the following morning, two hours before daybreak, word was brought by the scouts that the combined commandos of Delarey, Kemp, Liebenberg, and Potgeiter, 2,000 strong, with four field guns and two pom-poms (those captured from Col. von Donop's convoy six weeks previously) were halted 6 miles away on the right. Col. von Donop's column, being on the extreme right, was the first to move, the 21st M. I. being ordered to furnish the screen and supports of the advanced guard. At about 6 a.m. the screen came over a rise, and was at once face to face with Delarey's commandos, who were partially concealed in large mealie patches less than 4,000 yards away. Although apparently surprised, the enemy quickly formed into two or three long lines, and riding almost knee to knee, charged through the screen, shouting, and firing from the saddle. The 21st M. I. dismounted, and those horses which were not shot were galloped to the rear, the men lying in the grass and firing at the Boers as they galloped through. Many of the latter and of their horses were shot as they passed von Donop's main body, which by this time had had sufficient warning, and received the charge with a very heavy fire. At the same time Gen. Rawlinson, whose column had come up, met and repulsed an attempted turning movement. The Boers were now effectively stopped, their casualties being very large. Col. von Donop's Scottish Horse were then ordered to charge the enemy, who made a big wheel to the left towards some hills covered with scrub and small trees. The British guns then opening fire caused the whole force of Boers to break and scatter in all directions, though their guns still replied in a desultory way. The British pursued throughout the day, the Boers with their guns and wagons scattering in parties all over the country. By 4 p.m. all their guns and many prisoners had been captured. The 21st M. I. suffered more casualties than any other corps in this engagement, losing two officers and a colour-sergeant killed, and five out of nine officers dangerously or severely wounded, including Major Roy, of the Sherwood Foresters, then in command.

APPENDIX B.

The Boer casualties were given as forty-five killed and many wounded, Potgeiter being killed and Kemp badly wounded. The next day Col. von Donop received the following message from General Ian Hamilton :—"My best congratulations to you and your gallant troops. I shall have great pleasure in telling Lord Kitchener of their steadiness when attacked and their dashing pursuit."

The combined columns moved rapidly back to Brakspruit (near Klerksdorp) in order to rest horses and troops and procure remounts. Many of the horses had been killed or had given out from exhaustion.

On May 5th von Donop's column halted for a week at Rooijantjesfontein, 40 miles west of Klerksdorp. They started from here on the last big drive into the Mafeking Line, which occupied five days, through an almost waterless tract of country. The columns commanded by Col. Kekewich were again posted on the extreme right of the driving line, which extended southward 30 miles to Vryburg and beyond. Their right, at the termination of the drive, rested on Saltpan Siding. During the last two days they captured about forty or fifty Boers, the total bag for the whole drive being 400.

The 21st M. I. then returned to Klerksdorp, whence, after peace was declared, it was sent out to bring in many of the surrendered parties of Boers.

During June and July, and up to the 24th August, the 21st M. I. were camped 4 miles outside Klerksdorp, subsequently marching to Bloemfontein, which town was reached on the 28th August. Here Lieutenants Beeton and Drinan, together with all N.C.O.'s and men of the Royal Sussex Regiment, rejoined the Regiment.

APPENDIX C.

Names of officers and numbers of men sent out to South Africa by the Volunteer Battalions of the Royal Sussex Regiment.

1st Volunteer Battalion :—
    Capt. S. W. G. Tamplin ... (1st Active Service Coy.),
    Lieut. W. H. Findlay ... ... (2nd ,, ,, ,,),
    Lieut. J. G. Cockburn ... (2nd ,, ,, ,,),
    Lieut. T. O. B. Ruthven ... (3rd ,, , ,,),
    and 105 N.C.O.'s and men in all.

2nd Volunteer Battalion :—
    Capt. and Hon. Maj. Sir W. G. Barttelot (1st Active Service Coy.),
    Lieut. B. J. D'Olier ... ... (1st ,, ,, ,,),
    Capt. S. W. P. Beale ... ... (2nd ,, ,, ,,),
    and 81 N.C.O.'s and men in all.

[N.B.—Col. the Duke of Norfolk, E.M., K.G., served in South Africa with the Sussex Imperial Yeomanry; Capt. Lord Zouche served with the Rough Riders; Surgeon-Capt. G. Black served with the R.A.M. Corps].

1st Cinque Ports :—
    Lieut. A. F. A. Howe ... ... (1st Active Service Coy.),
    and 128 N.C.O.'s and men in all.

APPENDIX D.

Honours and rewards bestowed upon officers and men of the Royal Sussex Regiment for the South African War :—

C.B. ... ... Col. the Earl of March, A.D.C., (3rd Battn.)
    Lt.-Col. B. D. A. Donne.
Brevet Lt.-Col. ... ... Major L. E. du Moulin.
Brevet Major ... ... Capt. A. R. Gilbert,
    Capt. E. H. Montresor,
D.S.O. ... ... Lieut. and Adjt. R. Bellamy,
    Major A. R. Gilbert,
    Capt. F. Robinson,
      ,, E. L. Mackenzie,
    Lieut. E. F. Villiers,
      ,, C. E. Bond.

Lieut. A. R. Hopkins was specially promoted for services in the field to a Captaincy in the Manchester Regiment.

Medals for Distinguished Conduct in the field:—

Sergt.-Major S. S. Thwaits,   Sergt. T. Gates,
Color-Sergt. T. Jones,   Lc.-Sergt. A. Ockleford,
  ,,   A. Nye,   Corpl. P. Hoad,
  ,,   A. Weston,   Pte. J. Gill,
  ,,   H. Snaith,   ,, T. Say,
Q.-M. Sergt. C. Pittman,   ,, C. Nevill,
Sergt. G. Weston,   ,, T. Scrase.

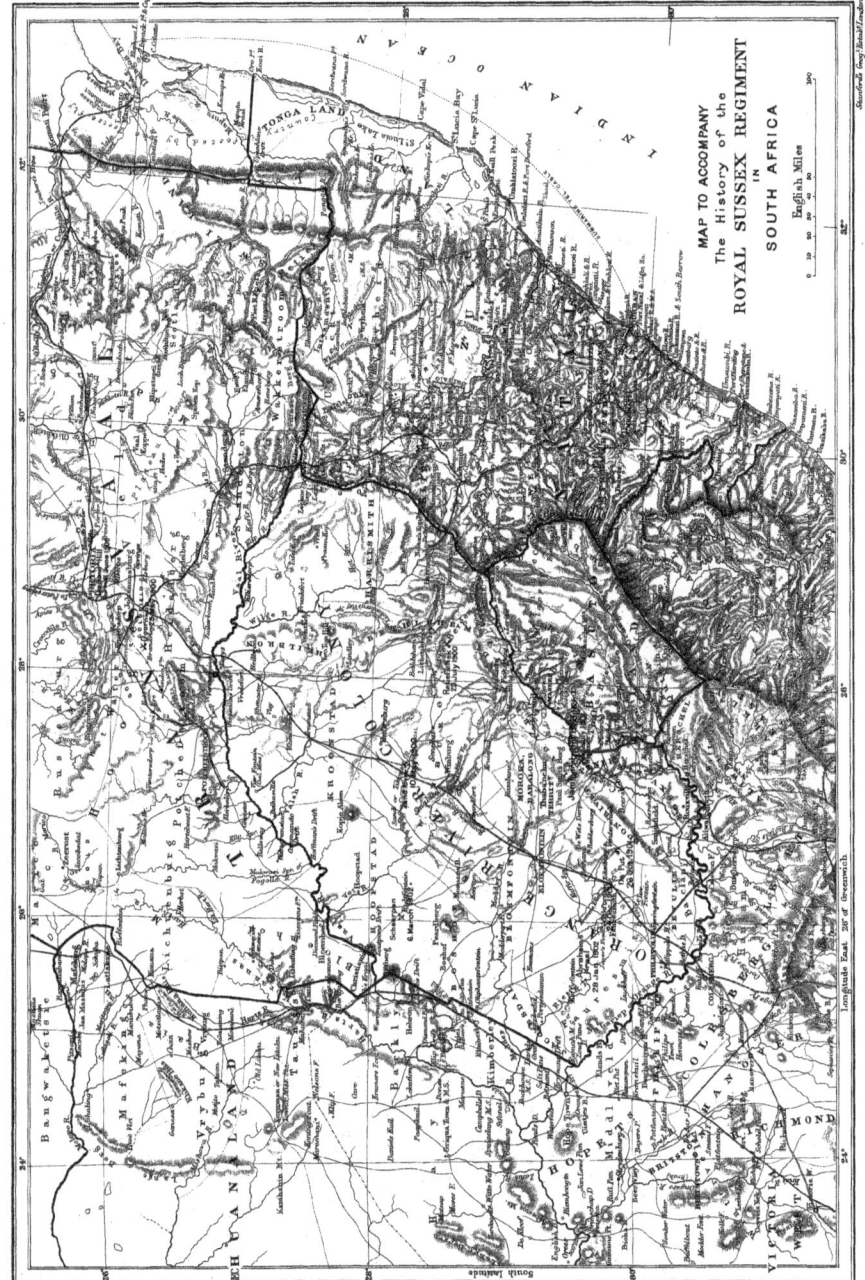

www.ingramcontent.com/pod-product-compliance
Lightning Source LLC
Chambersburg PA
CBHW031132160426
43193CB00008B/117